reading images

'Fresh and stimulating. The sociocentric approach is by far the most penetrating approach to the subject currently available.'
Paul Cobley, *London Guildhall University*

'A useful text for all students who are involved in areas which rely on both language and visual images for their expression and articulation of ideas.'
Catriona Scott, *Middlesex University*

'This is the best detailed and sustained development of the "social semiotic" approach to the analysis of visuals. Clear, informative and theoretically developmental.'
Dr S. Cottle, *Bath HE College*

'Excellent – wide ranging – accessible – tutors' "Bible".'
Jan Mair, *Edge Hill University College of Higher Education*

'Extremely attractive and well laid out. Very useful bibliography.'
Dr M. Brottman, *East London University*

'Very clearly written – it makes good connections between different areas of visual practice – especially useful for students from a variety of backgrounds attempting "mixed" coursework.'
Amy Sargeant, *Plymouth University*

Reading Images provides the first systematic and comprehensive account of the grammar of visual design. By looking at the formal elements and structures of design – colour, perspective, framing and composition – Gunther Kress and Theo van Leeuwen examine the ways in which images communicate meaning.

Drawing on an enormous range of examples – children's drawings, textbook illustrations, photojournalism, advertising images and fine art, as well as three-dimensional forms such as sculpture and architecture – the authors demonstrate the differences and the similarities between the grammar of language and that of visual communication.

As we move from a culture dominated by language to one in which visual literacy becomes increasingly important, this book provides an invaluable 'tool-kit' for reading images. It will be an essential text for anyone interested in communication, the media and the arts.

Gunther Kress is Professor of English, Media and Drama at the Institute of Education, University of London. **Theo van Leeuwen** is at the London College of Printing.

reading images

GUNTHER KRESS and
THEO van LEEUWEN

THE GRAMMAR
OF VISUAL DESIGN

London and New York

First published 1996
by Routledge
11 New Fetter Lane, London EC4P 4EE

Simultaneously published in the USA and Canada
by Routledge
29 West 35th Street, New York, NY 10001

Reprinted 1998, 1999, 2000, 2001 (twice), 2003

Routledge is an imprint of the Taylor & Francis Group

Typeset in Bell Gothic by Solidus (Bristol) Limited

Printed and bound in Great Britain by
St Edmundsbury Press Limited, Bury St Edmunds, Suffolk

British Library Cataloguing in Publication Data
A catalogue record for this book is available from the British
Library.

Library of Congress Cataloguing in Publication Data
A catalogue record for this book has been requested.

ISBN 0-415-10599-4
    0-415-10600-1 (pbk)

CONTENTS

Preface

This book grew out of discussions about visual communication which spanned a period of seven years. Both of us had worked on the analysis of verbal texts, and increasingly felt the need of a better understanding of all the things that go with the verbal: facial expressions, gestures, images, music, and so on. This not only because we wanted to analyse the whole of the texts in which these semiotic modes play a vital role rather than just the verbal part, but also to understand language better. Just as a knowledge of other languages can open new perspectives on one's own language, so a knowledge of other semiotic modes can open new perspectives on language.

In 1990 we published a first version of our ideas on visual communication, *Reading Images*, with Deakin University Press. It was written for teachers, and we concentrated on children's drawings and school textbook illustrations, although we also included examples from the mass media, such as advertisements and magazine layout. Since then we have expanded our research to other fields of visual communication: a much wider range of mass media materials; scientific (and other) diagrams, maps and charts; and the visual arts. We have also made a beginning with the study of three-dimensional communication: sculpture,.children's toys, architecture and everyday designed objects. The present book therefore offers a much more comprehensive theory of visual communication than the earlier book.

In Australia, and increasingly elsewhere, our work has been used in courses on communication and media studies and discourse analysis, and as a methodology for research in areas such as media representation, film studies, children's literature and the use of illustrations and layout in school textbooks. The present book has benefited greatly from the suggestions and comments of those who have used our work in these ways, and of our own undergraduate and postgraduate students, initially at the University of Technology and Macquarie University in Sydney, later at the Institute of Education and the London College of Printing in London, and also at the Temasek Polytechnic in Singapore.

We began our work on visual communication in the supportive and stimulating environment of the Newtown Semiotics Circle in Sydney; discussions with our friends, the members of this Circle, helped shape our ideas in more ways than we can acknowledge. If any two people from that first period were to be singled out, it would be Jim Martin, who gave us meticulously detailed, extensive and challenging comments on several of the chapters of the earlier book, and Fran Christie, who had urged us to write it. But here we would also like to make a special mention of Bob Hodge, whose ideas appear in this book in many ways, even if not always obviously so.

Of those who used our book in teaching and research, and whose comments on the earlier book have helped us to rethink and refine our ideas, we would like to mention the research team of the Disadvantaged Schools Programme in Sydney, in particular Rick

Iedema, Susan Feez, Peter White, Robert Veel and Sally Humphrey; Staffan Selander, through whose Centre for Textbook Research in Härnösand our work came to be taken up by researchers in the field of textbook research in Sweden and several other European countries; the members of the 'Language and Science' research team at the Institute of Education, Isabel Martins, Jon Ogborn and Kieran McGillicuddy; Philip Bell; Basil Bernstein; Paul Gillen and Teun van Dijk.

Three writers influenced our ideas in different and fundamental ways. One is Roland Barthes. Although we see our work as going beyond his seminal writings on visual semiotics in several ways, he remains a strong inspiration. There is not a subject in semiotics on which Barthes has not written originally and inspiringly. He has provided for us a model of what semiotics can be, in the range of his interests, in the depth of his work, and in his engagement with the social and cultural world. Equally significant for us is Michael Halliday. His view of language as a social semiotic and the wider implications of his theories gave us the means to go beyond the structuralist approach of the 1960s Paris School semiotics, and our work is everywhere influenced by his ideas. Then there is Rudolf Arnheim. The more we read his work, the more we realize that most of what we have to say has already been said by him, often better than we have done it, albeit usually in commentaries on individual works of art rather than in the form of a more general theory. He is commonly associated with Gestalt psychology: we would like to claim him as a great social semiotician.

We would like to thank our editor, Julia Hall, for her encouragement and invaluable help in producing the book. Jill Brewster and Laura Lopez-Bonilla were involved in various stages of the book; their encouragement and help made the work possible and enjoyable.

Acknowledgements

Acknowledgement is due to copyright holders for their kind permission to include the following material in this book: Fig no. 1.1 reproduced from a former edition of the Ladybird title, *Baby's First Book,* with the permission of the publishers, Ladybird books; Fig no. 1.2 taken from Dick Bruna, *On My Walk.* Illustration by Dick Bruna, © Mercie, 1959, 1962, 1970 and 1972; Fig no. 1.4(a) front page of *The Sun,* reproduced with permission; Fig no. 2.2 by permission of National Australia Bank; Fig no. 2.14, reproduced from *The Sydney Morning Herald,* by permission of Fairfax Photo Library; Fig no. 2.16 Ben Hur, Wyler 1959, © 1959, Turner Entertainment co., all rights reserved; Fig no. 2.18 taken from Saussure, F. (1974), *Course in General Linguistics,* Peter Owen, London, by permission of the publishers; Fig no. 2.20 by permission of *Vittel* mineral water; Fig no. 2.26 taken from Sale, C. *et al.* (1987) *Our Changing World Book One,* Longman, Australia, by permission of the publishers; Fig no. 2.30 *The Big Knife* 1995 © United Artists Corporation, all rights reserved; Fig no. 3.12 reproduced by permission of *Vogue* magazine; Fig no. 3.15 taken from Pask and Bryant (1982) *People in Australia: A Social Geography,* Jacaranda Wiley, by permission of the publishers; Fig no. 3.18 taken from Coupe, S. and Andrews, M. (1984) *Their Ghosts May be Heard,* Longman, by permission of the publishers; Fig no. 3.25 taken from Hill, J. (1980) *Introductory Physics,* Thomas Nelson Australia, by permission of the publishers; Fig 3.28 taken from Modley, R. and Lowenstein, D. *Pictographs and Graphs,* © 1952 by Harper and Bro., copyright renewed 1980 by Peter M. Modley and Marion E. Schling. Reprinted by permission of HarperCollins Pub Inc; Fig nos 3.40 and 3.41 by permission of the children of Adelaide School; Fig no. 3.37 *Sheer Magic,* reproduced by permission of Dodwell and Co, Australia; Fig no. 4.2 reproduced with permission of the Imperial War Museum; Fig no. 4.12 by permission of the Mitchel Library, State Library of South Wales, photo by G.N. Wilson; Fig no. 5.11 taken from Jennings, T. (1986) *The Young Geographer Investigates,* Oxford University Press. Reprinted by permission of the publishers; Fig no. 5.12 by permission of Warden and Fellows, New College Oxford; Fig no. 5.16 taken from Gregory, R.L. (1982) *The Eye and Brain,* Oxford University Press, by permission of the publishers; Fig no. 5.4 reproduced by permission; Fig no. 6.12 © Camera Press; Fig no. 6.14 The Louvre, Paris/Bridgeman Art Library; Fig nos 6.15 and 6.16 Musee d'Orsay, Paris/Lauros-Giraudon/Bridgeman Art Library, London; Fig no. 6.17 taken from Arnheim (1982), *The Power of the Centre: A Study of Composition in the Visual Arts,* UCLA Press, reproduced by permission of the publishers; Fig no. 6.23 Brett Whitley, *Art Life and the Other Thing* 1978 Collection: The Whitely Studio Museum NSW; Fig no. 6.27 taken from *Observer* Newspaper, © David Wiley; Fig no. 8.1 reproduced with kind permission of Playmobil; Fig no. 8.13 statue by Charles Ray and photographed by Peter Muscato; Fig no. 8.2 1950, Bronze reproduced by kind permission of Kenneth Armitage; Fig no. 8.8 by permission of the Granada Foundation; Fig nos: 8.11 and 8.12 – the works illustrated on pp. 255 and 257 are reproduced by permission of the Henry Moore foundation; Fig nos 8.5 and 8.15 (Winter catalogue 1994) reproduced by permission of Argos; Plate 2 reproduced with the permission of Unifoods, NSW. Suprematist Composition by Kasimir Malevich (1878–1935) Stedelijk Museum, Amsterdam/Bridgeman Art Library, London.

While every effort has been made to contact owners of copyright of material which is reproduced in this book, we have not always been successful. In the event of a copyright query, please contact the publishers.

Introduction: the grammar of visual design

The subtitle of this book is 'the grammar of visual design'. We hesitated over this title. Extensions of the term 'grammar' often suggest the idea of rules. In books with titles like *The Grammar of Television Production* one learns, for instance, about the rules of continuity; knowing these rules is then what sets the 'professional' apart from the 'amateur'. What we have sought to express is a little different. In our view, most accounts of visual semiotics have concentrated on what linguists would call 'lexis' rather than 'grammar', on the 'vocabulary' – for instance, on the 'denotative' and 'connotative', the 'iconographical' and 'iconological' significance of the individual people, places and things (including abstract 'things') depicted in images. In this book we will concentrate, by contrast, on 'grammar', on the way in which these depicted people, places and things are combined into a meaningful whole. Just as grammars of language describe how words combine in clauses, sentences and texts, so our visual 'grammar' will describe the way in which depicted people, places and things combine in visual 'statements' of greater or lesser complexity and extension.

We are not the first to deal with this subject. But where the study of visual 'lexis' has emphasized 'denotative', 'connotative', 'symbolic' meanings, the study of visual 'grammar' has not paid much attention to this, at least not in explicit or systematic ways. The focus has either been on the formal, aesthetic description of images, sometimes on the basis of the psychology of perception, or sometimes on more pragmatic descriptions, for instance of the way the composition can be used to attract the viewer's attention to one thing rather than another.

These approaches are entirely valid; however, they do not tell the whole story. The 'grammar of visual design' plays an equally vital role in the production of meaning, and it is this aspect we seek, above all, to describe in our book. We intend to provide inventories of the major compositional structures which have become established as conventions in the course of the history of visual semiotics, and to analyse how they are used to produce meaning by contemporary image-makers.

What we have said about visual 'grammar' is true also of the mainstream of linguistic grammar: grammar has been and still is formal. It has generally been studied in isolation from meaning. However, the linguists and the school of linguistic thought from which we draw part of our inspiration have taken issue with this view, and see grammatical forms as resources for encoding interpretations of experience and forms of social (inter)action. Benjamin Lee Whorf argued the point in relation to languages from different cultures. In what we call 'Standard Average European' languages, terms like *summer, winter, September, morning, noon, sunset* are coded as nouns, as though they were things. Hence these languages make it possible to interpret time as something you can count, use, save, etc. In Hopi, a North American Indian language, this is not possible. Time can only be expressed as 'subjective duration-feeling'. You cannot say 'at noon', or 'three summers'.

You have to say something like 'while the summer phase is occurring' (Whorf, 1956). The critical linguists of the East Anglia School, with which one of us was connected, have shown that such different interpretations of experience can also be encoded within the same language, on the basis of different ideological positions. Tony Trew (1979: 106–7) has described how, when the Harare police, in what was in 1975 still Rhodesia, fired into a crowd of unarmed people and shot thirteen of them, *The Rhodesia Herald* wrote 'A political clash has led to death and injury' while the *Tanzanian Daily News* wrote 'Rhodesia's white suprematist police . . . opened fire and killed thirteen unarmed Africans.' In other words, the political views of newspapers are not only encoded through different vocabularies (of the well-known 'terrorist' vs 'freedom fighter' type), but also through different grammatical structures, that is, through the choice between coding an event as a noun ('death', 'injury') or a verb ('kill') which, for its grammatical completion requires an active subject ('police') and an object ('unarmed Africans').

> Grammar goes beyond formal rules of correctness. It is a means of representing patterns of experience. . . . It enables human beings to build a mental picture of reality, to make sense of their experience of what goes on around them and inside them.
>
> (Halliday, 1985: 101)

The same is true for the 'grammar of visual design'. In the course of this book we will constantly elaborate and exemplify this point.

The analogy with language does not imply, however, that visual structures are like linguistic structures. The relation is much more general. Visual structures realize meanings as linguistic structures do also, and thereby point to different interpretations of experience and different forms of social interaction. The meanings which can be realized in language and in visual communication overlap in part, that is, some things can be expressed both visually and verbally; and in part they diverge – some things can be 'said' only visually, others only verbally. But even when something can be 'said' both visually and verbally the *way in which* it will be said is different. For instance, what is expressed in language through the choice between different word classes and semantic structures, is, in visual communication, expressed through the choice between, for instance, different uses of colour, or different compositional structures. We will elaborate and exemplify this point throughout the book.

As for other resonances of the term 'grammar' – 'grammar' as a set of rules one has to obey if one is to speak or write in 'correct', socially acceptable ways, linguists often protest that they are merely describing; but they are of course also involved in producing knowledge which others will transform from the descriptive into the normative, for instance in education. When a semiotic mode plays a dominant role in public communication its use will inevitably be constrained by rules, rules enforced through education, for instance, and through all kinds of written and unwritten social sanctions. Only a small elite of experimenters is allowed to break them – after all, breaking rules remains necessary to keep the possibility of change open. We believe that visual communication is coming to be less and less the domain of specialists, and more and more crucial in the domains of public communication. Inevitably this will lead to new, and more rules, and to more formal, normative teaching. Not being 'visually literate' will begin to attract social sanctions. 'Visual literacy' will begin to be a matter of survival, especially in the workplace.

We are well aware that work such as ours can or will help pave the way for developments of this kind. This can be seen negatively, as constraining the relative freedom which visual communication has so far enjoyed, albeit at the expense of a certain marginalization by comparison to writing; or positively, as allowing more people greater access to a wider range of visual skills. And it does not, of course, have to stand in the way of creativity. Teaching the rules of writing has not meant the end of creative uses of language in literature and elsewhere, and teaching visual skills will not spell the end of the arts. Yet, just as the grammar creatively employed by poets and novelists is, in the end, the same grammar we use when writing letters, memos, reports, so the 'grammar of visual design', creatively employed by artists is, in the end, the same grammar we need when producing attractive layouts, images, diagrams, for our course handouts, reports, brochures, communiques, and so on.

It is worth asking here what a linguistic grammar is a grammar of. The conventional answer is to say that it is a grammar of 'English' or 'Dutch' or 'French'. A slightly less conventional answer would be to say that a grammar is an inventory of elements and rules underlying culture-specific *verbal* communication. Of what is our 'visual grammar' a grammar? We would say, first of all, that it is a grammar of 'visual design', because we need a term that can encompass oil painting as well as magazine layout, the comic strip as well as the scientific diagram. And we would also say that it is a grammar of contemporary visual design in 'Western' cultures, and hence an inventory of the elements and rules underlying a culture-specific form of *visual* communication. We have confined our examples to visual objects from 'Western' cultures, and we have assumed that this communication system has a history, that it has evolved, over the past five centuries or so, alongside writing, as a 'language of visual design'. Its boundaries are not those of nation states (although there are, of course, cultural/regional variants), rather, it has spread wherever global Western culture is the dominant culture.

This means, first of all, that it is not a 'universal' grammar. Visual language is not transparent and universally understood, but culturally specific. We hope our work will provide some ideas and concepts for the study of visual communication in non-Western forms of visual communication. To give the most obvious example, Western visual communication is deeply affected by our convention of writing from left to right (in chapter 6 we will discuss this more fully). Other cultures write from right to left, or from top to bottom, and will consequently attach different values and meanings to these key dimensions of visual space. Such valuations and meanings will exert their influence beyond writing, and inform the meanings accorded to different compositional patterns, the amount of use made of them, and so on. In other words, we assume that the elements such as 'centre' or 'margin', 'top' or 'bottom', will be elements used in the visual semiotics of any culture, but with meanings and values which are likely to differ from those of Western cultures. We will comment on this issue from time to time. Here we merely want to signal that our investigations have been restricted, by and large, to Western visual communication, and that we make no specific claims for the relevance of our ideas to visual communication in other cultures. Within Western visual design, however, we believe that our theory applies to all forms of visual communication. We hope that the wide range of examples we use in the book will convince the reader of this proposition.

Our stress on the unity of Western visual communication does not exclude the possibility of regional and social variation. The unity of Western design is not some intrinsic feature of visuality, but derives from the global power of the Western mass media and culture industries, and their technologies. In many parts of the world, Western visual communication exists side by side with more traditional forms, with Western forms used, for instance, in public communication, such as in the press and in advertising, and traditional forms in other domains, for instance the visual arts, or interior decoration. And where Western visual communication begins to exert pressure on traditional forms, there will be transitional stages in which the two cultures mix. In looking at advertisements in English-language magazines from the Phillipines, for instance, we were struck by the way in which entirely conventional Western iconographical elements were integrated into a design following the rules of a local visual semiotic.

Within Europe, increasing regionality counterbalances increasing globalization. So long as the European nations and regions still retain different ways of life and a different ethos, they will use the 'grammar of visual design' differently. It is easy, for example, to find examples of the contrasting use of the left and right in the composition of pages and images in the British media. It is harder to find such examples in, for instance, the Greek or the Spanish media, as students from these countries assured us after trying to do the assignments we set them at home, during their holidays. In the course of our book we will give some examples of this, for instance in connection with newspaper layout in different European countries. However, we are not able to do more than touch on the subject; and the issue of different 'dialects' and 'inflections' needs to be explored more fully in the future.

In any case, the unity of languages is a social construct, a product of theory and of social and cultural histories. When the borders of a language are not policed by academies, and when languages are not homogenized by education systems and mass media, people quite freely combine elements from the languages they know to make themselves understood. Mixed languages ('pidgins') develop in this way, and in time can become the language of new generations ('creoles'). Visual communication, not subject to such policing, has developed more freely than language, but there has nevertheless been a dominant language, 'spoken' and developed in centres of high culture, alongside less highly valued regional and social variants (e.g. 'folk art'). The dominant visual language is now controlled by the global cultural/technological empires of the mass media, which disseminate the examples set by exemplary designers, and, through the spread of image banks and computer-imaging technology, exert a 'normalizing' rather than explicitly 'normative' influence on visual communication across the world. Much as it is the primary aim of this book to describe the current state of the 'grammar of visual design', we will also discuss the broad historical, social and cultural conditions that make and remake the visual 'language'.

A SOCIAL SEMIOTIC THEORY OF REPRESENTATION

We see our work as part of 'social semiotics', and it is therefore important to place it in context of what 'semiotics' is, and has been, in this century. Three schools of semiotics have applied ideas from the domain of linguistics to other, non-linguistic modes of communication. The first was the Prague School of the 1930s and early 1940s. It developed the work of Russian Formalists by providing it with a linguistic basis. Notions such as 'foregrounding' were applied to language (e.g. the 'foregrounding' of phonological or syntactic forms through 'deviation' from standard forms, for artistic purposes) as well as to the study of art (Mukarovsky), theatre (Honzl), cinema (Jakobson) and costume (Bogatyrev). Each of these semiotic systems could fulfil the same communicative functions (the 'referential' and the 'poetic' functions). The second was the Paris School of the 1960s and 1970s, which applied ideas from de Saussure and other linguists (Schefer), photography (Barthes, Lindekens), fashion (Barthes), cinema (Metz), music (Nattiez), comic strips (Fresnault-Deruelle), etc. The ideas developed by this school are still taught in countless courses of media studies, art and design, often under the heading 'semiology', despite the fact that they are at the same time regarded as overtaken by post-structuralism. Everywhere students are learning about 'langue' and 'parole'; the 'signifier' and the 'signified'; 'arbitrary' and 'motivated' signs; 'icons', 'indexes' and 'symbols' (these terms come from Peirce, but are incorporated in the framework of 'semiology'); 'syntagmatics' and 'paradigmatics'; and so on – generally without being given access to alternative theories of semiotics (or of linguistics). We will compare and contrast this kind of semiotics with our own approach, in this introduction as well as elsewhere in the book. The third fledgling movement of this kind is 'social semiotics', which began in Australia, where the ideas of Michael Halliday inspired studies of literature (Threadgold, Thibault), visual semiotics (O'Toole, ourselves) and music (van Leeuwen), as well as of other semiotic modes (Hodge and Kress).

The key notion in any semiotics is the 'sign'. Our book is about signs, or, as we would rather put it, about sign-making. We will be discussing forms ('signifiers') such as colour, perspective and line, as well as the way in which these forms are used to realize meanings ('signifieds'). But our conception of the sign differs somewhat from that of 'semiology', and we wish therefore to compare the two views explicitly. In doing so we use the term 'semiology' to refer to the way in which the Paris School semiotics is generally taught in the Anglo-Saxon world, through the mediation of influential textbooks such as the series of media studies textbooks edited by John Fiske (Fiske and Hartley, 1978; Dyer, 1982; Fiske, 1982; Hartley, 1982; O'Sullivan *et al.*, 1983). In doing this we do not seek to repudiate those who went before us. We see a continuity between their work and ours, as should be clear from our main title, *Reading Images*, which echoes that of the first volume in Fiske's series, *Reading Television* (Fiske and Hartley, 1978).

We would like to begin with an example of what we understand by 'sign-making'. The drawing in figure 0.1 was made by a three-year-old boy. Sitting on his father's lap, he talked about the drawing as he was doing it: 'Do you want to watch me? I'll make a car . . . got two wheels . . . and two wheels at the back . . . and two wheels here . . . that's a funny wheel. . . .' When he had finished, he said 'This is a car.' This was the first time he had named a drawing, and at first the name was puzzling. How was this a car? Of course he had provided the key himself: 'Here's a wheel.' A car, for him, was defined by the criterial characteristic of 'having wheels', and his representation focused on this aspect. What he represented was in fact, 'wheelness'. And wheels are a plausible criterion to choose for three-year-olds, and the wheel's action, on toy cars as on real cars, is a readily describable feature. In other words, a three-year-old's *interest* in cars is most plausibly condensed into and expressed as an interest in wheels. Wheels, in turn, are most plausibly represented by circles, both because of their visual appearance and because of the circular motion of the hand in representing the wheel's action of 'going round and round'.

In other words, we see representation as a *process* in which the makers of signs, whether child or adult, seek to make a representation of some object or entity, whether physical or semiotic, and in which their interest in the object, at the point of making the representation, is a complex one, arising out of the cultural, social and psychological history of the sign-maker, and focused by the specific context in which the sign is produced. *Interest* guides the selection of what is seen as the criterial aspects of the object, and this criterial aspect is then regarded as adequately or sufficiently representative of the object in the given context. In other words, it is never the 'whole object' but only ever its criterial aspects which are represented.

These criterial aspects are represented in what seems to the sign-maker, at the moment, the most apt and plausible fashion, and the most apt and plausible representational mode (e.g. drawing, lego blocks, painting). Sign-makers thus have a meaning, the signified, which they want to express, and then express it through the semiotic mode which makes available the subjectively most plausible, most apt form, the signifier. This means that, to us, the sign is not the pre-existing conjunction of a signifier and a signified, to be recognized and used *en bloc*, in the way that signs are usually defined in 'semiology', but

⬯ **Fig 0.1 Drawing by a three-year-old child**

a process of sign-making in which the stratum of the signifier and the stratum of the signified are relatively independent of each other. To put it in a different way, the process of sign-making is the process of the constitution of metaphor in two steps: 'a car is (most like) wheels' and 'wheels are (most like) circles'. Signs thus result from a double metaphoric process in which analogy is the constitutive principle. And analogy, in turn, is a process of classification: X is like Y (in criterial ways). Which metaphors carry the day and pass into the semiotic system as 'natural', neutral classifications, is then governed by social relations. Like adults, children are ceaselessly engaged in the construction of metaphors. Unlike adults, they are, on the one hand, less constricted by culture, by already existing metaphors, but, on the other hand, usually in a position of less power, so that their metaphors are less likely to carry the day.

It follows that we see signs as *motivated* conjunctions of signifiers (forms) and signifieds (meanings). In 'semiology' motivation is usually not related to the act of sign-making, but defined in terms of an intrinsic relation between the signifier and the signified. It is here that Peirce's 'icon', 'index' and 'symbol' make their appearance, incorporated into 'semiology' in a way which in fact contradicts some of the key ideas in Peirce's semiotics. The 'icon' is the sign in which 'the signifier–signified relationship is one of resemblance, likeness' (Dyer, 1982: 124) – i.e. objective likeness, rather than analogy motivated by interest establishes the relation; and the 'index' is the sign in which 'there is a sequential or causal relation between signifier and signified' (Dyer, 1982: 125) i.e. a logic of inference, rather than analogy motivated by interest. The third term in the triad, 'symbol', by contrast, *is* related to sign production, as it 'rests on convention, or "contract"' (Dyer, 1982: 125), but this very fact makes it 'arbitrary', 'unmotivated', a case of meaning by decree rather than of active sign-making. In our view signs are never arbitrary, and 'motivation' should be formulated in relation to the sign-maker and the context in which the sign is produced, and not in isolation from the act of producing analogies and classifications. Sign-makers use the forms they consider apt for the expression of their meaning, in any medium in which they can make signs. When children treat a cardboard box as a pirate ship, they do so because they consider the material form (box) an apt medium for the expression of the meaning they have in mind (pirate ship), because of their conception of criterial aspects of pirate ships (containment, mobility, etc.). Language is no exception to this. All linguistic form is used in a mediated, non-arbitrary manner in the expression of meaning. For children in their early, pre-school years there is both more and less freedom of expression: more, because they have not yet learnt to confine the making of signs to the culturally and socially facilitated media, and because they are unaware of established conventions and relatively unconstrained in the making of signs; less, because they do not have such rich cultural semiotic resources available as do adults. So when a three-year-old boy, labouring to climb a steep hill, says 'This is a heavy hill', he is constrained by not having the word 'steep' as an available semiotic resource. The same is the case with the resources of syntactic and textual forms.

'Heavy', in 'heavy hill', is, however, a motivated sign: the child has focused on particular aspects of climbing a hill (it takes a lot of energy; it is exhausting) and uses an available form which he sees as apt for the expression of these meanings. The adult who corrects by offering 'steep' ('Yes, it's a very steep hill') is, from the child's point of view, not so much offering an alternative as a synonym for the precise meaning which he, the child, had given to 'heavy' in that context. Both the child and the parent make use of 'what is available'. But to concentrate on this is to miss the central aspect of sign-making, especially that of children. 'Availability' is not the issue. Children, like adults, make their own resources of representation. They are not 'acquired', but made by the individual sign-maker. In 'semiology', countless students across the world are introduced to the terms 'langue' and 'parole', with 'langue' explained, for instance, as 'the abstract potential of a language system ... the shared language system out of which we make our particular, possibly unique, statements' (O'Sullivan *et al.*, 1983: 127), or in our terms, as a system of available forms already coupled to available meanings; and with 'parole' defined as:

> an individual utterance that is a particular realization of the potential of *langue*. . . . By extension we can argue that the total system of television and film conventions and practices constitutes a *langue*, and the way they are realized in each programme or film a *parole*.
>
> (O'Sullivan *et al.*, 1983: 127)

We clearly work with similar notions, with 'available forms' and 'available classifications' ('langue') and individual acts of sign-making ('parole'), and we agree that such notions can usefully be extended to semiotic modes other than language. But for us the idea of 'potential' (what you can mean and how you can 'say' it, in whatever medium) is not limited by a system of 'available meanings' coupled with 'available forms', and we would like to use a slightly less abstract formulation: a semiotic 'potential' is defined by the semiotic resources available to a specific individual in a specific social context. Of course, a description of semiotic potential can amalgamate the resources of many speakers and many contexts. But the resulting 'langue' (the langue of 'English' or of 'Western visual design') is in the end an artefact of analysis. What exists, and is therefore more crucial for understanding representation and communication are the resources available to real people in real social contexts. And if we construct a 'langue', a meaning potential for 'Western visual design', then it is no more and no less than a tool which can serve to describe a variety of sign-making practices, within boundaries drawn by the analyst. It follows that we would not draw the line between 'langue' and 'parole' as sharply as it is usually done. Describing a 'language' is describing what people do with words, or images, or music.

Here are some antecedents of the car drawing. Figure 0.2 is a drawing made by the same child, some ten months earlier. Its circular motion is expressive of the child's exuberant, enthusiastic and energetic actions in making the drawing. In figure 0.3, made about three months later, the circular motion has become more regular. The exuberance and energy are still there, but the drawing has acquired more regularity, more interest in shape: 'circular motion' is beginning to turn into 'circle'. In other words, the meanings of drawing 0.2 persist in drawing 0.3, transformed, but nevertheless with significant

⬤　**Fig 0.2 Drawing by a two-year-old child**

continuity: figure 0.3 gathers up, so to speak, the meanings of figure 0.2, and then transforms and extends them.

Figure 0.4, finally, shows a series of circles, each drawn on a separate sheet, one circle to each sheet. The movement from figure 0.2 to figure 0.4 is clear enough, as is the conceptual and transformative work done by the child over a period of fourteen months (figure 0.4 dates from the same period as figure 0.1). Together the drawings show how the child *developed* the representational resources available to him, and why circles seemed such an apt choice to him: the expressive, energetic physicality of the motion of figure 0.2 persisted as the child developed this representational resource, so that the circular *motion* remained part of the meaning of circle/wheel. But something was added as well: the transformation of representational resources was also a transformation of the child's subjectivity, from the emotional, physical and expressive disposition expressed in the act of representing 'circular motion' to the more conceptual and cognitive disposition expressed in the act of representing a 'car' – a quite fundamental change.

Children, then, make their 'own' representational resources, and do so as part of a constant production of signs, in which previously produced signs are transformed into new signs. More generally, signs are motivated conjunctions of meaning (signified) and form

Fig 0.3 Drawing by a two-year-old child

Fig 0.4 Drawing by a three-year-old child

(signifier) in which the meanings of sign-makers lead to apt, plausible, motivated expressions, in any medium which is to hand. This process rests on the *interest* of sign-makers, which leads them to select particular features of the object to be represented as criterial, at that moment, and in that context. This transformative, productive stance towards sign-making is at the same time a transformation of the sign-makers' subjectivity – a notion for which there was little place in a 'semiology' which described the relation between signifiers and signifieds as resting on inference or objective resemblance, or on the decrees of the social 'contract'.

We have used children's drawings as our example, because we believe that the production of signs by children provides the best model for thinking about sign-making, and that it applies also to fully socialized and acculturated humans, with this exception: as mature members of a culture we have available the culturally produced semiotic resources of our societies, and are aware of the conventions and constraints which are socially imposed on our making of signs. However, adult sign-makers, too, are guided by interest, that complex condensation of cultural and social histories and of awareness of present contingencies. They produce signs out of that interest, and always as transformations of existing semiotic materials, therefore always in some way newly made, and always motivated conjunctions of meaning and form.

One of the now taken-for-granted insights of socially orientated theories of language is the variation of language with the variation of social context. The accounts of this variation differ, ranging from correlation ('language form *x* relates to social context *y*') to determination ('language form *x* is produced by social actors *y* or in social context *y*'). A social semiotic approach takes the latter view, along the following lines.

(1) Communication requires that participants make their messages maximally understandable in a particular context. They therefore choose forms of expression which they believe to be maximally transparent to other participants. On the other hand, communication takes place in social structures which are inevitably marked by power differences, and this affects how each participant understands the notion of 'maximal understanding'. Participants in positions of power can force other participants into greater efforts of interpretation, and their notion of 'maximal understanding' is therefore different from that of participants who do their best to produce messages that will require a minimal effort of interpretation, or from that of participants who, through lack of command of the representational system, produce messages that are harder to interpret (e.g. children, learners of a foreign language). The other participants may then either make the effort required to interpret these messages or refuse to do so, whether in a school or in a railway station in a foreign country.

(2) Representation requires that sign-makers choose forms for the expression of what they have in mind, forms which they see as most apt and plausible in the given context. The examples above instantiate this: *circles* to stand for *wheels*, and *wheels* to stand for *cars*; *heavy* to stand for *significant effort*, and *significant effort* to stand for *climbing a steep slope*. Speakers of a foreign language use exactly the same strategy. They choose the nearest most plausible form they know for the expression of what

they have in mind. The requirements of communication are no different in more usual circumstances, they are only less apparent. The interest of sign-makers, at the moment of making the sign, leads them to choose an aspect or bundle of aspects of the object to be represented as being criterial, at that moment, for representing what they want to represent, and then choose the most plausible, the most apt form for its representation. This applies also to the interest of the social institutions within which messages are produced, and there takes the form of the (histories of) conventions and constraints.

APPLICATIONS

In the previous section we have focused on the theoretical background of our work, but our aims are not just theoretical. They are also descriptive. We seek to develop a descriptive framework that can be used as a tool for visual analysis. Such a tool will have its use for practical as well as critical purposes. To give some examples of the former, educationalists everywhere have become aware of the increasing role of visual communication in learning materials of various kinds, and they are asking themselves what kind of maps, charts, diagrams, pictures and forms of layout will be most effective for learning. To answer this question they need a language for speaking about the forms and meanings of these visual learning materials. Our previous work has already been applied in a number of projects of this kind (Veel *et al.*, 1992; Selander, 1994; van Leeuwen, 1992; van Leeuwen and Humphrey, in press) and as input into the design of curricula for 'arts literacy' (Disadvantage Schools Programme, 1991) and 'media literacy' (Iedema, 1993).

Within the media, visual design is still the province of specialists who generally see little need for methodical and analytically explicit approaches, and rely on creative sensibilities honed through experience. But where media forms are relatively recently introduced, as in the case, for example, with advertising in Eastern Europe and parts of Asia, there is no such resistance to combining systematic analysis and practice. And with the advances of desk-top publishing, visual design (layout, the production of diagrams and charts, etc.) becomes less of a specialist activity, something many people will do alongside other activities. This has already led to rapid growth in the number of courses in this area – and designing such courses requires more of an analytical grasp of principles than learning on the job, by example and osmosis.

Analysing visual communication is, or should be, an important part of critical disciplines. Although, in this book, we focus on the system of visual communication rather than its uses, we see images of whatever kind as entirely within the realm of ideology, as means – always – for the emergence of ideological positions, with all the complexities of that argument. The growing enterprise of 'critical discourse analysis' seeks to show how the apparently neutral, purely informative discourses of newspaper reporting, government publications, social science reports, and so on, may in fact convey ideological attitudes just as much as discourses which more explicitly editorialize or propagandize, and how language is used to convey power and status in contemporary social interaction. To start with the former, we constantly hear that the quantity of information has increased enormously, but the diversity of that information may, at the same time, have decreased, so that it becomes all the more important to be able to 'read between the lines', in order to glimpse at least the possibility of an alternative view. It is this kind of 'reading between the lines' for which critical discourse analysis seeks to provide the ways and means. Similarly, the traditional signs of power differences themselves have not gone away, and are expressed in increasingly subtle ways which are not always brought to consciousness easily. So far, however, critical discourse analysis has mostly been confined to verbal texts, or to verbal parts of texts which also use other semiotic modes to get their message across. We see our book as a contribution to a broadened critical discourse analysis, and we hope that our examples will demonstrate its potential for this kind of work.

Critical discourse analysis has tended to concentrate on 'informative' texts, rather than on the kinds of texts that are usually classified as 'entertainment' – movies, television series, literature, etc. Our examples include many works of art, not just because of the key role of art in the history of conventions and constraints, the formation of the 'grammar of visual design', but because art can and should be approached from the point of view of social critique – as has of course already been done by others, for instance by feminist writers on art. Finally, critical discourse analysis has concerned itself not only with text analysis, but also with broad trends in public communication. Fairclough (1992, 1993), for instance, has described how the language of advertising has spread to many institutions which formerly used more formal and bureaucratic forms of discourse. The incursion of the visual into many domains of public communication where formerly language was the sole and dominant mode, is, in our view, an equally significant theme for critical discourse analysis. For this reason, it is also a theme to which we will pay a great deal of attention in this book.

As is perhaps already obvious from what we have said so far, we believe that visual design, like language, indeed like all semiotic modes, fulfils two major functions. To use Halliday's terms, every semiotic fulfils both an 'ideational' function, a function of representing 'the world around and inside us' and an 'interpersonal' function, a function of enacting social interactions as social relations. Whether we engage in conversation, produce an advertisement or play a piece of music, we are simultaneously communicating, doing something to, or for, or with others in the here and now of a social context (swapping news with a friend; persuading the reader of a magazine to buy something; entertaining an audience) and representing some aspect of the world 'out there', be it in concrete or abstract terms (the content of a film we have seen; the qualities of the advertised product; a mood or melancholy sentiment or exuberant energy conveyed musically). The structure of our book reflects this. Chapters 2 and 3 deal with the *patterns of representation* which the 'grammar of visual design' makes available, and hence with the ways we can encode experience visually. Chapters 4 and 5 deal with the *patterns of interaction* which the 'grammar of visual design' makes available, and hence with the things we can do to or for each other with visual communication, and with the relations between the makers and viewers of visual 'texts' which this entails. Chapter 6 deals with what Halliday calls the 'textual' function, with the way in which representations and communicative acts cohere into the kind of meaningful whole we call 'text'. Chapter 7 deals with the materiality of visual signs — the tools we make them with (ink, paint, brushstrokes, etc.) and the materials we make them on (paper, canvas, computer screens, etc.): these, too, contribute to the meaning of visual texts. Chapter 8 extends the previous chapters into the domain of three-dimensional visuals. Again we assume that there is something like a Western 'grammar of three-dimensional visual design', a set of available forms and meanings used in sculpture as well as, for instance, in three-dimensional scientific models, or in children's toys. We see our work as a tool for practical as well as critical applications in a range of fields.

We will begin, however, by discussing some of the broader themes we have touched on in this introduction.

1 The semiotic landscape: language and visual communication

In the early years of schooling, children are constantly encouraged to produce images, and to illustrate their written work. Teachers comment on these illustrations as much as they do on the written part of the text, though perhaps not quite in the same vein: unlike writing, illustrations are not 'corrected' or subjected to detailed criticism ('this needs more work', 'not clear', 'poor expression', and so on). They are seen as self-expression, rather than as communication: as something which the children can do already, spontaneously, rather than as something they have to be taught.

By the time children are beyond their first two years of secondary schooling, illustrations have largely disappeared – from the children's own texts as well as from the texts produced for them. Whereas texts produced for the early years of schooling are richly illustrated, later on visual images give way to a greater and greater proportion of verbal, written text. In as much as visual images continue, they have become maps, diagrams or representations with a technical function – photographs illustrating a particular landform or estuary or settlement type, in a geography textbook, for instance.

Outside school, however, images continue to play a very important role, and not just in texts for children. Newspapers, magazines, public relations materials, advertisements and many kinds of books today involve a complex interplay of written text, images and other graphic elements, and what is more, these elements combine together into *visual* designs, by means of layout. The skill of producing texts of this kind, however important their role in contemporary society, is not taught in schools. In terms of this new visual literacy, education produces illiterates.

Writing itself is of course also a form of visual communication. Indeed, and paradoxically, the sign of the fully literate social person is the ability to treat writing completely as a visual medium – for instance, not moving one's lips and not vocalizing when one is reading, not even 'subvocalizing' (a silent 'speaking aloud in the head', to bring out the full paradox of this activity). Readers who move their lips when reading, who subvocalize, are regarded as still tainted with the culturally less advanced mode of spoken language. This kind of visual literacy (the 'old' visual literacy) has, for centuries now, been one of the most essential achievements and values of Western culture, and one of the most essential goals of education, so much so that one major and heavily value-laden distinction made by Western cultures has been that between literate (advanced) and non-literate (oral and primitive) cultures. No wonder that the move towards a new literacy, based on images and visual design, can come to be seen as a threat, a sign of the decline of culture, and hence a particularly potent symbol and rallying point for conservative and even reactionary social groupings.

The fading out of illustrations in texts by and for children, then, is not a straight-forward disvaluation of visual communication, but a valuation which gives particular prominence to one kind of visual communication, writing, and to one kind of visual literacy, the 'old' visual literacy. Other visual communication is either treated as the domain of a very small elite of specialists, or disvalued as a possible form of expression for articulate, reasoned communication, seen as a 'childish' stage one grows out of. This is not a valuation of *language* as such over visual communication. Even now the structures, meanings and varieties of spoken language are largely misunderstood, and certainly not highly valued in the education system (with some exceptions, such as in formal 'debating') or in public forums of power.

To sum up: the opposition to the emergence of a new visual literacy is not based on an opposition to the visual media as such, but on an opposition to the visual media in situations where they form an alternative to writing and can therefore be seen as a potential threat to the present dominance of verbal literacy among elite groups.

In this book we want to take a fresh look at the question of the visual. We want to treat forms of communication employing visual images more seriously than they have hitherto been treated. We have come to this position because of the overwhelming evidence of the importance of visual communication, and the staggering inability on all our parts to talk and think in any way seriously about what is actually communicated by means of images and visual design.

In doing so, we have to move away from the position which Roland Barthes took in his essay 'Rhetoric of the image' (1977). In this essay (and elsewhere, as in the introduction to *Elements of Semiology*, 1967a) Barthes argued that the meaning of images (and of other semiotic codes, like dress, food, etc.) is always related to, and, in a sense, dependent on, verbal text. By themselves, images are, he thought, too 'polysemous', too open to a variety of possible meanings. To arrive at a definite meaning, language must come to the rescue. Visual meaning is too indefinite, it is a 'floating chain of signifieds'. Hence, Barthes said, 'in every society various techniques are developed intended to *fix* the floating chain of signifieds in such a way as to counter the terror of uncertain signs; the linguistic message is one of these techniques' (1977: 39). He distinguished between an image–text relation in which the verbal text *extends* the meaning of the image, or vice versa, as is the case, for example, with the speech balloons in comic strips, and an image–text relation in which the verbal text *elaborates* the image, or vice versa. In the former case, which he calls *relay*, new and different meanings are added to complete the message. In the latter case, the same meanings are restated in a different (e.g. more definite and precise) way, as is the case, for example, when a caption identifies and/or interprets what is shown in a photograph. Of the two, elaboration is dominant. Relay, said Barthes, is 'more rare'. He distinguished two types of elaboration, one in which the verbal text comes first, so that the image forms an *illustration* of it, and one in which the image comes first, so that the text forms a more definite and precise restatement or 'fixing' of it (a relation he calls *anchorage*).

Before approximately 1600 (the transition is of course very gradual), Barthes argued, 'illustration' was dominant. Images elaborated texts, more specifically the founding texts of the culture – mythology, the Bible, the 'holy writ' of the culture – texts, therefore, with which viewers could be assumed to be familiar. This relation, in which verbal texts formed a source of authority in society, and in which images disseminated the dominant texts in a particular mode to particular groups within society, gradually changed to one in which nature, rather than discourse, became the source of authority. In the era of science, images, ever more naturalistic, began to function as 'the book of nature', as 'windows on the world', as 'observation', and verbal text served to identify and interpret, to 'load the image, burdening it with a culture, a moral, an imagination'.

This position does, of course, explain elements of communication. Any one of the image–text relations Barthes describes may at times be dominant, although we feel that today there is a move away from 'anchorage': compare for example the 'classic' documentary film in which the viewer is first confronted with 'images of nature', then with the authoritative voice of a narrator who identifies and interprets the images, with the modern 'current affairs' item, in which the viewer is first confronted with the anchor-person's verbal discourse, and only then with the 'images of nature' that illustrate, exemplify and authenticate the discourse. But Barthes' account misses an important point: the visual component of a text is an independently organized and structured message – connected with the verbal text, but in no way dependent on it: and similarly the other way around.

One important difference between the account we develop in this book, and that of earlier semioticians, is our use of work in linguistics. Although this book would not have been possible without the achievements of linguistics, we do not import the theories and methodologies of linguistics into the domain of the visual. We take the view that language and visual communication both realize the same more fundamental and far-reaching systems of meaning that constitute our cultures, but that each does so by means of its own specific forms, and independently.

To give an example. The distinction between 'subjective' and 'objective' meanings has played an important role in our culture ever since the physical sciences began to develop in the sixteenth century. This distinction can be realized (that is, given concrete, material expression, hence made perceivable and communicable) in linguistic as well as in visual codings. The terms 'subjective' and 'objective' can therefore be applied to both. But the *way* the distinction is realized in language is quite different from the way it is realized in images. In language, an idea can, for example, be realized subjectively by using a 'mental process verb' (like *believe*) in the first person (e.g. *We believe that images have their own grammar*); or, objectively through the absence of such a form (e.g. *the grammar of images*). In images the same things can be represented subjectively, through the presence of a perspectival angle, or objectively, through its absence, a point which will be discussed more fully in chapter 4. Mental process clauses and nominalization are unique to language. Perspective is unique to images. But the kinds of *meaning* expressed are from the same broad domain in each case; and the forms, different as they are, were developed in the same period, in response to the same cultural changes. Both language and visual communication express meanings belonging to and structured by cultures in the one society and this results in a considerable degree of congruence between the two.

At the same time, however, each medium has its own possibilities and limitations of meaning. Not everything that can be realized in language can also be realized by means of images, or vice versa. As well as a broad cultural congruence, there is significant difference between the two (and other semiotic codes, of course). The two sets of meaning are therefore neither fully conflated, nor entirely opposed: unlike the view of those who see the meaning of language as inherent in the forms and the meaning of images as derived from the context, or the meanings of language as 'conscious' and the meanings of images as 'unconscious'.

Our approach to communication starts from a social base. In our view the meanings expressed by speakers, writers, printmakers, photographers, painters and sculptors are first and foremost social meanings even though we acknowledge the effect and importance of individual differences. They are meanings which arise out of the society in which individuals live and work. Given that societies are not homogeneous, but composed of groups with varying, and often contradictory, interests, the messages produced by individuals will reflect the differences, incongruities and clashes which characterize social life. It is likely, and in our experience often the case, that the different media through which texts are constructed show these social differences in contrasting encodings – so that in a multimodal text using images and writing, the writing may carry one set of meanings and the images another. In an advertisement, for instance, it may be that the verbal text is studiously 'non-sexist', while the visual text encodes overtly sexist stereotypes.

Our examples in this book are drawn from very many domains, quite deliberately; from different cultures, and from different historical periods. We hope that our ideas will help anyone interested in communication to see in images not only the aesthetic and expressive, but also the structured social, political and communicative dimensions. We will draw examples from the kinds of texts which are already fully based on the new visual literacy and play a dominant role in any public sphere, magazine articles, advertisements, recipe books and so on. This is not because we want to promote these texts as a kind of model which should replace other kinds of texts, but because their role in the lives of children and adults is so important that we simply cannot afford to leave the ability to think and talk about them (and indeed, to produce them) to a handful of specialists. We have a particular interest in the place of the visual in the lives of children, and we hope to show that children very early on, and with very little help (despite all the encouragement), develop a surprising ability to use elements of the visual 'grammar' – an ability which, we feel, should be understood better and developed further, rather than being cut off prematurely as is, too often, the case at present; and an ability that should be available to adults too.

AN UNCONVENTIONAL HISTORY OF WRITING

The dominance of the verbal, written medium over other visual media is firmly coded and buttressed in conventional histories of writing. These go something like this. Language in its spoken form is a natural phenomenon, common to all human groups. Writing, however, is the achievement of only some, historically by far the minority of, cultures. At a particular stage in the history of certain cultures, there developed the need to make records of transactions of various kinds, associated usually with trade, religion or (governing) power. These records were initially highly iconic, that is, the relation between the object to be recorded and the forms and means of recording was close and transparent. For instance, the number of notches in a stick would represent the number of objects stored or traded or owed. The representation of the object would usually also be transparent: a wavy line eventually becomes the Chinese ideogram for 'water'; the hieroglyphic image of the ox's head which initially 'stands for' 'ox' eventually becomes the letter aleph (**א**), alpha (α), *a*. This last example illustrates that rarest of all achievements, the invention of alphabetic writing. In alphabetic writing the image of the object represented has come, over time, to stand at first for the object, then for the abbreviation of the name of the object and eventually for its initial letter: namely, *aleph* – 'ox', to alpha – the letter *alpha*, eventually *a*. This is clearly a step of considerable abstraction, so much so that, seemingly, alphabetic writing has been invented only once in the history of human cultures. All present alphabetic scripts, from Korea, via India, to the Middle East to Europe, are developments of that initial step from Egyptian hieroglyphic representation to the Phoenician alphabet (and from there to Greek, or Sanskrit, or Arabic).

This is indeed impressive; and certainly impressive enough to have stood as the accepted historical account of the achievement of writing unquestioned for centuries. Within this account, all cultures with forms of visual representation that are not directly connected to language are treated as cultures without writing. However, it is worth investigating this history, and in particular the crucial step from visual representation to the link with language, a little more closely. Prior to this step (in reality a development spanning millennia) there are two forms or media of representation. One is language in the form of speech, the other the visual image, or visual marks. Each serves a particular set of purposes (recording/construction of histories, myths, interactions, etc.; recording of objects, transactions, etc.). In the case of some cultures, however, the one form of representation 'takes over' the other, as a means of recording. That is, visual representation becomes specialized to function as a means of the visual representation of speech: perhaps in highly organized and bureaucratized societies. The visual has then been subsumed, taken over, by the verbal. Consequently its former possibilities and its potential for independent representation decline and wither away.

In the case of other cultures, however, this development did not occur. Here the visual continued, along with the verbal means of representation. Instances of this abound: from the one extreme of the Inca quipu strings (an instance very nearly of yet another mode of representation, the tactile) to Australian Aboriginal drawings, sand-paintings and carvings. These encode, in a manner not at all directly dependent on, or a 'translation' of, verbal language, aspects of culture which are deemed to be best represented in visual form. They are, of course, *connected with* language, or, language with them, so that wall-paintings or sand-paintings, for instance, are accompanied by verbal representations of geographical features, journeys, myths, and so on. There is, however, in these cases no question of the priority of the one over the other medium, and the visual has certainly not become subsumed to the verbal as its form of representation.

In this connection it is interesting to consider the history of two words which in a sense are synonymous with Western notions of literacy, the words *grammar* and *syntax*. *Grammar* derives from the Greek *grammatike* ('the art of reading and writing', 'grammar', 'alphabet'); related words were *gramma* ('sign', 'letter', 'alphabet'), *grammatikos* ('literate', '(primary) teacher', 'grammarian'). This etymology records the state of things in the Hellenistic period (from approximately 300BC); in earlier times the meaning 'sign', as in 'painted or drawn (etc.) mark' was the primary meaning. In Homer, for example, the verb *graphein* still means 'scratch', 'scratch in', as in engraving, and from there it comes to mean *both* 'writing' and 'drawing', 'painting'. *Syntaxis*, in pre-Hellenistic times, meant 'contract', 'wage', 'organization', 'system', 'battle formation', with *syntagma*, for instance 'contingent of troops', 'constitution (of a state)', 'book or treatise'. Only in the Hellenistic period does *syntaxis* come to mean (among its other meanings) 'grammatical construction'. The verb *syntasso*, again, means *both* 'arrange battle formations' and 'concentrate (one's thoughts)', 'organize', 'write', 'compose'.

While we do not wish to place too much emphasis on etymology, nevertheless the history of these two words which are so crucial to our notions of literacy, points to forms of social *organization* and *order*, on the one hand, and to *'markings' in the visual media* on the other. Together they indicate the initially quite independent organization of the medium of images and the medium of verbal language. At the same time, the history of the word *grammar* brings out clearly the subordination of the visual medium to the medium of verbal language.

Cultures which still retain the full use of both media of representation are, from the point of view of 'literate cultures', regarded as illiterate, impoverished, underdeveloped, when in fact they have a richer array of means of representation than that overtly and consciously available to literate cultures. Nevertheless, as we pointed out earlier, literate cultures do make use of means of visual communication other than writing, be it that they are seen as uncoded replicas of reality or as a means of individual expression. In other words, they are not treated as either the expressions of, or accessible to means of reading based on, articulated, rational and social meanings.

Our unconventional history of writing is one that treats the coming together of visual and verbal representation as only one possibility, and one, furthermore, that brings with it not just those benefits of writing which are well enough understood, but also the negative aspects incurred in the loss of an independent form of representation, the diminution of modes of expression and representation. From that point of view cultures such as Australian Aboriginal cultures are seen as having both modes of representation: the visual (or perhaps a whole set of visual forms of representation) and the verbal. The point of this history is not only the political one of undermining the notion of 'illiterate culture' (or, 'merely oral culture'), but also the attempt to see to what extent the conventional history blinds us to the facts and uses of visual communication in so-called literate cultures.

In this book we proceed, therefore, to develop the hypothesis that in a literate culture the visual means of communication are rational expressions of cultural meanings, amenable to rational accounts and analysis. The problem which we face is that literate cultures have systematically suppressed means of analysis of the visual forms of representation, so that there is not, at the moment, an established theoretical framework within which visual forms of representation can be discussed.

THE 'OLD' AND THE 'NEW' VISUAL LITERACY IN BOOKS FOR THE VERY YOUNG

So far we have distinguished two kinds of visual literacy: one in which visual communication has been made subservient to language and in which images have come to be regarded as unstructured replicas of reality; another in which (spoken) language exists side by side with, and independent of, forms of visual representation which are openly structured, rather than viewed as more or less faithful duplicates of reality. We have looked at these kinds of visual literacy as historical and cultural alternatives. But they also exist side by side in our own culture, and we suggest that we are in the middle of a shift in valuation and uses from the one mode to the other, from the 'old' to the 'new' visual literacy, in many important social contexts. The examples we will now discuss suggest that the very first books children encounter may already introduce them to particular kinds of visual literacy.

Figure 1.1 shows a typical two-page spread from *Baby's First Book*, a book from the widely distributed Ladybird series which, on its inside cover, declares that 'the text and illustrations, though oversimple to grown-ups, will satisfy their [i.e. the toddlers'] cravings

▲ **Fig 1.1 My bath (from *Baby's First Book*, Ladybird)**

for the repetition of what they already know, and will help them associate the words with the objects'.

Figure 1.2 shows a typical page from Dick Bruna's *On My Walk*. This book is one of a set of four, the others being *In My Home, In My Toy Cupboard* and *On the Farm*. It consists of eight pages, and, with the exception of the front and back covers, the pages contain no words whatsoever.

Compared to the picture of the bird in the tree, the picture of the bath is realistic, detailed and complex. If we were to analyse it into its components, if we were to try and identify all the different elements of this picture, we might encounter problems. Are the ripples in the water to be counted as components? Are the shadows, cast by the tub and towel? And if we were to try and identify the relations between these components, what would we have to say, for example, about the relation between the duck and the soap? We ask these questions because they are the sort of questions with which one might start if one wanted to show that images are structured messages, amenable to constituent analysis. Isn't the structure here that of the cultural object 'bathroom', rather than one imposed by the conventions of a visual code? Isn't this picture unproblematically, transparently readable (recognizable), provided one knows what bathrooms look like?

This is the line Paris School semioticians such as Roland Barthes and Christian Metz took in the 1960s. Commenting on photography, Barthes said:

○   **Fig 1.2 Bird in tree (Bruna, 1988)**

> In order to move from the reality to its photograph it is in no way necessary to divide up this reality into units and to constitute these units as signs, substantially different from the object they communicate. . . . Certainly, the image is not the reality but at least it is its perfect *analogon* and it is exactly this analogical perfection which, to commonsense, defines the photograph. Thus can be seen the special status of the photographic image: *it is a message without a code.*
>
> (Barthes, 1977: 17)

And he extends this argument to other pictorial modes, albeit with a qualification:

> Are there other messages without a code? At first sight, yes: precisely the whole range of analogical reproductions of reality – drawings, paintings, cinema, theatre. However, each of those messages develops in an immediate and obvious way a supplementary message . . . which is what is commonly called the *style* of the reproduction.
>
> (Barthes, 1977: 17)

The picture of the bird in the tree, on the other hand, is much less naturalistic, much less detailed and much simpler than the picture of the bath. It is stylized and conventional, and quite clearly a *coded* image. No depth, no shadows, no subtle nuances of colour: everything is plain and bold and simple. And the structure of the image, with its one central and four marginal images, does not imitate anything in the real world. It is a conventional visual arrangement, based on a visual code. As a result the components of the whole stand out as separate, distinct units, and the picture would seem quite amenable to constituent analysis. This is not just a matter of style: the structure of this picture could also be realized in more detailed styles. Bruna's book dates from 1953, well before the era of computer 'imaging', but the picture of the bird in the tree could have been composed with a computer, aligning ready-made simple icons in a compositional configuration – it is in fact quite similar to the computer-drawn dinner invitation in figure 1.3 – and in computer imaging naturalistic details (texture, depth, etc.) can now be added or subtracted as independent variables.

Second, the picture of the bathroom is accompanied by words. Language comes first, authoritatively imposing meaning on the image, turning it into a typical instance of a bathroom by means of the generic label 'Bath'. As a result the picture could be replaced by other images of bathrooms without much loss of meaning (one verbal text, many images, many possible illustrations). Language bestows similarity and order on the diverse, heterogeneous world of images. Thus the book presents, on the one hand, an 'uncoded', naturalistic representation ('the world as it is' – empirical, factual, specific) and, on the other hand, a specific, authoritatively prescribed way of reading this 'uncoded' naturalistic picture. We will show later that, contrary to what Barthes and others argued in the 1960s, pictures of this kind are also structured, whether they are photographs, drawings, paintings or other kinds of pictures. For the moment, however, the important point is that they are not usually interpreted as such, that awareness of the structuredness

Fig 1.3 Computer-drawn dinner invitation

of images of this kind is, in our society, suppressed and not part of 'commonsense'.

In Dick Bruna's *On My Walk*, by contrast, there are no words to authoritatively impose meaning on the image, and the image is no longer an illustration: the words, rather than the image, come second. Parents who read this book with their children could all tell a different story, even use different languages (one image, many verbal texts). The world of 'one image, many different verbal texts' ('commentaries') imposes a new mode of control over meaning, and turns the image, formerly a record of nature or a playground for children and artists, into a more powerful, but also more rigorously controlled and codified public language, while it gives language, formerly closely policed in many social institutions, a more private and less controlled, but also less powerful status. The 'readings' which parents produce when they read *On My Walk* with their children may all be different, yet these different readings will necessarily have common elements, deriving from their common basis – the elements included in the image, and the way these elements are compositionally brought together. Whatever story parents will tell about the page with the bird in the tree, it will necessarily have to be a story that creates a relation between, for instance, birds and aeroplanes (nature and technology) and birds and cats (prey and predator). It will also have to be a story in which the bird, safely in its tree, is the central character, literally and figuratively. In how many ways can cats and birds be related? Not that many, at least not if one assumes that books like *On My Walk* serve to introduce children to the world around them, rather than to the possible worlds of fantasies and utopias.

Cats can 'hunt', 'torture', 'kill' and 'eat' birds. Birds can 'escape' cats or fail to do so. There are not that many stories to choose from. On the other hand, parents and their children can choose the order in which they want to deal with the various elements: the page is 'non-linear'. It does not impose a sequential structure. And they can choose whether to tell the story of the bird and the cat as a political story, a story of powerful predators coming from another continent and native birds killed and threatened with extinction (as might be done, for instance, in Australia), or as a story that legitimizes the survival of the fittest. The story of the bird and the aeroplane, similarly, may be told from an environmentalist point of view, as a story of evolutionary triumphs and human technological progress. Even where such discourses are not explicitly invoked, they will still communicate themselves to children through the parents' attitudes towards the characters and the actions.

Not only the elements on the individual pages, but also the pages themselves must be brought in relation to each other. The book as a whole must be readable as a coherent sequence. This is prompted by the title (*On My Walk*) as well as by the picture on the front cover, which shows all the elements together. We have investigated this a little further in connection with another book in the Bruna series, *On the Farm*. This book contains the following central pictures: house, farmer, cat, dog, apple tree, rooster, lamb, cow. Listing the ways in which these pictures can plausibly be linked to each other, we found that some (e.g. the apple tree and the house) can only be linked in spatial, locative terms (e.g. the apple tree is next to the house). Others (e.g. the animals and the house) can be related by verbs of 'dwelling' (e.g. the cow lies under the apple tree) or by the verbs of 'motion' (e.g. the cat climbs up the apple tree). Two of the animals (the cat and the dog) can relate to the other animals and to each other by means of antagonistic or co-operative actions (e.g. the dog barks at the cow; the dog leads the sheep). Only the farmer can relate to all the other elements in an agentive way. He can buy them, own them, build them, grow them, keep them, raise them, harvest them, shear them, slaughter them, and so on. In other words, whatever way the parents read these pictures, they will, in the end, have to deal with the theme of spatial order, the theme of social interaction (projected onto animals) and the theme of human mastery over nature (as well as, via the marginal pictures, with the theme of procreation), and they will have to do all this in terms of the elements preselected by the book. An analysis of the way the elements can be opposed to each other shows that, whatever the classifications parents may construct, they will not be able to avoid engaging with the Western cultural distinctions between 'untamed nature', 'domesticated/cultivated nature' and 'human technology'. And they will also have to recognize the distinction between animate and inanimate, flora and fauna, and between pets, farm animals and wild animals.

It should be noted, however, that every page in the book (and in Bruna's other books) contains at least one relation that does not easily fit the received classifications, that forms somewhat of a challenge and a puzzle. What, for example, is the relation between a rabbit and a basket of flowers? A beetle and a fence? Such visual enigmas can challenge parents and children to exercise their imagination, to include in their thinking elements that do not easily fit in with the traditional order of things, to tolerate some ambiguity, to allow the inclusion of the 'other' in their construction of the world.

The two books, then, are very different in their stance towards the image. The Bruna stance presents highly processed, highly essentialized, highly idealized representations, and provides parents and, later, children, with the opportunity to talk about the images in ways which are or seem appropriate to them, to apply specific values, specific discourses to highly abstracted images. The Ladybird stance presents ostensibly less processed, more naturalistic representations and provides parents (and, later on, children) with a specific prescribed way of reading the image. The one book presents itself as open and interactive, the other as closed and authoritarian. Yet, as we have seen, there is closure in the Bruna text too, even though less explicitly and visibly so. This closure lies in the limits which the selection and structure of the images impose on the apparently open readings, as well as in the discourses which are already 'in' the socialized parents, and which, once orally transmitted to the children, will appear spontaneous and 'natural' to parents and children alike. Are they not, after all, merely engaged in an innocent reading of 'what is there' in the pictures? Thus the two books represent two different forms of social control over meaning, one which is openly and explicitly located in the text itself, and one which, more covertly and implicitly, lies in the way the book is less like a text than like a language, a system with which to *make* texts, and in the parental discourses that structure the way texts are made with this language.

These discourses, however, are not themselves part of Bruna's books, of the public text meant to transcend their diversity. Instead they are relegated to the realm of more private or subcultural 'lifestyles' where they do not powerfully threaten the order of the larger social world. There is never just 'heteroglossia' (many meanings), nor ever just 'homoglossia' (one authoritative meaning). Instead there is a role distribution among the different semiotics, a role distribution in which some semiotics are given a great deal of social power, but at the price of being subjected to greater institutional (and techno-logical) control, while others are allowed relative freedom from control, but pay for this with diminished power. Today, we seem to move towards a decrease of control over language (e.g. the greater variety of accents allowed on the public media, the increasing problems in enforcing normative spelling), and towards an increase in codification and control over the visual (e.g. the use of image banks from which ready-made images can be drawn for the construction of visual texts, and, generally, the effect of computer imaging technology).

The two forms of control over meaning can be found elsewhere also. Compare, for example, the classic documentary film, in which an authoritative 'voice of God' narrator explains and interprets images of recorded reality, to the more modern 'direct cinema' documentary in which control over meaning lies in the selection of images and in the sometimes hardly noticeable ways in which these images are edited together. Or think of the way in which, in the field of 'cultural studies', an emphasis on analysing 'what the text says' is gradually being replaced by an emphasis on 'how different audiences read the same text', an emphasis, in other words, on the apparent freedom of interpretation which, by diverting attention away from the text itself, allows the limitations which the text imposes on this 'freedom of reading' to remain invisible, and therefore, perhaps, all the more efficacious and powerful. Or perhaps more insidiously, the transfer from 'what the text says' to 'what this theory constructs this text to be'.

It is interesting, in this connection, to consider the background of the Bruna books. They were first printed in 1953, in Amsterdam, and reprinted many times in their country of origin. The first British printing was in 1978. The time lag is perhaps no accident. Unlike the British, the Dutch have, for most of this century, recognized that their country does not have a 'common culture', but is divided into groups characterized by different and often opposing ideologies, *zuilen* (literally 'columns', 'pillars'), as the Dutch have called them. Dutch broadcasting, for example, had from its inception in the late 1920s a system in which different *levensbeschouwelijke* (i.e. 'orientated towards a particular view of life') groups ran broadcasting organizations which were allotted air time according to the size of their membership. Thus the same events would, on radio and later on television, be interpreted from a variety of different discursive ideological positions, while most other European countries had centralized, usually government-run, broadcasting organizations with one authoritative message. For a message to reach, in this context, the whole population, it had to be adaptable to a variety of cultural and ideological constructions, and, as we have seen, the Bruna books use the visual medium to achieve exactly that. Perhaps the belated success of the series in countries like Britain and Australia shows that there is now, in these countries too, beginning an awareness that they no longer have a 'common culture', and that, instead, they have become complex, diverse and discursively divided, and therefore in need of new forms of communication.

The changing role of distribution between language and image, which, we suggest, is now being implemented, was first attempted in the 1920s in the Soviet Union. While linguists and literary scholars like Volshinov and Bakhtin wrote of language as socially divided, 'multi-accentual' and 'heteroglossic', constructivist artists like Malevich, El Lissitzky and Rodchenko, and film-makers like Eisenstein, rejected naturalism and began to elaborate a new visual language, capable of communicating new, revolutionary ideas visually. Then, as now, images became more stylized, more abstract and more obviously *coded*: the new visual language was explicitly compared with language, with hieroglyphic writing, with the stylized masks of Kabuki theatre. Then, as now, visual communication was also seen as *transparent*: colours and shapes were thought to have a direct, unmediated, 'psychological' impact, a non-semiotic capacity for stirring the emotions of the 'masses'. Then, as now, visual communication was to be *removed from the sphere of art*, to become part of the more powerful and more public sphere of industrial production, of typography, design, architecture. This semiotic revolution was allied to the political revolution: constructivist posters and films had a propagandistic purpose – they sought to help bring about a cultural revolution, and they had to get their message across to a socially and linguistically heterogeneous population. The visual, able to transcend an emotive immediacy, was to be the medium that could achieve this. In the end, the new semiotic order failed to establish itself permanently. It was crushed by Stalin. Old-fashioned centralist and repressive control over meaning (and with it a return to naturalist, 'bourgeois' art) prevailed over control by means of a form of propaganda that

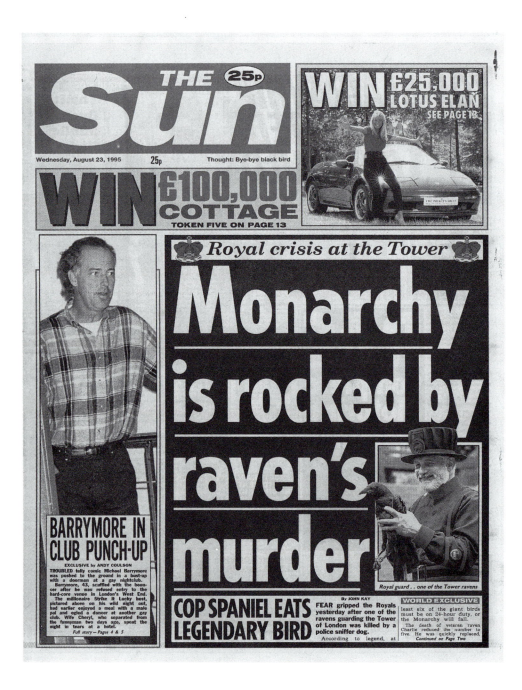

Fig 1.4 Front pages of △ (a) *The Sun* and ▷ (b) *Frankfurter Allgemeine*

(b)

Frankfurter Allgemeine

ZEITUNG FÜR DEUTSCHLAND

2,00 DM   D 2954 A

Dienstag, 22. August 1995, Nr. 194/34 D   Herausgegeben von Jürgen Jeske, Hugo Müller-Vogg, Günther Nonnenmacher, Johann Georg Reißmüller, Frank Schirrmacher

Russische Truppen stürmen Milizgebäude in Tschetschenien

MOSKAU, 21. August (dpa). Russische Elite-Truppen haben am Montag nach Angaben der staatlichen Nachrichtenagentur Itar-Tass das Milizgebäude der tschetschenischen Stadt Argun gestürmt. Dort hatten sich am Sonntag etwa 250 tschetschenische Separatisten verschanzt und vier Polizeibeamte in ihrer Gewalt gehabt, so am Montag aber freigelassen. Wie Itar-Tass unter Berufung auf das russische Oberkommando weiter meldete, war das Gebäude zuvor mit Artillerie beschossen worden. ... (Siehe Seite 5.)

Fünf Tote und hundert Verletzte bei einer Bombenexplosion in Jerusalem

Arafat verurteilt das Attentat / Ministerpräsident Rabin suspendiert die Verhandlungen mit der PLO

jöh. JERUSALEM, 21. August. Bei einem Bombenanschlag auf einen Linienbus in Jerusalem sind am Montag morgen fünf Menschen getötet und etwa hundert verletzt worden. ...

Die Koalitionsparteien streiten über das Kruzifix-Urteil

Gerhardt: Entscheidungen des Verfassungsgerichts akzeptieren / Aufruf zu zivilem Ungehorsam

han. BONN, 21. August. Zwischen den Bonner Koalitionsparteien ist es zu heftigen Auseinandersetzungen über das Kruzifix-Urteil des Bundesverfassungsgerichts gekommen. ...

UN gegen Abschiebung von Abdić-Anhängern nach Bosnien

Flucht von Muslimen und Kroaten aus Banja Luka geht weiter / Vorwürfe gegen Kroatien

ZAGREB, 21. August (dpa/Reuter). Einen Tag nach der Entscheidung Kroatiens, Anhänger des Vereinten Nationen die kroatische Regierung aufgefordert, die in den ehemals besetzten Gebieten Kroatiens festsitzenden 20 000 Muslime aus dem bosnischen Region Bihać nicht gewaltsam nach Bosnien-Herzegowina abzuschieben. ...

Basisentscheid

G.H. Macht ist oft nicht mehr als die Freiheit in der Wahl, wenn man sich unterordnet. ...

Und wenn das Urteil falsch wäre?

Von Friedrich Karl Fromme

Kaum ist je eine Entscheidung der Bundesverfassungsgerichts auf so viel Widerspruch gestoßen wie die, daß die Ausstattung der Schulzimmer in bayerischen Schulen mit Kreuzen gegen das Grundgesetz verstoße. ...

China läßt weiter nach dem neuen Pantschen Lama suchen

PEKING, 21. August. Die Suche nach dem zehnten Pantschen Lama, das nach dem Dalai Lama höchstbuddhistischen Würdenträgers Tibets, ist nach offizieller Pekinger Darstellung längst nicht abgeschlossen. ...

Rühe sagt Litauen deutsche Hilfe zu

VILNIUS, 21. August (AFP). Zum Auftakt seiner Reise durch die baltischen Staaten ist Bundesverteidigungsminister Rühe am Montag in der litauischen Hauptstadt Vilnius (Wilna) eingetroffen. ...

Herzog unterzeichnet das neue Abtreibungsgesetz

BONN, 21. August (AFP). Bundespräsident Herzog hat am Montag in Bonn das neue Abtreibungsgesetz unterzeichnet. ...

Amnestie in Südkorea angekündigt

SEOUL, 21. August (AP). Der südkoreanische Präsident Kim Young-sam hat am Montag eine umfangreiche Amnestie angekündigt. ...

Manfred Donike gestorben

F.A.Z. FRANKFURT, 21. August. Professor Manfred Donike, der Leiter des Instituts für Biochemie der Deutschen Sporthochschule in Köln, ist am Montag, zwei Tage vor seinem 62. Geburtstag, auf einer Dienstreise in den Afrikaspielen in Zimbabwe gestorben. ...

Frankfurter Allgemeine Zeitung GmbH; 60267 Frankfurt am Main; Telefon (069) 7591-0; Telefax 41223; Telefax Anzeigen 7591-2184; Redaktion 7591-1743; Vertrieb 7591-2180 could allow pluralism and ideological cohesion to coexist. This time it may not fail.

The semiotic shift we have exemplified in our discussion of the two children's books can be observed also in other forms of public communication, for instance in newspapers, and in particular on their front pages. Take, as two contrasting examples, the front pages of the German *Frankfurter Allgemeine* and the British *The Sun* (figure 1.4). The examples make the case without further argument, but it is worth remembering how recent these changes are. In the early 1970s, the front pages of *The Sun* were still covered in written language, with only a few, small images – a history already forgotten by most readers of *The Sun*. Such changes have an effect, not only on habits of reading, but also on readers themselves. The reader of *The Sun* is addressed through the medium of the visual (photographs, screamer headlines, colour), with only a small proportion of the page given over to written language. Pleasure, entertainment and immediacy of apprehension determine how 'reading' is constructed here. There is usually only one story on the front page: implicitly this is a statement either that the world is a simple, straightforward place, or that, at the very least, it can be made simple by *The Sun* for its readers. The contrast with the *Frankfurter Allgemeine* hardly needs elaboration. The point is that both sets of readers are habituated to a complex set of practices, which, we would suggest, have far-reaching effects on the formation of their subjectivity and identity. If each of these papers is felt to be reader-friendly by its readers, then each is a very specific kind of friend – and each set of readers a very specific set. Of course, the facts of class and culture intrude here as well. However, a comparison of the *Frankfurter Allgemeine* with either the *Daily Telegraph* or the *Guardian* reveals more similarities between the latter two than between either and the German paper. Like language, the visual is formed in, and produced by, particular cultures.

As another example, consider a page from a science textbook for the lower years of highschool (figure 1.5). Language has here been displaced by the visual as decisively as on the front page of *The Sun* or in the Bruna book: instead of the major medium of information, with the visual as 'illustration', it has become a medium for comment, with the visual as the main source of information. As with the newspapers, two questions need asking: one is the question of implicit changes in notions of reading, and of reading science in particular; the other is the question of changes in the very constitution of science itself. Students of science are no longer addressed in the hierarchically complex structures of scientific writing, with its specific demands for cognitive processing. They are addressed, seemingly, as people whose interests need to be solicited and *won*, who need to be entertained, humoured; a very different notion of reading science from that implicit in the page in figure 1.6, taken from a science textbook published in the 1930s.

More complex is the question whether, in this dramatic shift from the verbal to the visual, the very constitution of the school subject science is undergoing a transformation. Can everything that was communicable in the formation of scientific writing be said in these visually constructed pages? Conversely, are there possibilities of scientific communication in the visual which were not available in the medium of writing? And which of these is a more apt medium for scientific theory? Will scientific theories change as the form of expression shifts from the written to the visual medium? We cannot take up these

Using stored chemical energy

⬭ **Fig 1.5 Contemporary science textbook (*Suffolk Coordinated Science*, 1978)**

questions here, but if we are to make ourselves conscious of the far-reaching implications of these changes in the semiotic landscape, they need at least to be asked.

This is a central question, and it needs to be put openly, and debated seriously: is the move from the verbal to the visual a loss, or a gain? Our answer at this stage in our thinking is multiple. There are losses, and there are gains. Our argument throughout this book will be that different semiotic modes – the visual, the verbal, the gestural, etc. – each have their potentialities, and their limitations. A move from a central reliance on one to a central reliance on another will therefore inevitably have both kinds of effect. But that is not the end of the story. We also have to consider what is represented. It may be that visual representation is more apt to the stuff of science than language was, or even, that a science which is constructed visually will be a different kind of science. The world represented visually in the mass media is a different world – and produces different citizen/subjects – from the world represented in language.

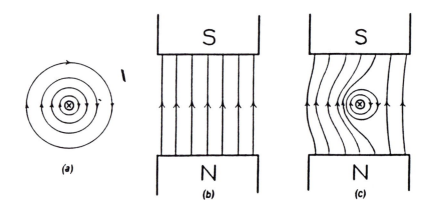

⬤   Fig 1.6 Early twentieth-century science textbook (McKenzie, 1938)

More far-reaching questions would ask about the changing nature of societies – as we did in the comparison of the Bruna and Ladybird books – and would ask about the different economic/technological world of tomorrow. Could it be the case that information is now so vast, so complex that, perhaps, it *has* to be handled visually, because the verbal is no longer adequate?

Mere nostalgia, mere social and cultural regrets or pessimism cannot help here. We, all of us, have our particular standpoints, values from yesterday or from the day before yesterday. The first most important challenge is to understand this shift, in all of its detail, and in all of its meaning. From that understanding, we can hope to begin the task of constructing adequate new value systems.

To summarize:

(1) Visual communication is always coded. It *seems* transparent only because we know the code already, at least passively – but without knowing what it is we know, without having the means for talking about what it is we do when we read an image. A glance at the 'stylized' arts of other cultures should teach us that the myth of transparency is indeed a myth. We may experience these arts as 'decorative', 'exotic', 'mysterious' or 'beautiful', but we cannot understand them as communication, as forms of 'writing' unless we are, or become, members of these cultures.

(2) Societies tend to develop ways for talking about codes only with respect to codes that are highly valued, that play a significant role in controlling the common under-standings any society needs in order to function. Until now, language, especially written language, was the most highly valued, the most frequently analysed, the most prescriptively taught and the most meticulously policed code in our society. If, as we have argued, this is now changing in favour of visual communication, educationalists should perhaps begin to rethink what 'literacy' ought to include, and what should be taught under the heading of 'writing' in schools. If schools are to equip students adequately for the new semiotic order, if they are not to produce people unable to use

the 'new writing' actively and effectively, then the old boundaries between 'writing' on the one hand, traditionally the form of literacy without which people cannot adequately function as citizens, and, on the other hand, the 'visual arts', a marginal subject for the specially gifted, and 'technical drawing', a technical subject with limited and specialized application, should be redrawn. This will have to involve modern computer technology, central as it is to the new semiotic landscape. But, above all, it is crucially dependent on having the means of analysis, the means for talking about the 'new literacy', about what it is we do when we produce and read images. As Iedema (1994: 64) notes, in the 'post-Fordist' workplace:

> Workers must be multi-skilled, articulate and 'self-steering'. . . . [They] nego-
> tiate their jobs as members of 'quality circles' and consultative committees.
> This requires that workers are not merely capable of *doing* their work, but also
> that they are capable of talking and thinking about their work and its
> effectiveness.

Given the importance of visually displayed information in so many significant social contexts, there is an urgent need for developing adequate ways of talking and thinking about the visual, and it is to this end that we hope to make a contribution with this book.

THE SEMIOTIC LANDSCAPE

The place of visual communication in a given society can only be understood in the context of, on the one hand, the range of forms or modes of public communication available in that society, and, on the other hand, their uses and valuations. We refer to this as 'the semiotic landscape'. The metaphor is worth exploring a little, as is its etymology. Just as the features of a landscape (a field, a wood, a clump of trees, a house, a group of buildings) only make sense in the context of their whole environment ('waste land' has meaning only in that context, as has 'field' or 'track'), so particular modes of communication should be seen in *their* environment, in the environment of all the other modes of communication which surround them, and of their functions. The use of the visual mode is not the same now as it was even fifty years ago in Western societies; it is not the same from one society to another; and it is not the same from one social group or institution to another.

Each feature of a landscape has its history, as does the landscape as a whole, and each is subject to constant remaking. It is here that the etymology of the word *landscape* is revealing. While to the casual beholder a landscape simply *is*, and may even have a timeless appearance ('the timeless beauty of the English, or Spanish, countryside'), it is in fact a product of social action and of a social history, of human work on the land, on nature: *-scape*, with its relatives *to shape* in English and *schaffen* (both 'to work' and 'to create') in German, indicates this. And this applies also to the 'semiotic landscape'. Metaphoric excursions of this kind can be stretched too far; however, we will allow ourselves one other point of comparison. Landscapes are the result, not just of human social work, but also of the characteristics of the land itself. The flat land by the river is most suitable for the grazing of cattle or the growing of wheat; the hillsides for vineyards or forestry. At the same time, the characteristic values of a culture may determine which of the potential uses of the land are realized, whether the hillsides are used for vineyards or forestry, for example. And cultural values may even induce people to go against the grain of the land, to use the steep hillside for growing rice, for example, which opposes the 'natural potential' of the land almost to the limit.

Semiotic modes, similarly, are shaped both by the intrinsic characteristics and potentialities of the medium and by the requirements, histories and values of societies and their cultures. The characteristics of the medium of air are not the same as those of the medium of stone, and the potentialities of the speech organs are not the same as those of the human hand. Nevertheless, cultural and social valuations and structures strongly affect the uses of these potentialities. It is not an accident that in Western societies written language has had the place which it has had for the last three or four millennia, and that the visual mode has in effect become subservient to language, as its mode of expression in writing. Linguistic theories have more or less naturalized the view that the use of air and the vocal organs is the natural, inevitable semiotic means of expression. But even speech is, in the end, cultural. We are not biologically predisposed to use speech as our major mode of communication. Indeed, there is some evidence that the adaptation to speech of the physical organs which developed initially to prevent humans from choking while breathing *and* eating, have begun to lead to some ineffectiveness of these organs for their original task. When the need arises, we *can* and do use other means of expression, as in the highly articulated development of gesture in sign languages, and also in theatrical mime and certain Eastern forms of ballet. And while these are at present restricted to relatively marginal domains, who is to say that this will always remain so in the future development of humankind?

The new realities of the semiotic landscape are, as we have already indicated, primarily brought about by social and cultural factors: by the intensification of linguistic and cultural diversity within the boundaries of nation states, and by the weakening of these boundaries, due to multiculturalism, electronic media of communication, technologies of transport and global economic developments. Global flows of capital and information dissolve not only cultural and political boundaries but also semiotic boundaries. This is already beginning to have the most far-reaching effects on the characteristics of English (and Englishes), globally, and even within the national boundaries of England.

The place of language in public forms of communication is changing. Language is moving from its former, unchallenged role as *the* medium of communication, to a role as *one* medium of communication, and perhaps to the role of the medium of comment, albeit more so in some domains than in others, and more rapidly in some areas than in others. Although this is a relatively new phenomenon in public communication, children do this quite 'naturally'.

New modes of thinking are needed in this field. Here we use, once more, the metaphor of children's representation to suggest some directions. The drawings reproduced in figure 1.7 were made by a five-year-old boy. On a summer Sunday afternoon, while his parents were entertaining friends, the child took a small, square notepad from near the telephone, and drew a picture on each of six pages. His father had not noticed this until he came across him in the hall of their house, where the child was putting the cards 'in order', as shown in figure 1.7. Asked what he was doing, the child's account was as follows: for pictures 1 and 2 together 'Me and the dog are in life, so they're in the correct order'; on pictures 3 and 4 'The flying bomb is in the air and the plane is in the air, so they're in the correct order'; and on 5 and 6 'The patterns are in the correct order'.

Clearly, these acts, involving sign-making, representation and classification, had proceeded through the visual medium. It was only when the parent came along with his question that the child was forced to use words. The metaphoric processes of sign-making, involving complex analogies and acts of classification, took place in the visual, and so did the act of representation. Language, in the spoken mode, entered the situation when communication with the parent became necessary, after the child was asked a question.

Some two weeks later, at the end of the summer term of his primary school, the child

1   2

"ME AND THE DOG ARE IN LIFE, SO THEY'RE IN THE CORRECT ORDER"

3   4

"THE FLYING BOMB IS IN THE AIR AND THE PLANE IS IN THE AIR, SO THEY'RE IN THE CORRECT ORDER"

5   6

"THE PATTERNS ARE IN THE CORRECT ORDER"

Fig 1.7 Six drawings by a five-year-old boy

Draw a line to join the things which are the same.

○ **Fig 1.8 School exercise book of a five-year-old boy**

brought home some of his exercise books. Among these was the page shown in figure 1.8. The task was clearly one of classification, and it had been undertaken at school, prior to the making and ordering of the drawings in figure 1.7, at home. A whole sequence of semiotic activities is thus involved, a sequence of production, transformation and development, moving from the relatively simple classificatory, cognitive, conceptual, semiotic and manual task of joining similar image categories, to that of producing complex and dissimilar images, and finding likeness in them (or imposing likeness on them) through an intermediary task of abstraction and generalization. The child's production of metaphoric signs involved a series of distinct semiotic modes, and translations between such modes: first the teacher *spoke* with the children about the task (language/speech); then she introduced the book and *showed* them what was at issue (physical object/visual mode); then the children used their pencils to *draw* the connecting lines (a manual action as much as a semiotic act – as anyone will appreciate who has seen a five-year-old holding a pen and making a line). All this took place in a particular affective, emotional state which affected how the activity was 'read' and taken up by the child – in other words, the affective acted continuously as a modality on cognitive semiotic processes. Next, the teacher engaged the children in *spoken* discussion, and made evaluatory comments. This was followed by a long period of 'silence' – a fortnight or so when nothing was seen or heard, but when, we assume, the series of transformative acts of the child continued 'internally', 'mentally'. Finally the internal activity became visible, literally, through the child's unprompted production of the drawings, his unprompted classificatory activity and his spoken commentary in response to his father's question.

The child, in part in response to the representational, semiotic and cognitive resources made available by the teacher, used a series of different representational media (including, of course, 'internal representations') in a constantly productive, constantly transformative sequence of semiotic activities, which, in turn, transformed his subjectivity. And these activities were not at all confined to the medium of language. Indeed, the visual, rather than language, was his central representational and cognitive resource. And language was used, not for cognition, but for communication with adults, as a translation medium, a medium of comment. It may well be that the complexities realized in the six images and their classification were beyond the child's capacity of expression, of conception and formulation, in spoken language, and that the visual medium offered semiotic and cognitive resources which were not available to him in the verbal medium. However, once expressed in the visual medium, and once classified *through* the visual medium, the meanings which the child had produced became available, in some part at least, for verbal expression.

This incessant 'translation', or 'transcoding', between a range of semiotic modes, represents, we suggest, a better, a more adequate understanding of representation and of communication. In the example we have discussed here, language is not in the centre. In many areas of public communication the same is either the case already, or rapidly coming to be the case. And clearly, it matters which semiotic modes of representation and communication are dominant, most frequent, most valued in the public domains in which we act.

Figure 1.9 comes from a science textbook for children in the early to middle years of secondary schooling in England. Two questions can be asked. The first: 'What is the effect of the mode of representation on the epistemology of science?', 'Do different modes of representation facilitate, or rule out, different accounts of natural phenomena?' The second question is, again, the question of subjectivity: the implied reader of this page is a fundamentally different reader from that of the older textbook shown in figure 1.6. Readers who have become habituated to the contemporary textbook page not only have a different conception of what science is, but also of what (being) a scientist is. They have different notions of authority relations, of the status of science as a discipline, of epistemological positions, and so on – just as the designers of this page have different conceptions of these questions to those of the page shown in figure 1.6.

Again, what is the status of written language in these pages? In figure 1.6 it is the

Fig 1.9 Science textbook (*Suffolk Coordinated Science*, 1978)

central medium, the medium of information. Images have the function of illustrating an argument carried by the written word, that is, of presenting ('translating') the contents of the written language in a different medium. The subjectivity of the reader is here formed in, and implied by, the hierarchic organization of the mode of (scientific) writing. It is a subjectivity which treats language naturally as the medium of information, the medium of truth, and of truth transmitted relatively transparently in the syntax of the writing; and it is a subjectivity habituated to sustained, concentrated analysis, attention, reflection. In figure 1.5, by contrast (shown again on this page, in figure 1.9), images are the central medium of information, and the role of language has become that of a medium of commentary. Images (and this includes the layout of the page) carry the argument. The subjectivity of the reader is formed in a mix of semiotic modes in which the visual is clearly dominant. It is a subjectivity which relies on the visual rather than on the verbal, as a medium of entertainment as much as a medium of information; information in fact becomes relatively marginal as an aim, both on the part of the student and on the part of the textbook designer, though for different reasons. It is also a subjectivity habituated to the more ready apprehension of the transparently presented visual. The apprehension of facts displaces the concern with truth, and the emphasis is not on sustained, concentrated analysis, but on the quick apprehension of facts and information.

The shift is based on changed relations of power in two distinct areas: in the area of social valuations of scientific knowledge, where the authority of science can no longer be taken for granted; and in the area of education, where the authority of the transmitters of social values can no longer be taken for granted, but has to be *achieved*. In this set of relations the subjectivity of the student readers in relation to power and authority is changed. They no longer accept the social valuations of science and education accepted by most earlier students, even if many of them turned away from internalizing them as their own.

As before, we wish to avoid a negative evaluation here. The earlier notions of language, truth and authority have, over the last two decades, been shown, quite decisively to have been ideological constructs, serving the interests of certain groups and not of others. A nostalgic yearning for these older verities is as misguided as a quick dismissal, or worse, of the facility of the new forms. The question is and remains: what social changes are at work here, and how can we understand them in their interrelations with larger social, economic and technological changes?

These changes in the semiotic landscape also reveal what has in fact always been the case: language, whether in speech or writing, has always existed as just one mode in the totality of modes involved in the production of any text, spoken or written. A spoken text is not just verbal but also visual, combining with 'non-verbal' modes of communication such as facial expression, gesture, posture and other forms of self-presentation. A written text, similarly, involves more than language: it is written *on* something, on some *material* (paper, wood, vellum, stone, metal, rock, etc.) and it is written *with* something (gold, ink, (en)gravings, dots of ink, etc.); with letters formed in systems influenced by aesthetic, psychological, pragmatic and other considerations; and with a layout imposed on the material substance, whether on the page, the computer screen or a polished brass plaque. The multimodality of written texts has, by and large, been ignored, whether in educational contexts, in linguistic theorizing or in popular common sense. Today, in the age of 'multimedia', it can suddenly be perceived again.

We can summarize this discussion in the form of a set of hypotheses: (a) human societies use a variety of modes of representation; (b) each mode has, inherently, a different representational potential, a different potential for meaning-making; (c) each mode has a specific social valuation in particular social contexts; (d) different potential for meaning-making may imply different potentials for the formation of subjectivities; (e) individuals use a range of representational modes, and therefore have available a range of means of meaning-making, each affecting the formation of their subjectivity; (f) the different modes of representation are not held discretely, separately, as autonomous domains in the brain, or as autonomous communicational resources in a culture, nor are they deployed discretely, either in representation or in communication; rather, they intermesh and interact at all times; (g) affective aspects of human behaviour and being are not discrete from other cognitive activity, and therefore never separate from representational and communicative behaviour; (h) each mode of representation has a continuously evolving history, in which its semantic reach can contract or expand or move into different areas as a result of the uses to which it is put.

As modes of representation are made and remade, they contribute to the making and remaking of human societies and of the subjectivities of their members. None of these hypotheses would, we imagine, attract significant disagreement, especially when put singly. Together, however, they represent a challenge to the existing common sense on the relations between language and thought, and on mainstream theories and practices in all areas of public communication. This is a crucial feature of the new semiotic landscape. In the pages and chapters which follow we will attempt to describe the contours of this landscape in detail, focusing on the potentialities of its characteristic features as well as on the work that has gone into its making.

A NOTE ON A SOCIAL SEMIOTIC THEORY OF COMMUNICATION

The visual, like all semiotic modes, has to serve several communicational (and representational) requirements, in order to function as a full system of communication. We have adopted the theoretical notion of 'metafunction' from the work of Michael Halliday for the purpose of dealing with this factor. The three metafunctions which he posits are the *ideational*, the *interpersonal* and the *textual*. In the form in which we gloss them here they are not specific to any one semiotic mode: for instance, they are not specific to the linguistic.

The ideational metafunction

Any semiotic system has to be able to represent, in a referential or pseudo-referential sense, aspects of the experiential world outside its particular system of signs. In other words, it has to be able to represent objects and their relations in a world outside the representational system. That world may of course be, and most frequently is, the world of other semiotic systems.

In doing so, semiotic systems offer an array of *choices*, of different ways in which objects can be represented, and different ways in which they can be related to each other. Two objects may be represented as involved in a process of interaction which could be visually realized by vectors:

A ⟶ B

○ **Fig 1.10 Vector**

But objects can also related in other ways, for instance in terms of a classification. They would be connected, not by a vector, but, for instance, by a 'tree' structure:

◐ **Fig 1.11 Tree structure**

In chapters 2 and 3 we will investigate precisely which ideational choices are available for visual sign-making in this way.

The interpersonal metafunction

Any semiotic system has to be able to project the relations between the producer of a sign or complex sign, and the receiver/reproducer of that sign. That is, any semiotic system has to be able to project a particular social relation between the producer, the viewer and the object represented.

As in the case of the ideational metafunction, semiotic systems offer an array of different 'interpersonal' relations, some of which will be favoured in one form of visual representation (say, in the naturalistic image), others in another (say, in the diagram). A depicted person may address viewers directly, by looking at the camera. This conveys a sense of interaction between the depicted person and the viewer. But depicted persons may also be turned away from the viewer, and this conveys the absence of a sense of interaction. It allows the viewer to scrutinize the represented characters as though they were specimens in a display case.

In chapters 4 and 5 we will discuss these and other interpersonal choices, both in terms of the kinds of interactions that can be represented, and in terms of the pictorial characteristics that realize these interactions.

The textual metafunction

Any semiotic system has to have the capacity to form *texts*, complexes of signs which cohere both internally and with the context in and for which they were produced. Here, too, visual grammar makes a range of resources available: different compositional arrangements to allow the realization of different textual meanings. In figure 1.1, for example, the text is on the left and the picture on the right. Changing the layout (figure 1.12) would completely alter the relation between text and image, and cause the image, rather than the text, to come first, and to serve as point of departure, as 'anchor' for the message. In chapter 6 we will discuss such left–right relationships and other compositional resources.

Our focus, then, is on the description of these ideational, interpersonal and textual

Bath

Every night
I have my bath
before I go
to bed.

Fig 1.12 Altered layout of figure 1.1 (left–right reversal)

resources. But as we have noted already, we recognize that in doing this work of 'mere description' we are ourselves participating in the reshaping of the semiotic landscape; and we realize also that this is by no means an unproblematic activity, but a highly political enterprise.

2 Narrative representations: designing social action

INTRODUCTION

The pictures shown in figure 2.1, are taken from an Australian primary school social studies textbook (Oakley *et al.*, 1985). One represents the traditional technology of the Australian Aborigines, the other the superior technology of those who invaded their territory ('The British had a technology that was capable of changing the face of the earth. Their tools were able to work faster than those of the Aborigines and their weapons were much more powerful'). The former has three main elements (an axe, a basket and a wooden sword), the latter four (the 'British', as they are called in the caption, their guns, the Aborigines and the landscape). But the two pictures differ not only in what each includes and excludes (the left picture, for instance, excludes the *users* of the technology, the right picture includes them), they differ also in structure: they relate their elements to each other differently. The elements of the left picture are arranged symmetrically, against a neutral background: axe, basket and wooden sword are represented as equal in size, placed at equal distance from each other and orientated in the same way towards the horizontal and the vertical axes, so that the picture as a whole creates a relation of similarity between the three elements. The picture says, as it were: this axe, this basket and this wooden sword all belong to the same overarching category (a category,

^ The British used guns

< Stone axe, bark basket and wooden sword

○ **Fig 2.1 The British Used Guns (Oakley *et al.*, 1985)**

incidentally, which is only implied, and which conflates the notion of 'tools' and the notion of 'weapons').

The right picture represents technology in action. Where the left picture is impersonal, this picture is personal. Where the left picture is static, this picture is dynamic. Where the left picture is dry and conceptual, this picture is dramatic. It relates the British and the Aborigines through a transactional schema in which the British play the role of 'Actor', the element that does the deed, and the Aborigines the role of 'Goal', the element to which the deed is done – the British *stalk* the Aborigines, one could say. It also relates the landscape to the British and the Aborigines in a 'locative' way (the British and the Aborigines are *in* the landscape), and the gun to the British in an 'instrumental' way (the British stalk the Aborigines *with* their guns).

These relations can be transformed into linguistic form, as we have just done, but the point is that here they are realized by pictorial means. The transactional relation between the British and the Aborigines is realized by the vector that links them, namely the oblique lines formed by the glances and outstretched arms of the British and by their guns. The locative relation is realized by overlapping, by the gradients of focus, by colour saturation and so on, which create the contrast between foreground and background. And the instrumental relation is realized by the gesture of holding, where the object held is a tool.

The important point at this stage is not the detail of the analysis, but the observation that the semiotic code of language and the semiotic code of pictures each have their own quite particular means of realizing what in the end are perhaps quite similar semantic relations. What in language is realized by words of the category 'action verbs' is in pictures realized by elements that can be formally defined as *vectors*. What in language is realized by locative prepositions, is realized in pictures by the formal characteristics that create the contrast between foreground and background. This is not to say that all the relations that can be realized in language can also be realized in pictures, or vice versa, that all the relations that can be realized in pictures can also be realized in language. Rather, a given culture has a range of general, possible relations which is not tied to expression in any particular semiotic code, although some relations can only be realized in pictures and others only in words, or some more easily in pictures and others more easily in words. This distribution of realization possibilities across the semiotic codes is itself determined historically and socially as well as by the inherent potentialities and limitations of a semiotic medium.

To return to the two pictures in figure 2.1, they can be said to represent an aspect of the experiential world, technology. But through the different design patterns selected in each, through the manner in which each brings its individual elements together into a coherent and meaningful whole, they represent the technology of Aborigines very differently from the technology of the British. Nothing about Aboriginal technology necessitates it to be represented as a static, conceptual taxonomy, nor is there anything intrinsic about British technology that requires it to be represented in a personalized and dramatized way. British technology is just as capable of being represented by a classificatory scheme as is Aboriginal technology, and it is just as possible to tell dramatic stories of Aborigines stalking their invaders with spears or wooden swords as it is to tell such stories about the British, even if the former kind of story does not usually form part of mainstream Australian history. In other words, the representation is mediated, visually, through two distinct discourses: that of anthropology for Aboriginal people – who know no history; and that of history for the whites – who are not subjects of anthropology.

Imagine a reversal of those relations. Imagine on the left a catalogue of British tools and weapons, and on the right a picture in which Aborigines point their wooden swords at a small group of British in the background. Suddenly a representation of colonization as the transition from a fixed, stable ('primitive') order of things to the dynamic unfolding of history is changed into something like the revenge of the 'primitive' on the West's technological order. Suitable for a fiction film, perhaps, set safely in an apocalyptic future, but not for a primary school textbook.

The two design patterns in figure 2.1, the classificatory pattern and the transactional pattern, are only two of several possible patterns. In the course of this chapter we will introduce others, and try to give an overview of the visual structures that can realize ways of representing the world. Our emphasis will not therefore be on depiction in the first place, nor on the question of how we can recognize configurations of pencil marks or brush strokes or pixels as pictures of trees, nor on how pictures of trees may connote or symbolize meanings and values over and above what they literally represent. This aspect of the pictorial has already received a good deal of attention in the writings of philosophers (e.g. Goodman, 1969; Hermeren, 1969), semioticians (e.g. Eco, 1976a; Barthes, 1977), media analysts (Williamson, 1978) and art historians (e.g. Panofsky and Bryant, 1970). At this stage of our work on visual communication we have little to add to what they have said in these areas.

The question of visual structuring, on the other hand, has, in our opinion, been dealt with less satisfactorily. Visual structuring has either been treated as simply reproducing the structures of reality (e.g. Metz, 1974a, 1974b), rather than as creating meaningful propositions by means of visual syntax, or it has been discussed in formal terms only (e.g. Arnheim, 1974, 1982, who in his actual analyses offers many insights about the semantic dimension of visual structuring). Our example of the representation of Aboriginal and British technology has, we hope, made clear why neither of these approaches satisfies us. Pictorial structures do not simply reproduce the structures of 'reality'. On the contrary, they *produce* images of reality which are bound up with the interests of the social institutions within which the pictures are produced, circulated and read. They are ideological. Pictorial structures are never merely formal: they have a deeply important semantic dimension.

PARTICIPANTS

In chapter 1 we defined the ideational metafunction as the ability of semiotic systems to represent objects and their relations in a world outside the representational system or in the semiotic systems of a culture. In the introduction to the present chapter we tried to show how two design patterns can produce two different representations of broadly the same aspect of the world. Instead of 'objects' or 'elements' we will, from now on, use the technical term 'participants', or more precisely, 'represented participants'. The term has two advantages: it points to the relational characteristic of 'participant *in* something'; and it draws attention to the fact that there are two kinds of participant involved in every semiotic act, the *interactive participants* and the *represented participants*. The former are the participants in the act of communication – who speak and listen or write and read, make images or view them; the latter are the participants who are the subject of the communication, that is, the people, places and things (including abstract 'things') represented in and by the speech or writing or image, the participants *about* whom or which we are speaking or writing or producing images.

The situation is of course more complex than this, for the real interactive participants, the real image-producers and -viewers, cannot be taken to be identical with the 'implied' producer who 'silently instructs us, through the design of the whole' (Chatman, 1978: 148) and the 'implied' viewer. It may also be that the producers and/or viewers are themselves explicitly represented in the image, causing the two categories to shade into each other, complexities which have been studied extensively in the field of literary narratology (e.g. Iser, 1978; Bal, 1985; Rimmon-Kenan, 1983). We will return to these in the next chapter; for the purposes of this chapter the basic distinction will suffice.

In the case of highly abstract pictures such as diagrams, it does not seem too difficult to determine who or what the represented participants are. Shannon and Weaver's famous 'communication model' (figure 2.2), for instance, is made up of boxes and arrows. The boxes represent participants (people and/or things, the distinction being blurred by objectivating labels like 'information source' and 'destination'); the arrows represent the processes that relate them. If we wanted to transform this into language, we could say that the boxes are like nouns, the arrows like verbs (e.g. 'send' or 'transmit'), and that, together, they form clauses (e.g. 'an information source sends [information] to a transmitter').

In the case of more detailed naturalistic images, however, it may be difficult, even futile, to try and identify the represented participants. Take 'The British used guns', for instance (figure 2.1). Do we include the hats and kerchiefs worn by the two men? Every single tree, every single one of the rocks strewn about in the foreground? The analogy with language loses its relevance here. In language words such as *man, gun, tree, rocky ground*

⬦ **Fig 2.2 Shannon and Weaver's communication model**

abstract away from details of this kind. In naturalistic images this does not happen. They are 'worth a thousand words'.

Yet we think that naturalistic images can be analysed into participants and processes much in the same way as diagrams. There are two different, but in the end compatible, ways of arguing this. The first is the way of formal art theory (e.g. Arnheim, 1974, 1982). The language of this kind of theory is, for the most part, formalistic, and grounded in the psychology of perception. Participants are called 'volumes' or 'masses', each with a distinct 'weight' or 'gravitational pull'. Processes are called 'vectors' or 'tensions' or 'dynamic forces'. But, and this is what matters for the purpose of identifying participants, these 'volumes' are perceived as distinct entities which are salient ('heavy') to different degrees because of their different sizes, shapes, colour, and so on. Thus the two men in figure 2.1 stand out as a distinct entity because of the tonal contrast between their silhouettes and the light of the fire. And what is more, we recognize their shapes on the basis of visual schemas not unlike those that are realized in diagrams. Artists have long learned their craft by reducing the visible world to simple geometric forms (see Gombrich, 1960). According to Arnheim (1974: Ch. 4), children learn to draw in the same way, building up a repertoire of basic forms, and then, gradually, 'fusing the parts'. If the perception of pictures does indeed operate on the basis of the same principles as the production of pictures, we might grasp the overall structure of a picture like 'The British used guns' according to a schema (as in figure 2.3) not so different from that of Shannon and Weaver's communication model.

The second way of identifying participants is that of functional semiotic theory (see Halliday, 1978, 1985). The conceptual apparatus of this kind of theory has, so far, been

⬤   Fig 2.3 Schematic reduction of figure 2.1, showing vector

applied only to language, the most frequently and methodically analysed semiotic system. It is orientated towards the semantic functions rather than towards the forms of the participants. It uses terms like 'Actor', 'Goal' and 'Recipient', rather than terms like 'volume' and 'mass'. Yet the two approaches are compatible. The most salient 'volumes' in 'The British used guns' are not only perceptually most conspicuous, they also play the most crucial *roles* in the grammatical structure that constitutes the meaning of the picture: the two men (the participant from which the vector en:anates) have the role of *Actor*, and the Aborigines (the participant at which the vector points) have the role of *Goal* in a structure that represents their relation as a *Transaction*, as something *done by* an Actor *to* a Goal. The same terms ('Actor', 'Goal', 'Transaction') are used in functional linguistics. This is possible because they are semantic-functional, rather than formal terms. Our use of these terms does not imply that images work in the same way as language, only that they can 'say' (some of) the same things as language – *in very different ways*: what in language is realized by means of syntactic configurations of certain classes of nouns and certain classes of verbs is in pictures realized, made perceivable and communicable, by the vectorial relations between volumes. In Arnheim's words: 'We shall distinguish between volumes and vectors, between being and acting' (1982: 154).

The transactional structure is not the only kind of structure which images can realize. We have already discussed an example of a classificatory structure (a subject which we will take up in more detail in a later section, pp. 81–8). In the picture in figure 2.4, taken from the same social studies textbook as figure 2.1 (Oakley *et al.*, 1985), the structure

▲   **Fig 2.4 Antarctic explorer (Oakley *et al.*, 1985)**

is 'analytical'. Here the participants have the roles not of 'Actor' and 'Goal' but of 'Carrier' and 'Attribute'. This picture is not about something which participants are *doing* to other participants, but about the way participants *fit together* to make up a larger whole. It has the structure of a map. Just as in maps a larger participant, the 'Carrier', represents the 'whole' (say, Australia), and a number of other participants, the 'Possessive Attributes', represent the 'parts' (say, the states of Australia), so the Antarctic explorer functions as 'Carrier', and the balaclava, the windproof top, the fur mittens, etc. function as 'Possessive Attributes', as the parts that make up the whole. The closest linguistic transcoding here is not an action clause like 'The British point their guns at the Aborigines', but a 'possessive attributive' clause like 'The outfit of the Antarctic explorer *consists of* a balaclava, a windproof top, fur mittens . . .' (etc.).

We can now look at the abundance of detail in naturalistic images in a new way. The naturalistic image, whatever else it may be about, is always also about detail. It contains a multitude of *embedded* 'analytical' processes. It may, at the most salient level, say 'The British point their guns at the Aborigines', but it will also, at less immediately conspicuous levels, say things like 'The men's outfits consist of hats, kerchiefs . . . (etc.)' and 'The trees have clumps of leaves.' In language, prepositional phrases (*two men* **with hats and kerchiefs**) and subordinate clauses (*two men,* **wearing hats and kerchiefs**) fulfil the same function of adding detail at a 'secondary' or even more deeply embedded level.

Embedding can also occur in diagrams. Take the 'communication model' in figure 2.5, a model drawn up, not by two telecommunication engineers, as in the case of Shannon and Weaver (figure 2.2), but by two sociologists, Riley and Riley (1959). As a whole, the diagram is 'analytical'; it is a kind of abstract map. It shows that the 'over-all social system' consists of 'larger social structures' which in turn consist of 'primary groups'. It also features two individuals, 'C' ('Communicator') and 'R' ('Recipient'). These are depicted as half in, half out of the 'larger social structures' and they are connected to, though not part of, the 'primary groups'. Embedded within this analytical structure is a transactional structure: the 'larger social structures' and the individuals 'C' and 'R' are

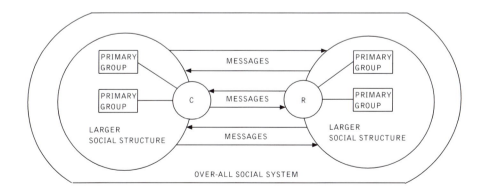

●   **Fig 2.5 Communication model (from Watson and Hill, 1980: 143)**

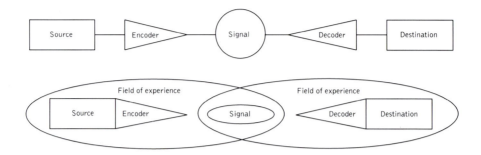

⬤ **Fig 2.6 Two communication models (from Watson and Hill, 1980: 147)**

represented as involved in an active process of communication, realized by vectors.

When we look at 'The British used guns' (in figure 2.1) as a transactional structure, the two men form one participant: together they have the role of 'Actor'. When we look at the two men as an 'analytical' structure, they form two distinct participants, linked by the lines formed by the hand of the man on the right and the gun of the man on the left. Diagrams allow further possibilities, as can be seen in the two communication models in figure 2.6, both drawn by Schramm (1954), a social psychologist writing about mass communication. In the first model, 'source' and 'encoder' are separate entities, *conjoined* by a line, just as are the two men in 'The British used guns' – we will argue later that lines without arrowheads realize a particular kind of 'analytical' structure:

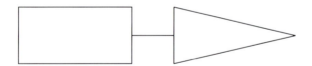

⬤ **Fig 2.7 Conjoining participants**

In the second model, 'source' and 'encoder' are *compounded*, welded together yet still distinct components of the whole:

⬤ **Fig 2.8 Compounding of participants**

The third possibility is a complete *fusion* between 'source' and 'encoder'; we have not found an actual example of this as yet.

⬤ Fig 2.9 Fusion of participants

However, the shape of Riley and Riley's 'overall social system' (figure 2.5) can be interpreted as such a fusion – a fusion of two circles and a box. Apparently participants can lose their separate identity to different degrees. When they are conjoined, the process, the act of connecting them, is still explicit, realized by a line. When they are compounded, their identities remain distinct, but there is no longer an explicitly expressed process to connect them. When they are fused, even their separate identities have disappeared. In language, similarly, we can move from, say, *The bird is black*, which has two distinct participants as well as a connecting process (*is*); to *the black bird*, which has *black* and *bird* still as different words, but removes the process; to *the blackbird*, in which two words have been fused to become one noun. Each step further obscures the act of predication, the explicit act of bringing the two participants together, until the structure is no longer 'analytical', no longer analysed or analysable.

As with many other kinds of diagram, the communication models we have used to illustrate this section are explained or paraphrased in the verbal texts that accompany them. Yet not everything that is expressed in the diagrams is also expressed in the verbal texts. Not all of the meanings conveyed visually are also conveyed verbally. The meanings of the visual shapes, the boxes and circles and triangles that give the participants their volume, for example, are almost always left unexplained. Older, commonsense or theoretical notions, such as 'illustration' (images 'illustrating' verbal texts) or 'explanation' (words 'explaining' diagrams) are no longer an adequate account of the relations between words and pictures, here as in other instances. Why, in figure 2.6, is the 'signal' a circle, the 'source' a rectangle, the 'encoder' a triangle? Why, in figure 2.5, is the 'primary group' a rectangle, while the 'larger social structure' and the individuals 'C' and 'R' are circles? Why do Shannon and Weaver (figure 2.2) prefer angularity, while Riley and Riley prefer curvature (figure 2.5)?

There can be little doubt that such choices are charged with meaning. The basic geometrical shapes have always been a source of fascination, even of religious awe. Our scientific age is no exception. Circles, squares and triangles have been regarded as pure, quasi-scientific 'atoms' of the visible world, a 'pure manifestation of the elements', the 'universal-as-the-mathematical', as Mondriaan said (quoted in Jaffé, 1986: 54–5). And they have been thought to have the power to directly affect our nervous system, for instance by the constructivist artist Gabo: 'The emotional force of an absolute shape is unique and not replaceable by any other means. . . . Shapes exult and shapes depress, they elate and make desperate' (quoted in Nash, 1974: 54). As we are here primarily concerned with the relations between participants, this subject falls somewhat outside our main concern, and really deserves a separate study. But it may still be worth while at least to indicate the issues with which such a study might be concerned.

In our society, squares and rectangles are the elements of the mechanical, techno-logical order, of the world of human construction. They dominate the shape of our cities, our buildings, our roads. They dominate the shape of many of the objects we use in daily life, including our pictures, which nowadays rarely have a round or oval frame, though other periods were happy to use these to frame more intimate portraits in particular. Unlike circles, which are self-contained, complete in themselves, rectangular shapes can be stacked, aligned with each other in geometrical patterns: they form the modules, the building blocks with which we construct our world, and they are therefore the dominant choice of builders and engineers, and of those who think like builders and engineers. In art, they are the choice of geometrical abstractionists, artists for whom art has to be, above all, rational. As Mondriaan wrote in the 1920s:

> In all fields life grows increasingly abstract while it remains real. More and more the *machine* displaces natural power. In fashion we see a characteristic tensing of form and intensification of colour, signifying the departure from the natural.
>
> *In modern dance steps* (boston, tango, etc.) the same tensing is seen: the curved line of the old dance (waltz etc.) has yielded to the straight line, and each movement is immediately neutralized by a counter-movement – signifying the search for equilibrium. Our *social life* shows this too: autocracy, imperialism with its (natural) rule of power, is about to fall – if it has not fallen already – and yields to the (spiritual) power of law.
>
> Likewise the new spirit comes strongly forward in *logic, science and religion*. The imparting of veiled wisdom yields to the wisdom of pure reason; and knowledge shows increasing exactness. The old religion, with its mysteries and dogmas, is increasingly thrust aside by a clear relationship to the universal.
>
> (quoted in Jaffé, 1967: 64)

Glosses in 'dictionaries of visual symbols' and similar publications tend to express the meaning of geometrical shapes in terms of intrinsic, abstract qualities, but they point in the same direction. According to Dondis (1973), the square represents 'honesty, straightness and workmanlike meaning' (p. 44); according to Thompson and Davenport (1982: 110), it 'represents the world and denotes order'.

Circles are glossed very differently in such dictionaries, as denoting 'endlessness, warmth, protection' (Dondis, 1973: 44), or as 'the traditional symbol of eternity and the heavens' (Thompson and Davenport, 1982: 110). But such descriptions can be multiplied endlessly: the more abstract the sign, the greater its semantic extension; or, to put it in our terms, the greater its potential range of uses as a signifier in signs. We need to look for the principles that unite these meanings, and for the fundamental oppositions between square and circle, between the angular and the curved. In organic nature, squareness does not exist.

Mondriaan admitted that his method of 'abstracting the curve' made it difficult to represent nature: 'In painting a tree, I progressively abstracted the curve; you can understand that very little "tree" remained' (quoted in Jaffé, 1967: 120). Circles and curved forms generally are the elements we associate with an organic and natural order, with the world of organic nature – and such mystical meanings as may be associated with them derive from this. Angularity we associate with the inorganic, crystalline world, or with the world of technology, which is a world we have made ourselves, and therefore a world we can, at least in principle, understand fully and rationally. The world of organic nature is not of our making, and will always retain an element of mystery. Curved forms are therefore the dominant choice of people who think in terms of organic growth rather than mechanical construction, in terms of what is natural rather than in terms of what is artificial. In art, it is the choice of what is sometimes called 'biomorphic abstractionalism' – the curves, blobs and bulges in the paintings of Hans Arp or the sculptures of Henry Moore.

The values attached to these poles of meaning – that is, the actual signs produced with the signifiers of the 'technological' and the 'natural' – do of course differ. The square can connote the 'technological' positively, as a source of power and progress, or negatively, as a source of oppression which, literally and figuratively, 'boxes us in'. In Riley and Riley's communication model (figure 2.5) society is represented as a natural order, organically evolved rather than humanly constructed. But the 'primary groups' are depicted as rectangles. Perhaps this betrays an unconscious bias in favour of modern urban society, a view in which the small, close-knit community in which everyone knows everything about everyone, is seen as oppressive, and the 'larger social structure' as liberating, providing the individual with anonymity, and thereby with autonomy and self-containment, choice and freedom. For Riley and Riley, individuals hail from 'primary groups' (and are still connected to them, albeit tenuously), but then go their own way, leaving the 'primary groups' behind, and moving freely in and out of the 'larger social structures', in a socially mobile world. This example shows that diagrams, rational and scientific as they may seem, can convey meanings visually that are not necessarily also conveyed verbally.

The triangle is angular, like the square – an element of the mechanical, technological order. But, unlike the square, the triangle, especially when tilted, is a (fused structure of) a participant and a vector, because it can convey directionality, point at things. The meanings it attracts are therefore less like 'qualities of being' than like processes, as in the well-known revolutionary poster by El Lissitzky (figure 2.10), in which the revolution, represented by a red triangle, is an active, dynamic force, wedging itself into the inert, self-contained, 'organic' society of White Russia.

In diagrams, triangles can similarly introduce a sense of process. The triangles in figure 2.6, for instance, could be seen as 'focusing' or 'aiming' the 'message' (we have already indicated why it is so difficult to give verbal transcodings of visual processes and we will discuss this more fully later). Not surprisingly, glosses of the meanings of triangles in visual dictionaries reflect this dynamic quality. Triangles are 'a symbol of generative power' (Thompson and Davenport, 1982: 110), and represent 'action, conflict, tension' (Dondis, 1973: 44).

⬭ **Fig 2.10** *Beat the Whites with the Red Wedge* **(El Lissitzky, 1919) (from Nash, 1974)**

The meanings of the basic geometrical shapes, then, are motivated in two ways. First, they derive from the properties of the shapes, or rather, from the values given to these properties in specific social and cultural contexts. The straight line, for instance, means what it, literally, is: 'straight'. This 'straightness' may then be used to carry any one of a vast range of meanings compatible with that. It may be positively valued in one context (e.g. the 'straight and narrow path', or Mondriaan's association of straightness with the 'spiritual power of law'), less positively in another (e.g. 'the straight man' as opposed to the 'funny man', or 'straight' as opposed to 'gay'). The producers of an image have their interests in making the visual sign, and this makes the meaning of the image quite specific for the producer, it colours in and makes specific the abstract meanings that derive from the cultural properties of the shapes. Rectangles can be stacked – and, again, this may be positively valued in one context, say in urban planning, or in geometric abstractionism, less positively in another, say in countercultures that dream of living in geodesic domes, or in biomorphic abstractionism. Second, these meanings derive from the common qualities we may detect in such objects in our environment as would be circular or rectangular when abstracted to their underlying basic shape, and from the values attached to these qualities in different social contexts. The sun, the moon, the belly of the pregnant woman, are curved. The skyscraper, the executive desk, the expensive briefcase, are rectangular. Such common qualities as we may see in these groups of objects (say, 'nature's cycles' and 'male power') will evidently be read and valued differently in different social contexts – and the groupings of objects from which we derive these meanings are likely to be made selectively, so as to obtain the common qualities sought. Finally, our argument suggests that the semiotic genesis of diagrams lies, not just in technical drawing, but also in art, and specifically in the abstract art movements of our century, which no longer fill out and corporealize the schematic reductions which naturalistic artists have used for centuries, and which, if the Gestaltists are right, underlie all visual representation.

From the basic shapes other geometrical shapes can be derived: square, circle and triangle can be horizontally or vertically elongated to different degrees; and the square, the triangle, and all elongated shapes can be tilted, either towards the right, or towards the left. *Vertical elongation* creates a more pronounced distinction between top and bottom, and hence a bias towards hierarchy, and towards 'opposition' generally (what is most important or otherwise dominant goes on top, what is less important or dominant is relegated to the bottom). *Horizontal elongation* causes a shape to lean towards the kind of structure in which what is positioned on the left is presented as 'Given', as information that is already familiar to the reader and serves as a 'departure point' for the message, while what is positioned on the right is presented as 'New', as information not yet known to the reader, and hence deserving his or her special attention. The shape of Schramm's 'field of experience' and 'signal' in the second diagram of figure 2.6, for instance, suggests that these participants are, at least potentially, endowed with such an information structure. *Tilting*, finally, creates oblique lines and hence a sense of vectoriality. In Malevich's *Red Square and Black Square* (figure 2.11) the participants are represented as squares. But because the red square is tilted, the painting is structurally more similar to El Lissitzky's *Beat the Whites with the Red Wedge* (figure 2.10) than, for instance, to Mondriaan's compositions of red, yellow and blue squares: it is about dynamic action, whereas Mondriaan's compositions are about a stable order, a 'search for equilibrium'.

Finally, it is important to stress the essential *interchangeability* of visual and verbal participants in diagrams, and, indeed, in many other visual genres. Although the *processes* and *structures* in diagrams are always visual, the participants which they relate to each other may be of different kinds: pictures, naturalistic or schematic; abstract shapes, with or without verbal labels; words, either enclosed or not enclosed in boxes or other shapes; letters; and so on. The same thing can be seen in page layout: the participants are heterogeneous. They can be verbal (headlines, blocks of copy, etc.), but the semiotic means which bring them together into a coherent semantic structure are always visual. The key to understanding such texts therefore lies above all in an understanding of the visual semiotic means which are used to weld these heterogeneous elements into a coherent whole, into a text. Visual structures relate visual elements to each other; these visual elements, however, may themselves be heterogeneous – a word as a visual element, a block of written text as a visual element, an image as a visual element, a number or an equation as a visual element.

○ Fig 2.11 *Suprematist composition: Red Square and Black Square* (Kasimir Malevich, 1914) (from Nash, 1974)

NARRATIVE PROCESSES

When participants are connected by a vector, they are represented as *doing* something to or for each other. From here on we will call such vectorial patterns *narrative* (in Kress and van Leeuwen, 1990, we used the term 'presentational') and contrast them to *conceptual* patterns (see figure 2.12). Where conceptual patterns represent participants in terms of their class, structure or meaning, in other words, in terms of their generalized and more or less stable and timeless essence, narrative patterns serve to present unfolding actions and events, processes of change, transitory spatial arrangements. In the following chapter we will discuss the three principal kinds of conceptual processes, namely classificational, analytical and symbolic processes. In this chapter we will concern ourselves with narrative processes.

○ Fig 2.12 Main types of visual representational structure

The hallmark of a narrative visual 'proposition' is the presence of a vector: narrative structures always have one, conceptual structures never do. In pictures, these vectors are formed by depicted elements that form an oblique line, often a quite strong, diagonal line, as in 'The British used guns' (in figure 2.1), where the guns and the outstretched arms of the British form such a line. The vectors may be formed by bodies or limbs or tools 'in action', but there are many other ways to turn represented elements into diagonal lines of action. A road running diagonally across the picture space, for instance, is also a vector, and the car driving on it an 'Actor' in the process of 'driving'. In abstract pictures such as diagrams, narrative processes are realized by abstract graphic elements, for instance lines with an explicit indicator of directionality, usually an arrowhead. Such features of directionality must always be present if the structure is to realize a narrative representation: connecting lines without an indicator of directionality form a particular kind of analytical structure, and mean something like 'is connected to', 'is conjoined to', 'is related to' (see chapter 3).

The 'Actor' is the participant from whom or which the vector departs, and which may be *fused* with the vector to different degrees. In *Beat the Whites with the Red Wedge* (figure 2.10), for instance, the red triangle is both participant and vector, and represents both the 'wedge' and the act of wedging in (or 'beating', as the title has it). In figure 2.13, taken from a factual children's book about France (Bender, 1988), the Actors are realized

⬖ Fig 2.13 *Gulf Stream and Mistral* (Bender, 1988)

by the colour of the arrows (the 'Gulf Stream' vector is red, the 'Mistral' vector blue), and the narrative processes are realized by the vectors themselves. In Shannon and Weaver's communication model (figure 2.2), on the other hand, Actor and process are realized by separate visual elements, the Actor by a box ('information source'), the process by an arrow. Pictures like 'The British used guns' (in figure 2.1) occupy, perhaps, an intermediate position.

In the case of pictures, the context usually makes clear what kind of action the vectors represent. 'The British used guns' (in figure 2.1) can be transcoded not so much with 'used', as the caption has it, as with something like 'The British stalk the Aborigines with their guns.' Other transcodings are of course possible, but the field of possibilities is limited. The vectors in abstract pictures are more difficult to transcode. One first needs to formulate what they, literally, formally, *do*. This can then help to circumscribe the field of possible readings. The triangle in El Lissitzky's *Beat the Whites with the Red Wedge* (figure 2.10) literally *wedges itself into* the white circle. This opens up a perhaps large, but by no means infinite range of possible readings: the triangle can be said to 'pierce' or 'infiltrate' or 'destabilize' the circle. In fact it does all these things: the process represents a field of possible meanings. In the case of Malevich's *Suprematist composition* (figure 2.11), the red square literally *tilts towards* the black square above it. How can we transcode this? Does the red square 'aspire to' or 'point at' or 'aim at' or 'direct its attention towards' or 'line up to move towards' the black square? All these readings are legitimate. The point is that each reading will have the small red square as the mobile and active participant, however much it is dominated by the big, heavy black square, and the black square as static, as motionless, and monolithic. The picture tells the story of an 'underling' going into action against the forces that keep him or her or it down. Who or what this underling or these forces are the readers will produce in the process of reading: although the shapes and colours will point them in a certain direction, make certain readings more plausible, more like those of the producer's than others.

In the case of diagrams it is also difficult to say in words just what kind of action the vectors represent. The commonsense view of the function of images as 'illustration' and 'explanation' would be that the accompanying verbal text explains what is not made clear visually. But usually this is not so. Usually the process is represented only visually, and the text either does not paraphrase it at all, or provides contradictory or misleading glosses. The Shannon and Weaver communication model has been 'quoted' and verbally explained in many books and articles, for instance in Watson and Hill's *Dictionary of Communication and Media Studies* (1980), which has a 250-word entry about the model, and in a *Scientific American* article by Pierce, a telecommunications engineer (1972). The first gives the following indications of the meaning of the vectors: the authors say that the model 'can be applied to any information *transfer* system' and they call it a '*process-centred model*' (p. 149, our italics). Two rather oblique references, one a broad gloss, 'process', the other only slightly more specific, 'transfer'. Pierce's explanations are contradictory. On the one hand, he calls the model a 'system' (as do Watson and Hill in the dictionary) and paraphrases it in terms of an analytical rather than a narrative structure: 'The system *consists of* an information source, a transmitter, a communication channel, a noise source, a receiver and a message destination' (p. 32, our italics) – note that he lists only the participants, not the processes. On the other hand, when he gives an example, he paraphrases the vectors by means of active verbs:

> A human being may *type* a message consisting of the letters and spaces on the keyboard of a teletypewriter. The teletypewriter *serves as* a transmitter that *encodes* each character as a sequence of electrical pulses, which may be 'on' or 'off', 'current' or 'no current'. These electrical pulses *are transmitted* by a pair of wires to another teletypewriter that *acts* as a receiver and *prints out* the letters and spaces.
>
> (Pierce, 1972: 33, our italics)

These are just two examples where others are possible. The meaning potential of diagrammatic vectors is broad, abstract and hence difficult to put into words. The accompanying texts tend to be much more explicit about participants, about things existing in space (or represented as though they are), than about processes, events and actions. Scientific and bureaucratic language, and many forms of expository writing generally, put most of their meaning in the nouns rather than in the verbs. Verbs, in these forms of language, remain restricted to a relatively small set of (logical) connectors ('is', 'has', 'leads to', 'causes', 'generates', 'develops into', and so on), almost as though they were 'function words', like articles and pronouns, rather than 'content words'. In his book *Factual Writing* (1985: 40), Martin gives an example:

> There is little doubt that television coverage of a domestic slaughtering operation, conducted in a government approved abattoir, which involved the slaughter of lambs, calves and swine, would generate a good deal of public revulsion and protest.

In this extract most of the specific actions appear in noun form, and some have been *nominalized*, that is, turned into nouns from prior full clausal forms ('doubt', 'coverage', 'slaughtering operation', 'slaughter', 'revulsion', 'protest'). In a text of thirty-seven words there are only two main verbs ('is' and 'generate'), both very general. Doings and happenings have been turned into things. The dynamic of action has been changed into the static of relations. Diagrams do something similar. They represent events which take place over time as *spatial configurations,* and so turn 'process' into 'system' – or into something ambiguously in between, something that can be called either 'system-centred' or 'process-centred'. Diagrams are in this respect akin to certain forms of nominalizing writing, while naturalistic images, with their human participants and their more concrete, specific processes, are akin to story-writing. Like many naturalistic images, stories are about human or animate beings and the things they do, and in stories much more meaning is put into verbs than in most non-narrative forms of writing.

Because their meaning is so abstract and general, vectors can represent fundamentally different processes as though they were the same (for instance, 'humans typing letters and spaces on a keyboard' and 'teletypewriters transmitting electrical pulses'). Diagrams of the Shannon and Weaver type can impose two models of interpretation on one situation or perhaps one model on many: here the two models are 'transport' and 'transformation'. The diagram represents what is going on either as *transport*, movement from one place to another, or as the more or less causally determined *transformation* from one thing into another. And because one sign, the arrow, can represent both, the two meanings often become conflated: movement, transport *is* transformation; mobility *is* the cause of and condition for change, growth, evolution, progress. The Shannon and Weaver model, for instance, represents communication as transport, as moving information from one place to another, but it also and at the same time represents communication as the transformation of messages into signals, of 'letters and spaces' into 'electrical pulses'. In the Gulf War diagram in figure 2.14, taken from the *Sydney Morning Herald* (14 February 1991), war planes *move* towards the town of Khafji. But there is also a transformation involved. The planes' movement effects a change of state: it recaptures the town.

The arrows in the 'system networks' of systemic–functional grammar (our diagram in

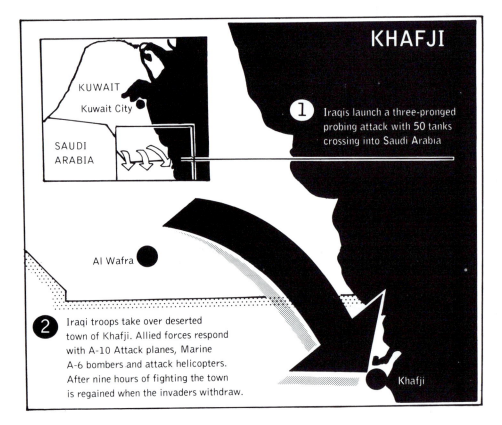

⬥ **Fig 2.14 Gulf War diagram (*Sydney Morning Herald*, 14 February 1991)**

figure 2.12 is such a 'system network') are usually transcoded by 'choose' or 'select' (e.g. '"Conceptual" selects "Classificational", "Analytical" or "Symbolical"'). But visually the process is, again, a combination of transport and transformation. And when such networks are turned into computer programs, as indeed they have been, the visual metaphor becomes a reality in which there are not people 'choosing' between 'options', but pulses transported to points at which a change of state occurs. At that point the schematic reduction of one semiotic reality has turned into a blueprint for another, new semiotic reality, and people will have been reduced to the role of 'source' and 'destination' in an autonomized and exteriorized semiotic process, just as they are in Shannon and Weaver's communication model.

Different kinds of narrative process can be distinguished on the basis of the kinds of vector and the number and kind of participants involved.

1 Action processes

The Actor is the participant from which the vector emanates, or which itself, in whole or in part, forms the vector (as with the triangle in figure 2.10). In pictures they are often also the most salient participants, through size, place in the composition, contrast against background, colour saturation or conspicuousness, sharpness of focus, and through the 'psychological salience', which certain participants (e.g. the human figure, and even more so, the human face) have for viewers. In figure 2.1, for instance, the British are larger than the Aborigines, and placed in the foreground. In the Shannon and Weaver communication model, the 'information source' and the 'noise source' are Actors (we will comment on their different position in the diagram, and on the different directionality of their arrows, in chapter 6):

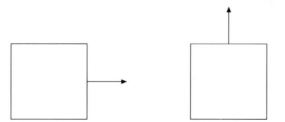

○ **Fig 2.15 Actors**

When diagrams have only one participant, this participant will always be the Actor. The resulting structure we call *non-transactional*. The action in a non-transactional structure has no 'Goal', is not 'done to' or 'aimed at' anyone or anything. The non-transactional action process is therefore analogous to the intransitive verb in language (the verb that does not take an object). In the picture in figure 2.16 the principal Actor is formed by Ben Hur (Charlton Heston) and his chariot, the process by the vector created by the diagonal line of action. Ben Hur 'races', but he does not race anything or

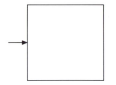

Fig 2.16 Charlton Heston in *Ben Hur* (Wyler, 1959)

anyone, at least not so far as we can see in this picture. The processes in figure 2.13 are also non-transactional: the water of the Gulf Stream does not move *something*, it just moves; and the wind of the Mistral does not blow *something*, it just blows. This visual representation is akin to the way meteorological processes are represented in English: *it rains*, or *it snows*. As Halliday has pointed out (1985: 102), other languages do not necessarily do this. In one Chinese dialect, for instance, one has to say something like 'The sky is dropping water', in other words, raining has to be represented as a transactive process.

When a narrative visual proposition has two participants, one is the Actor, the other the *Goal*. The Goal is the participant at whom the vector is directed, hence it is also the participant *to whom* the action is done, or *at whom* the action is aimed:

Fig 2.17 Goal

The Actor in such a *transactional* process is not so much the participant which moves (as in the non-transactional process) as the participant which instigates the movement, and if we were to give a verbal paraphrase of a transactional process, we would probably use a transitive verb, a verb that takes an object (e.g. 'transport' or 'send' instead of (intransitive) 'move').

In 'The British used guns' (in figure 2.1), the two men are the Actor, the Aborigines are the Goal. There is, in fact, a second transactional process: there are also vectors formed by lines that can be drawn from the heads of the Aborigines to the fire, and so constitute a process in which the Aborigines are Actor and the fire Goal. 'The Aborigines surround the fire', one could transcode. But the point is not to find a verbal equivalent, the point is to establish that the Aborigines are represented as Actor and the fire as Goal. Because of its smaller size and placement further towards the background, this process is a 'minor process', embedded in the major process. The whole could be transcoded as 'The British stalk the Aborigines, who surround the fire.'

It is possible that structures such as the Shannon and Weaver diagram have been affected by the structure of English, with its lexical distinction of verbs/processes and nouns/objects. So arrows as vectors/processes and boxes as participants/nouns may be a more or less unconscious translation from language into the visual. We feel that it is most important here to insist on the distinct organization of the two media. The visual structure of arrows and boxes conveys a strong sense of 'impacting' or 'targetting', which is quite absent in any of the verbal translations which come most immediately to mind. The visual structure foregrounds procedure over substantive content, the act of 'impacting' over what makes the impact, more or less in the way that, for instance, marketing experts are often more concerned about strategies for reaching consumers than about the goods and services that should reach them, or pedagogic experts more concerned about the format of classroom interaction than about the content of lessons.

Some transactional structures are bidirectional, each participant playing now the role of Actor, now the role of Goal, as for instance in de Saussure's well-known 'speech circuit' diagram (figure 2.18) in which 'A' and 'B' are now speaker, now listener. It is not always clear whether bidirectional transactions are represented as occurring simultaneously or in succession, although there is a tendency to use one arrow with two heads to signify simultaneity, and two arrows pointing in different directions to signify sequentiality. In

Fig 2.18 Speech circuit (de Saussure 1974 [1916])

○ Fig 2.19 Simultaneous bidirectionality ◑ Sequential bidirectionality

figure 2.18, for instance, sequentiality is realized by two separate dotted lines (line and arrowhead, connection and directionality, are separate elements in this diagram).

We will refer to the participants in such structures as *Interactors*, to indicate their double role.

2 Reactional processes

When the vector is formed by an eyeline, by the direction of the glance of one or more of the represented participants, the process is *reactional*, and we will speak, not of Actors, but of *Reacters*, and not of Goals, but of *Phenomena*. The Reacter, the participant who does the looking, must necessarily be human, or a human-like animal – a creature with visible eyes that have distinct pupils, and capable of facial expression. The Phenomenon may be formed either by another participant, the participant at whom or which the Reacter

○ Fig 2.20 Simultaneous and sequential bidirectionality (*Vittel* advertisement, from *New Idea*, 5 December 1987)

Fig 2.21 *Claire's Knee* (Rohmer, 1972)

is looking, or by a whole visual proposition, for example a transactional structure. In figure 2.20, for instance, an advertisement for mineral water, the man is Actor in a transactional action process in which the water is Goal ('the man drinks water', one might transcode): the whole angle of his body forms a strong vector between the two represented participants. This process ('man drinks water') then becomes the Phenomenon of a reactional structure in which the woman is Reacter: a vector, formed by the direction of her glance and the angle of her left arm, leads from her to the drinking man. She reacts to his action, with a smile of approval (the precise nature of reactions is coloured in by facial expression). The man as doer, the woman as faithful admirer of his actions is a distribution of roles which, as Goffman has shown in his *Gender Advertisements* (1976), is very common in advertisements (and not only in advertisements): 'When a man and a woman collaborate in an undertaking, the man is likely to perform the executive role' (Goffman, 1976: 32).

Figure 2.21, a still from Eric Rohmer's film *Claire's Knee* shows a subtle interplay of action and reaction. The woman's leg is Actor in a non-transactional action structure, and this structure becomes the Phenomenon of the man's admiring gaze. The man, in turn, becomes the Phenomenon of the girl's pensive look.

Like actions, reactions can be transactional or non-transactional. In the latter case there is no Phenomenon. We see someone looking at something outside the picture frame, but what it is he or she is looking at we cannot see. If the Reacters in such pictures are women, they often seem to gaze into the middle distance, as if they have mentally withdrawn from their immediate surroundings. If they are men, they tend to have their eyes firmly fixed on far horizons. It is then left to the viewer to imagine what they are thinking about or looking at, and this can create a powerful sense of empathy or identification with the represented participant (figure 2.22).

Sometimes photograph or picture editors crop photos back to close ups of non-

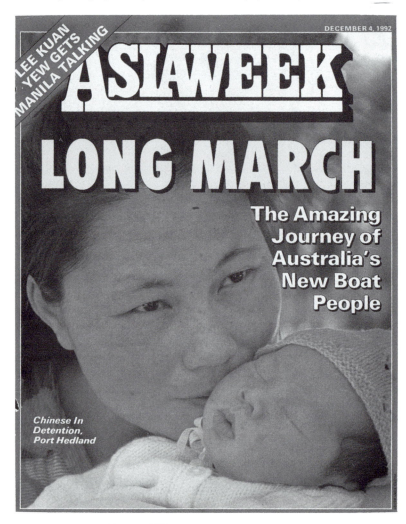

⬣　Fig 2.22　Cover of *Asiaweek*, 4 December 1992

transactional Reacters who look bored, or animated, or puzzled, at something we cannot see. This can become a source of representational manipulation. A caption may, for example, suggest what the Reacter is looking at, but, needless to say, it need not be what the Reacter was actually looking at when the picture was taken. Stuart Hall (1982) has described how this kind of manipulation is used in press photographs of politicians.

3 Speech process and mental process

A special kind of vector can be observed in comic strips: the oblique protrusions of the thought balloons and dialogue balloons that connect drawings of speakers or thinkers to their speech or thought. Until recently they were confined to the comic strips, although there have of course also been speech processes in medieval art, for instance in the form of ribbons emanating from the speaker's mouth. Today they increasingly crop up in other contexts too, for instance in connection with quotes in school textbooks, or on the screens of automatic bank tellers (figure 2.23). Like transactional reactions, these processes connect a human (or animate) being with 'content', but where in transactional reactions it is the content of a perception, in the case of thought bubbles and similar devices it is the content of an inner mental process (thought, fear, etc.) and in the case of speech vectors the content of the speech. Halliday (1985: 227ff.) calls this kind of structure 'projective'. The Phenomenon of the transactional Reaction, and the content of the dialogue balloon or thought balloon are not represented directly, but mediated through a Reacter, a 'Senser' (in the case of a thought balloon), or a 'Speaker' (in the case of the dialogue balloon).

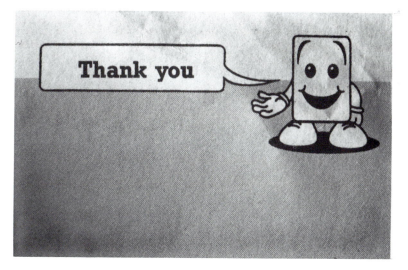

△ Fig 2.23 Cartoon character on ATM receipt

4 Conversion processes

The Shannon and Weaver communication model (figure 2.2) forms a *chain* of transactional processes. This chaining results in a third kind of participant, a participant which is the Goal with respect to one participant and the Actor with respect to another. Shannon and Weaver's 'transmitter' is such a participant, acting as Goal with respect to the 'information source' and as Actor with respect to the 'receiver'. We will call this kind of participant *Relay* (see figure 2.24; our use of this term obviously differs from that of Barthes, 1977, who uses it to denote an image-text relation in which the text extends, rather than elaborates ('anchors'), the visual information). Relays do not just pass on, in unchanged form, what they receive, they always also transform it, for instance from 'letters and spaces' into 'electrical pulses', or, as in figure 2.26, from 'grasses, sedges and flowers' into 'urine, droppings and dead carcasses'.

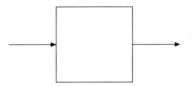

◐ Fig 2.24 Relay

While the Shannon and Weaver model represents communication as a chained process with a beginning and an end, hence as an agentive process, a process set into motion by an Actor, other models, such as that shown in figure 2.25, represent communication as a cycle, and in that case all the participants are Relays, and agency is more weakly signified. This kind of process, which we will call a *Conversion* process, is especially common in representations of natural events, for instance food chain diagrams or

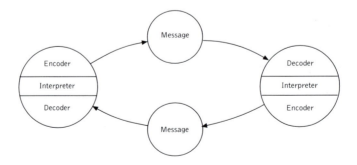

◐ Fig 2.25 Communication model (from Watson and Hill, 1980: 147)

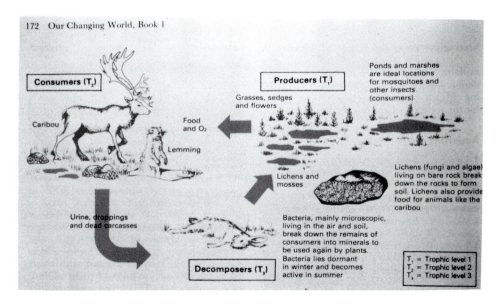

172 Our Changing World, Book 1

Consumers (T₂)

Caribou

Food and O₂

Lemming

Producers (T₁)

Grasses, sedges and flowers

Ponds and marshes are ideal locations for mosquitoes and other insects (consumers)

Lichens (fungi and algae) living on bare rock break down the rocks to form soil. Lichens also provide food for animals like the caribou

Lichens and mosses

Urine, droppings and dead carcasses

Decomposers (T₃)

Bacteria, mainly microscopic, living in the air and soil, break down the remains of consumers into minerals to be used again by plants. Bacteria lies dormant in winter and becomes active in summer

T_1 = Trophic level 1
T_2 = Trophic level 2
T_3 = Trophic level 3

◯ **Fig 2.26 Arctic tundra system (Sale *et al.*, 1954)**

diagrammatic representations of the hydrological cycle. But, as figure 2.25 shows, it can also be applied to human (inter)action, and when this happens human (inter)action is represented as though it was a natural process.

5 Geometrical symbolism

Figure 2.26, another 'communication model', does not include any participants. There is only a vector, indicating directionality by means of an 'infinity' sign, rather than by means of an arrowhead. Dance's diagram is in fact not so much a communication model as a 'metadiagram' which shows us a process in isolation, in order to discuss why *helical* vectors are more suitable for the representation of communication than, for instance,

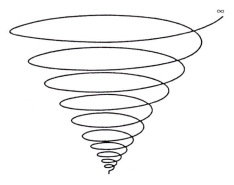

∞

◯ **Fig 2.27 Communication model (from Dance, 1967)**

straight or curved arrows. Dance does this by pointing at the symbolic meanings of intrinsic properties of the helix. According to Dance, the shape of the helix:

> combines the desirable features of the straight line and of the circle, while avoiding the weakness of either.... It gives testimony to the concept that communication, while moving forward, is at the same time coming back upon itself and being affected by its past behaviour, for the coming curve of the helix is fundamentally affected by the curve from which it emerges.
>
> (Dance, 1967)

Images of this kind use pictorial or abstract patterns as processes whose meanings are constituted by their symbolic values, and so extend the vectorial vocabulary by drawing our attention to possibilities beyond the diagonal action line or the simple arrow: coils, spirals, helixes.

Variants of the arrow may affect the meaning of the process in narrative diagrams. A curved arrow, for instance, partakes of the symbolic value of the circle, so that the process is represented as 'natural' and 'organic' (see figure 2.25). Vectors may also be *attenuated*, by the use of dotted lines, by making the arrowhead smaller or less conspicuous in other ways, or by placing it in the middle, rather than at the front of the line, which diminishes the sense of 'impacting' and 'targetting', and causes the meaning of the vector to move in the direction of mere connectivity (see figure 2.28).

Attenuated vectors

○ **Fig 2.28 Attenuated vectors**

The vectorial relation may also be *amplified*, by means of bolder arrows (see figure 2.29), which perhaps suggest a certain density of 'traffic', as in figure 2.14, the diagram of the attack on Khafji, or by the use of a number of arrows, which may suggest the frequency or multiplicity with which the process occurs.

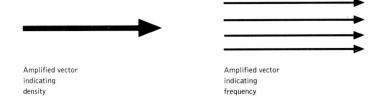

Amplified vector
indicating
density

Amplified vector
indicating
frequency

○ **Fig 2.29 Amplified vectors indicating density and frequency**

In pictures a similar effect can be achieved by making the diagonal action lines more or less conspicuous, more or less dominant in the composition as a whole.

6 Circumstances

As we indicated in our discussion of 'The British used guns' (in figure 2.1), narrative images may contain secondary participants, participants related to the main participants, not by means of vectors, but in other ways. We will refer to these participants, following Halliday (1985), as *Circumstances*. They are participants which could be left out without affecting the basic proposition realized by the narrative pattern, even though their deletion would of course entail a loss of information.

Locative Circumstances relate other participants to a specific participant we will call *Setting*. This requires a contrast between foreground and background which can be realized in one or more of the following ways: (1) the participants in the foreground overlap, and hence partially obscure the Setting; (2) the Setting is drawn or painted in less detail (or, in the case of photography, has softer focus); (3) the Setting is more muted and desaturated in colour, with the various colours all tending towards the same hue, for instance the blue of distance; (4) the Setting is darker than the foreground, or lighter, so that it acquires an 'overexposed', ethereal look. These formal features can occur in various combinations, and they are all gradients, 'more-or-less' rather than 'either–or' features.

◭　**Fig 2.30　Rod Steiger and Jack Palance in *The Big Knife* (Aldridge, 1955)**

Fig 2.31 Penguin with baby (Oakley, 1985)

In chapter 5 we will discuss their importance for the realization of pictorial modality. The Settings themselves can of course be read as embedded analytical processes ('the landscape consists of grass, trees and rocks').

The tools used in action processes are often represented as *Circumstances of Means*. If this is the case, there is no clear vector between the tool and its user. The tools themselves may of course constitute the vectors which realize the action processes, as with the guns in 'The British used guns' (in figure 2.1), and they need not be objects. For instance, we would interpret the visual process in figure 2.30 as transactional ('Rod Steiger addresses (or perhaps "implores") Jack Palance'), and Steiger's hands as a Circumstance of Means ('Rod Steiger implores Jack Palance *with* his hands'); we say 'the visual process' because in films the verbal processes are not realized in the visual semiotic as in comic strips, but through dialogue.

Figure 2.31 shows a penguin with her baby. There is, again, no vector to relate the two. Yet the penguin and her baby clearly form two distinct participants: this is a picture of a penguin *with* a baby. In such a case we will interpret the relation as a *Circumstance of Accompaniment*. As the picture contains no vector and displays the penguin more or less frontally, against a de-emphasised background, we interpret it as 'analytical', as the kind of picture more likely to illustrate a text giving descriptive information about penguins than a story about what penguins do. Figure 2.22 also shows a mother and her baby, but here we would interpret the angle of the woman's head as a vector, and the process, therefore, as a transaction in which the mother is Actor and the baby Goal ('the mother hugs the baby', perhaps). We have already indicated that the mother is at the same time also Reacter in a non-transactional reaction process.

SUMMARY

Figure 2.32 summarizes the distinctions we have introduced in this section. Following Halliday (1985), we have called processes that can take a whole visual (or verbal) proposition as their 'object' *projective,* and the others *non-projective.* The square brackets indicate a single choice, for instance 'a transactional action is either unidirectional or bidirectional'. Our claim is that the 'choices' in figure 2.32 chart the principal ways in which images can represent the world 'narratively', that is, in terms of 'doing' and 'happening'.

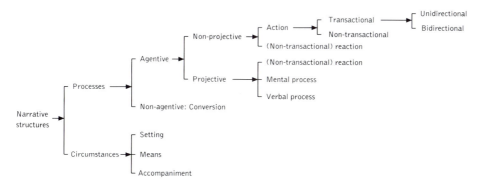

◆   **Fig 2.32 Narrative structures in visual communication**

REALIZATIONS

Unidirectional transactional action	A vector, formed by a (usually diagonal) depicted element, or an arrow, connects two participants, an Actor and a Goal.
Bidirectional transactional action	A vector, formed by a (usually diagonal) depicted element, or a double-headed arrow, connects two Interactors.
Non-transactional action	A vector, formed by a (usually diagonal) depicted element, or an arrow, emanates from a participant, the Actor, but does not point at any other participant.
Actor	The active participant in an action process is the participant from which the vector emanates or which is fused with the vector.
Goal	The passive participant in an action process is the participant at which the vector is directed.
Interactors	The participants in a transactional action process where the vector could be said to emanate from and be directed at both participants.
Transactional reaction	An eyeline vector connects two participants, a Reacter and a Phenomenon.
Non-transactional reaction	An eyeline vector emanates from a participant, the Reacter, but does not point at another participant.
Reacter	The active participant in a reaction process is the participant whose look creates the eyeline.
Phenomenon	The passive participant in a (transactional) reaction is the participant at which the eyeline is directed, in other words, the participant which forms the object of the Reacter's look.
Conversion	A process in which a participant, the Relay, is the Goal of one action and the

	Actor of another. This involves a change of state in the participant.
Mental process	A vector formed by a 'thought bubble' or a similar conventional device connects two participants, the Senser and the Phenomenon.
Senser	The participant from whom the 'thought bubble' vector emanates.
Phenomenon	The participant (verbal or non-verbal) enclosed by the 'thought bubble'.
Verbal process	A vector formed by the arrow-like protrusion of a 'dialogue balloon' or similar device connects two participants, a Sayer and an Utterance.
Sayer	The participant in a verbal process from whom the 'dialogue balloon' emanates.
Utterance	The (verbal) participant enclosed in the 'dialogue balloon'.
Setting	The Setting of a process is recognizable because the participants in the foreground overlap and hence partially obscure it; because it is often drawn or painted in less detail, or, in the case of photography, has a softer focus; and because of contrasts in colour saturation and overall darkness or lightness between foreground and background.
Means	The Means of a process is formed by the tool with which the action is executed. It usually also forms the vector.
Accompaniment	An Accompaniment is a participant in a narrative structure which has no vectorial relation with other participants and cannot be interpreted as a Symbolic Attribute (see chapter 3).

VISUAL STRUCTURES AND LINGUISTIC STRUCTURES

We have drawn attention to the fact that while both visual structures and verbal structures can be used to express meanings drawn from a common cultural source, we have insisted that the two media are not simply alternative means of representing 'the same thing'. In this brief final section we wish to exemplify this point in some detail.

Narrative visual structures have relatively clearcut equivalents in the English language. Like 'non-transactional actions', 'one-participant material processes' (Halliday, 1985: 103ff.) represent events as though they bear no relation to, and have no consequences for, participants other than the Actor. In *Many people migrated* one cannot add a second participant to this clause and say, for instance, *Many people migrated their relatives*, although one can of course add circumstances: *Many people migrated to Australia*. And like 'transactional actions', 'two-participant material processes' (Halliday, 1985: 103ff.) involve *two* participants (e.g. *Migrants invaded Australia*). But material processes allow a third option. Events can also be represented, not as things *done* by someone or something else ('transactions'), but as things *happening to* someone or something, hence as one-participant material processes taking a Goal rather than an Actor (e.g. *Many of my relatives died*) and this distinction cannot be realized visually. To show someone dying it is necessary to show someone being killed, or to show someone performing an action that represents his or her death. Also, while in English many processes can take a third participant, the 'Beneficiary' (traditionally 'indirect object' in e.g. *Mary gave him the book*), in images a third participant can never occur. What is a Beneficiary in English becomes a Goal in images ('she message-sends him' instead of 'she sends him a message').

On the other hand, English lacks structural devices to represent events as cyclical, as though linguistic participants can have a double role in English; for instance, examples like *He made them do it*, where *them* is Goal of *make do* as well as Actor of *do*. In this case, the participant *he* is then called 'Assigner' (Halliday, 1985: 153). Nor is there an 'interactional' process: to realize what we have called 'Interactors', English must make use of reflexive pronouns. Consider, for instance, the problem of transcoding figure 2.18, de Saussure's 'speech circuit' diagram, into English. A single process indicates something for which, in English we need at least four clauses: 'A speaks to B', 'B speaks to A', 'A listens to B', 'B listens to A'. How can one render this in one clause? 'A and B communicate with each other'? But that causes 'A' and 'B' to lose their separate identity, transforming a reciprocal, bidirectional transaction into a jointly authored *non-transactional* action.

What we have called the 'non-transactional reaction' is quite akin to what Halliday calls the *behavioural process* (1985: 128), a process type which can take only one participant (who must be human) and serves to realize a restricted field of action, the field of 'physiological and psychological behaving' (*ibid*.: 128). The meanings of visual 'non-transactional reactions' form, of course, a still more restricted field, tied up as they are with one kind of behaviour, looking.

Projective processes, that is, mental and verbal processes, play an important part in English, and it is possible to distinguish a number of different types of each on the basis of formal grammatical criteria (Halliday, 1985: 106ff.; 129). Mental processes, for instance, include processes of perception ('see', 'hear', etc.), processes of affection ('like', 'fear', 'wish', etc.) and processes of cognition ('know', 'think', 'believe', etc.). Each has a Senser, the person who does the seeing, or liking, or knowing (this has to be a person, or a participant represented *as* human), and a Phenomenon, someone or something seen or liked or known by the Senser. Phenomena may be realized by participants or whole structures, just as in the case of images. In *Many people want to migrate to Australia,* the clause *to migrate to Australia* is Phenomenon; this sets mental processes apart from actions and transactions, which cannot have a clause as Goal. What we have called the 'transactional reaction' can be seen as equivalent to a subset of the perception process, because non-visual Phenomena cannot be realized in the visual semiotic. Mental processes form, as we have shown, only a minor category in the visual semiotic; as far as we can see, there are no visual devices for distinguishing between 'cognition' and 'affection'. The cinema, however, has developed a fairly extensive set of projective conventions for realizing different kinds of mental processes such as memories, dreams, hallucinations, and so on.

Unlike mental processes, verbal processes do not need a human 'Sayer' (one can say *The document said that . . .* but not *The document thought that . . .*). Like mental processes, they can take whole clauses as their object, and this in two different ways, in the form of Reported Speech (as in *He said [that] he had no idea*) and in the form of Quoted Speech (as in *He said 'I have no idea'*). This distinction seems not to be realized in the visual representation of speech processes: 'dialogue balloons' always quote.

We have identified only three different types of circumstance in images: location, means and accompaniment. All three exist in English (Halliday, 1985: 137ff.) but there they are by no means the only types. English allows all kinds of information to be added to the basic narrative proposition conveyed by the process ('What happened?') and the participants ('Who or what was involved?'); information about time ('When did it happen?'; 'How long did it last?'); about purpose ('What did it happen for?'); cause ('Why did it happen?') and so on.

The following table gives an overview of some of the correspondences between linguistic and visual narrative processes:

Table 2.1 **Narrative process in language and visual communication**

Visual narrative processes	*Linguistic narrative clauses*
Non-transactional action	One-participant (Actor) material process ('action')
Unidirectional transactional action	Two-participant material process
–	One-participant (Goal) material process ('event')
Bidirectional transactional action	–
Non-transactional reaction	Behavioural process (field of looking)
Transactional reaction	Mental process: perception (visual only)
Mental process	Mental process (cognition and affection)
Verbal process	Verbal process (quotation)
–	Verbal process (affection)
Conversion	–

Comparisons such as these can highlight which ways of representing the world can be realized linguistically, which visually and which in both ways. And this, in turn, is useful as a background for analysing representation in multimodal texts: photographs and their captions, diagrams and their verbal glosses, stories and their illustrations. If, for instance, a diagram shows an arrow emanating from a participant labelled 'environment' and directed at another participant labelled 'message' (see figure 6.21), then a literal translation would be 'the environment acts upon the message'. If the accompanying text says that the 'communication process' is 'interacting with factors (or stimuli) from the environment' (Watson and Hill, 1984: 14), it mistranslates, and the mistranslation is not due to the limitations of either English or visual communication. A literal 'translation' of 'the source sends a message to the receiver', on the other hand, is not possible: the spatial representation of verbally conceived ideas changes these ideas, and vice versa. In the next chapter we will show further examples of this problem.

We wish to emphasize again that this role distribution, this distribution of what can be done with language and what with visuals, is not fixed, nor entirely given with the nature of the two modes of communication. Verbal processes, for instance, have until recently been restricted to the domains of comic strip and cartoon drawings, but 'dialogue balloons' and similar visual quoting devices are now becoming more common in other domains also, for instance in school textbooks and even in papers by linguists. In future this may well lead to the development of visual conventions for different types of 'saying'.

3 Conceptual representations: designing social constructs

CLASSIFICATIONAL PROCESSES

In the previous chapter we noted that visual structures of representation can either be narrative, presenting unfolding actions and events, processes of change, transitory spatial arrangements, or conceptual, representing participants in terms of their more generalized and more or less stable and timeless essence, in terms of class, or structure, or meaning.

Fig 3.1 Weapons of the ground war (*Sydney Morning Herald*, 20 February 1991)

⬥ **Fig 3.2 Revlon advertisement (*Women's Weekly*, December 1987)**

It is to the latter category of representational structures that we now turn, beginning with classificational processes.

Classificational processes relate participants to each other in terms of a 'kind of' relation, a taxonomy: at least one set of participants will play the role of *Subordinates* with respect to at least one other participant, the *Superordinate*. We have already come across an example in the left-hand picture of figure 2.1, where the three participants, the axe, the basket and the wooden sword, were represented as 'species' of the same 'genus', as all belonging to the same overarching category. In this example the overarching category was not shown or named. The structure was a *Covert Taxonomy*, a taxonomy in which the Superordinate is either only indicated in the accompanying text, or inferred from such similarities as the viewer may perceive to exist between the Subordinates.

One visual characteristic is crucial in the realization of covert taxonomies: the proposed equivalence between the Subordinates is visually realized by a symmetrical composition. The Subordinates are placed at equal distance from each other, given the same size and the same orientation towards the horizontal and vertical axes. To realize the stable, timeless nature of the classification, the participants are often shown in a more or less objective, decontextualized way. The background is plain and neutral. Depth is reduced or absent. The angle is frontal and objective. And frequently there are words inside the picture space. These features will be discussed in a later chapter under the heading 'modality'.

Classification processes do not, of course, simply reflect 'real', 'natural' classifications. For participants to be put together in a syntagm which establishes a classification *means* that they were judged to be members of the same class and are to be read as such. As in language, naturalization is not natural. The picture itself constitutes the relation. This makes it possible for the producer of an image to classify baskets and weapons as being of the same order, or, as in figure 3.1, to suggest that the ground weapons of the Allied and Iraqi forces in the Gulf War, were somehow the same, implying that the war was therefore a fair and equal one.

Covert taxonomies are often used in advertisements, where the photographs may, for instance, show arrangements of bottles that represent the variety of products marketed under a brand name, or arrangements of different people who all use the same product. Figure 3.2 is an example. What do the four women have in common? The text reveals it. They are all 'unforgettable' and they all 'wear Revlon'.

Other taxonomies include the Superordinate. The process usually takes the form of some kind of tree structure, and the orientation is vertical, with the Superordinate placed,

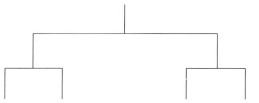

◆ **Fig 3.3 Classificational process (tree structure)**

not to the right or the left of the Subordinates, but above or below them, as in figure 3.3. The participants may be realized verbally, visually, or both verbally and visually, but the process is always visual (see figure 3.4).

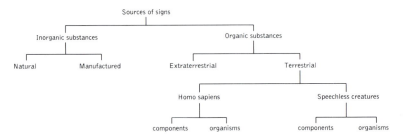

● **Fig 3.4 Sources of signs (Eco, 1976b: 177)**

Not all overt taxonomies are diagrammatic. A pictorial 'tree' may replace the diagrammatic tree structure, for instance, and figure 3.5, taken from Iedema *et al.* (1993), depicts the hierarchical structure of a company photographically. We reproduce the whole article to show how the picture contrasted with a picture representing the relation between management and personnel in another company as transactional rather

● **Fig 3.5 Photographic taxonomy**

than classificational. The article quotes the management of the former as being in favour of deregulating employment contracts, that of the latter as being against, and the size and placement of the classificational photo clearly privileges the pro-deregulation view.

Overt taxonomies are usually 'chained', so that the 'intermediate' participants (e.g. the 'inorganic objects' and 'organic substances' of figure 3.4) will be Superordinate with respect to some of the other participants, and Subordinate with respect to others. To indicate this we will coin the term *Interordinate*. In other words, overt taxonomies have levels, and participants at the same level are represented as being, in some sense, 'of the same kind'.

Tree structures, however, are not only used to realize 'kind of' relations. 'Reporting diagrams', showing the hierarchical structure of companies and other organizations, and genealogical or evolutionary trees use the same structure. This means that visual grammar conflates, or at least represents as very closely related, what would, in language, be expressed by different means. Conceptual classification is represented by the same structure as social hierarchy, that is, the more general *idea* is represented as similar to greater *power*. As Virginia Woolf has said: 'General ideas are always also Generals' ideas.' And second, hierarchies of concepts and hierarchies of social power are represented as similar to genealogies. In other words, the identity of an individual (or a species) is represented as being 'subordinate' to its 'origins' or 'ancestors' in the same way as specific concepts are subordinated to more general and abstract concepts, and lower employees or local bodies to managers or central organs. Diagrammatic tree structures can take

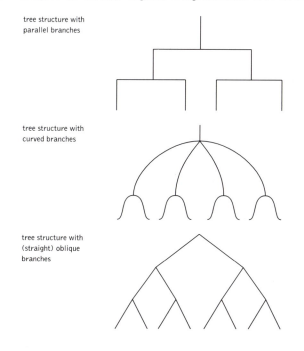

tree structure with
parallel branches

tree structure with
curved branches

tree structure with
(straight) oblique
branches

Fig 3.6 Tree structures with parallel, (straight) oblique and curved branches

different forms. The branches of the tree may be parallel or oblique, straight or curved (see figure 3.6).

Oblique branches abstract somewhat less from the shape of the tree than parallel branches, so that more of the symbolic meaning of the tree can be preserved. Hence they are common in contexts where a sense of 'generation' and 'growth' is connoted, as for instance in genealogies or in the diagrams used in 'generative grammar', a form of linguistics which posits that 'surface structures' are generated from innate and universal 'deep structures'. The contrast between straight and curved branches is perhaps similar to that between participants represented as boxes and participants represented as circles or ovals (see chapter 2), a contrast between the 'mechanical' and 'technological', and the 'natural' and 'organic'.

Most trees are inverted (bottom up), and when the branches are oblique, the overall shape will tend towards that of a pyramid. Such structures are concerned with hierarchy and hierarchical difference rather than with clarity about levels: a reading of levels is possible, but not readily facilitated. Not all trees, however, are inverted. Sometimes the specific, or, in the case of genealogies and evolutionary trees, the present, is placed on the top, depicting, for instance, humankind as the pinnacle of evolution, rather than as being forever dominated by its lowly origins.

Although classificational structures represent participants in terms of their place in a static order, the verbal labels and explanations which may accompany them do not always do so. The term 'reporting diagram', for instance, uses an active process ('report') rather than a static one such as 'is subordinate to'. Genealogies and evolutionary trees, similarly, may be glossed by verbs like 'generates', 'evolves into', 'begets' and so on. *Visually*, however, a hierarchical order is signified, a system. Thus the visual representation can blur the boundaries between the dynamic and the static. Is the dynamic in reality the instantiation or enactment of an underlying system? Or is the static the systemization and objectification of a dynamic and ever-changing reality? Such questions become difficult to answer in a language which has erased the boundaries between the schema and the blueprint.

A similar blurring may occur between analytical ('part of') and classificational ('kind of') processes. The 'stack diagram' in figure 3.7 could be called classificational, and is in fact so rendered in the accompanying text: 'to the Latin word /mus/ correspond two different things which we shall call x_1 and x_2' (Eco, 1976: 78). In other words, a 'mouse' is a kind of 'mus'. But it can also be seen as analytical. One can also say: the meaning 'mouse' is part of the meaning of 'mus'. And most importantly, Eco has chosen the form of the *analytical* diagram.

○ Fig 3.7 Semantic field diagram (Eco, 1976b: 78)

Finally, classificational diagrams may be rotated through 90° so that their main *orientation* is along the horizontal axis. They have then the orientation typical of narrative diagrams, and hence a dynamic connotation. But they retain the *process* of the classificational diagram. They still represent the relation between the participants as a system. Features from different types of process are abstracted and recombined to create patterns that are ambiguously in between the dynamic and the conceptual. When such diagrams acquire arrows, as, for example, in system networks (see figure 3.11) they become in fact dynamic and narrative. Yet they still move from the general to the specific, in contrast for example, to flowcharts such as figure 3.8.

Taxonomies and flowcharts clearly provide two different kinds of knowledge. The one represents the world in terms of a hierarchical order. Its main concern is the ranking of phenomena from the perspective of a single unifying term, be it that of the origin of things, the most generalizing generalization, or that of the highest power. The other describes the world in terms of an actively pursued process with a clear beginning and an end (or 'input' and 'output', 'source' and 'destination', 'raw materials' and 'finished product'). It has a sequential progression and is goal-orientated. And, as we have noted already, system networks such as we use in this book, attempt to combine the two perspectives.

Recently another kind of diagram has begun to gain ascendance, often referred to as 'digital network'. Such networks seek to show the multiple interconnections between participants. Any participant in a network ('node') can form an entry-point from which its environment can be explored, and the vectors or lines ('links') between these participants can take on many different values, the value of signification ('is a'), of

Fig 3.8 Uses of oil (Merritt, 1984)

combination ('goes with'), of composition ('contains a'): the essence of the link between two participants is that they are, in some sense, next to each other, or close to each other, associated with each other. To demonstrate the difference with a linguistic example, a taxonomy would show, for instance, a hierarchy of words, a 'flowchart', for instance, a way of generating a clause by following a precise sequence of 'instructions'; and a network might show the *collocation* of words – the other words with which any given word typically combines, regardless of the *structural* relations between the words (see figure 3.9).

Figure 3.10 shows a 'linear' (flowchart) and 'non-linear' (network) representation from an article on a 'writer's assistant' computer program. The network, its author says, allows the writer 'to form ideas into an associative network' (Sharples *et al.*, 1992: 22). The principle behind such networks clearly relates to the idea of the 'non-linear' text to

Taxonomy

Flowchart

Network

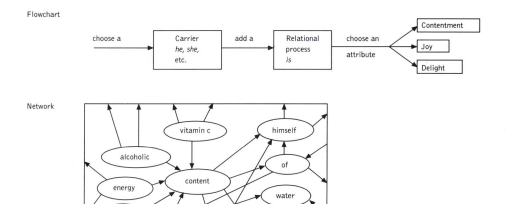

⬤ **Fig 3.9 Taxonomy, flowchart and network**

⬯ **Fig 3.10 Network (from Sharples and Pemberton, 1992)**

which we have alluded in our discussion of Dick Bruna's *On My Walk* (figure 1.2) and to which we will return in greater detail in chapter 6. In discussing a page from Bruna we stressed that such pages on the one hand provide the reader with many choices, many paths to follow, but on the other hand tend to obscure the fact that the range of choices is ultimately predesigned and limited. As such, networks are, in the end, just as much modelled on forms of social organization as taxonomies and flowcharts. The taxonomy is modelled on a static, hierarchical organization in which everything has its pre-ordained place in a grand scheme unified by a single source of authority. The flowchart is modelled on the principle of authoritatively prescribed, structured, goal-orientated activity. The network is modelled on a form of social organization which is a vast, labyrinthine network of intersecting local relations in which each node is related in many different ways to other nodes in its immediate environment, but in which it is difficult, if not impossible, to form a coherent view of the whole. Perhaps it is not accidental that this kind of network is coming to the fore in an age of increasing social fragmentation and regionalization. But regions are nevertheless connected to the whole and the network model may obscure the globalizing tendencies which are also and simultaneously at work in contemporary society. This is recognized by those who pioneer the application of this mode of representation, for instance in connection with 'hypertexts', which are also networks:

> Readers who browse hypertext networks become 'lost', unaware of where they are in relation to the document, and thus unable to achieve a sense of text, i.e. an intellectual feel for the substance of the document. This is analogous to starting at a particular word in a thesaurus and passing from one similar associative word to another. Soon it is likely that the reader would be examining a word that is completely different from the original word, with no notion of any meaning to the derivation that has just taken place.
>
> (Ghaoui *et al.*, 1992: 110)

In the pronouncements of digital-networks guru Kevin Kelly, as reported by Jim McClellan in the *Observer*, the political implications of the network become even clearer:

> The image of the atom ... stood for power and knowledge. Its sure, regular orbits and defined spaces represented 'law-abiding solar systems of energy' under central direction. In contrast the Net – a tangle of apparent disorder – was an icon of no beginning, no centre, no end (or all beginning, all centre, all end). It was the emblem of our new understanding of the complex logic of nature and computers; the banner of systems which, in some senses, organized themselves. The atom had been the icon of the 20th century (the Atom Age), he concluded, but the Net would be the archetype of the coming network culture of the 21st.
>
> (McClellan, *Observer Life Magazine*, 21 September 1994, p. 62)

In figure 3.11 we summarize the distinctions we have made in this section. Digital networks are not included in the summary as they are 'analytical' rather than 'classificational'. The difference between 'single-' and 'multi-levelled' is marked by the absence or presence of 'Interordinates'. Our discussion above has, we hope, made it clear that we see these distinctions as tools with which to describe visual structures rather than that specific, concrete visuals can necessarily always be described exhaustively and uniquely in terms of any one of our categories.

● **Fig 3.11 Classificational image structures**

REALIZATIONS

Covert taxonomy	A set of participants ('Subordinates') is distributed symmetrically across the picture space, at equal distance from each other, equal in size, and orientated towards the vertical and horizontal axes in the same way.
Single-levelled overt taxonomy	A participant ('Superordinate') is connected to two or more other participants ('Subordinates') through a tree structure with two levels only.
Multi-levelled overt taxonomy	A participant ('Superordinate') is connected to other participants through a tree structure with more than two

levels. The participants which occupy intermediate levels are Interordinates, those which occupy the lowest level (if the Superordinate is on top) or the highest level (if the Superordinate is at the bottom) Subordinates.

ANALYTICAL PROCESSES

Analytical processes relate participants in terms of a part–whole structure. They involve two kinds of participants: one *Carrier* (the whole) and any number of *Possessive Attributes* (the parts). We have already given an example of an analytical structure, the picture of the Antarctic explorer (figure 2.4) which analysed the explorer in terms of his 'outfit'. Fashion shots, too, are analytical. Like the picture of the Antarctic explorer, they label both the Carrier ('easy-wearing, inexpensive cottons teamed with the right accessories' – see figure 3.12) and the Possessive Attributes ('Laura Ashley trenchcoat, Stuart Membery sweater, Benetton jodhpurs'), albeit in a caption, rather than inside the picture space, and in the flowery language of fashion writing which has been described so well by Barthes (1967b).

○ Fig 3.12 *Easy-wearing Cottons* (*Vogue*, November 1987)

Different as they may seem at first sight, maps have the same structure: there is a Carrier, for instance 'Australia', and there are Possessive Attributes, for instance 'the states of Australia', and both are labelled, either inside the picture space, or in a legend or caption. Maps may provide quite distinct analyses of what seems to be the same Carrier. Some maps focus on geographical features such as waterways, altitude, etc.; others concentrate on social and political boundaries. Analysis always involves selection. Some attributes or characteristics of the Carrier are singled out as criterial in the given context, or generally, while others are ignored, treated as non-essential and irrelevant.

The difference between the map and the fashion shot lies not in their ideational but in their interpersonal structures, for instance in their modality (see chapter 5). Many analytical visuals have low modality, from the naturalistic point of view. Too much life-likeness, too much detail distracts from their analytical purpose. Only the essential features of the Possessive Attributes are shown, and for this reason drawings of various degrees of schematization are generally preferred over photographs or highly detail artwork. The representation of depth is reduced or absent, as is the detailed representation of light and shadow, and of subtle tonal distinctions. Colour, if it is used at all, is restricted to a reduced palette, or used conventionally, for instance to distinguish participants, such as different socio-economic groups, or landforms. Background is left out, or only sketched in lightly. And the Possessive Attributes are labelled. Note that the arrows in figure 2.4 do not realize narrative processes but a relation of identity between a verbal and a visual realization of the same Possessive Attribute. Yet photographs, particularly posed photographs, can also be analytical, as in the case of fashion shots, or of advertisements which give a detailed depiction of the advertised product, or of press 'mug shots' of politicians and other newsworthy persons. The school social studies textbook from which we took figure 2.4 shows, on the page opposite to that showing the drawing in figure 2.4, the two pictures reproduced in figure 3.13.

Both these pictures are analytical: there is neither a vector (narrative process) nor compositional symmetry and/or a tree structure (classificational process), and they serve to identify a Carrier and to allow viewers to scrutinize this Carrier's Possessive Attributes. Some minor degree of lowered modality is also present: the background is plain or very much out of focus, and the fact that the pictures are posed adds further artificiality. Yet, although they are analytical, their purpose is more interactional than representational. The interactional system of the *gaze* dominates: the gaze of represented participants directly addresses the viewers and so establishes an imaginary relation with them, while more schematic analytical pictures invite impersonal, detached scrutiny. A similar argument can be made about advertisements showing the advertised product: the overall impression of an abundance of parts (or ingredients, or varieties of the product), or the alluring sensory quality of the advertised product as a whole (the streamlined sheen of the car, the vivid colour and texture of the ingredients of a canned soup) take precedence over more dispassionate scrutiny of the Possessive Attributes. Persuasion is foregrounded, instruction and exposition are backgrounded. The textbook includes both figure 2.4 and figure 3.13. because it seeks not only to teach children objective facts about Antarctic exploration but also to make them emotionally identify with an adventurous hero. In the

Sir Douglas Mawson

One of the most famous of these Antarctic explorers was the Australian, Douglas Mawson.

Douglas Mawson was a scientist—a geologist. He wanted to find minerals and to claim some of this large continent for Australia. He first went to Antarctica as a member of the British Antarctic Expedition, led by Sir Ernest Shackleton, in 1907–1909. During this expedition, Mawson became one of the first men to climb Mount Erebus, a volcano and one of Antarctica's highest mountains. Mawson was so impressed by what he saw on his first journey that he made up his mind to go back again, as soon as he could. He wanted to discover more about this large, unexplored land.

Only two years later, Mawson was back in Antarctica with his own party of explorers. This time he was the leader.

Look at the clothes worn by explorers to Antarctica.

Mawson's second journey to Antarctica has been described as one of the greatest tales of human courage ever told. To find out why, read the story yourself or ask your teacher to tell you the story.

Journey into the unknown

Mawson's party set up their base camp at Commonwealth Bay, on the Antarctic coast south of Australia. They built a small hut on the narrow, stony beach, surrounded by cliffs of ice 80 metres high.

20

○ **Fig 3.13 Sir Douglas Mawson (Oakley, 1985)**

later years of education, scientific modality increases in frequency. Advanced textbooks address their readers as 'no longer needing pictures', as having been weaned off everyday naturalism, and as having acquired the abstract and impersonal attitude characteristic of higher learning and higher art appreciation in our culture. This difference has its counterpart in language. In primary school textbooks, as also in advertising language, 'you' is a key word; the reader is always directly addressed:

> Here is a picture of Antarctica. If you landed here in a spaceship, how would you describe this place?

In the language of the senior highschool textbook, as also in the language of science and the language of bureaucracy, the passive voice has come to be normal, realizing a more impersonal and detached form of address:

> These outlines may be abstracted from topographic maps and street directories.

Of course, some photographs are almost as objective and detached as diagrams and maps. This is the case, for instance, with aerial photographs: their top–down angle ensures the absence of depth and background, and depending on the height from which they are taken detail is more or less removed. The same is true of many scientific photographs. But in the main drawings are the preferred mode in scientific representations.

Abstract art may also be analytical. The structure of Theo van Doesburg's *Pure Painting*, for instance (figure 3.14), is like the structure of a map. It analyses reality in terms of Possessive Attributes, highly abstract ones: rectangles of different size and colour. But it does not label either the Carrier or the Possessive Attributes. It leaves it up to the viewer to do so, and, as a result, the painting can be read in many different ways. We could see it, quite concretely, as the map of the modern city (green for recreational areas, yellow for housing, red for industrial areas, and so on) – figure 3.15 *is* in fact a map of a city. We could also see it more abstractly, as a map of desirable human qualities or activities (green for contemplation, red for passion, etc.), and of the space they should occupy in our lives. The point is, the painting represents both these things, and many more. It is open to many readings, and that constitutes its power to shape reality, a power which,

Fig 3.14 *Pure Painting* (Theo van Doesburg, 1920) (from Jaffé, 1986)

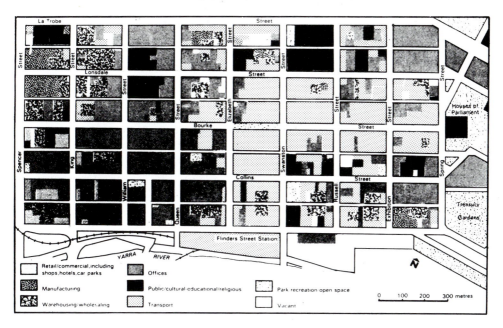

⬤ Fig 3.15 Map of the central business district of Melbourne (Pask and Bryant, 1982)

however, cannot be unleashed until the boxes are given concrete reference, so that the schema can be turned into a blueprint.

Lowered naturalistic modality, however, is not a defining characteristic of analytic visuals. Modality forms a separate (interactional) system which is present in visuals simultaneously with the kinds of structure we are describing in this chapter. At most we can say that in specific social contexts (cartography, education at different levels, advertising, fashion), there is a tendency for certain modality choices to go together with certain representational choices, certain kinds of processes. The defining characteristic of the analytical process is in fact a negative one. It lies in the absence of vectors and the absence of compositional symmetry and/or tree structures, and also in the absence of the features that mark the symbolic processes we will describe in the next section. There are more positive and specific characteristics, but these pertain to specific kinds of analytical process. As a whole, the analytical process is the usual, the 'unmarked' and therefore also the most elementary option in the visual system of representation: a visual 'this is'. Experimental studies of the production of drawings would seem to bear this out: the principal task drawers must master is the representation of objects in terms of their minimal defining characteristics, and the principal purpose for which non-specialists actually use drawing in everyday life is the production of pragmatically motivated 'descriptions', sketches of localities, clothes and hair styles, mechanical devices and so on, as well as the production of doodles, which often are also analytical (Van Sommers, 1984: 234ff.)

Fig 3.16 Resort wear (*Women's Weekly*, December 1987)

1 Unstructured analytical processes

Some analytical processes are *unstructured*, that is, they show us the Possessive Attributes of the Carrier, but not the Carrier itself, the parts, but not the way the parts fit together to make up a whole. The page reproduced in figure 3.16, for instance, is a kind of unstructured map, accurate in scale, but without any *visual* indication of the location of the Possessive Attributes relative to each other. We see the parts of the garment, but not the way they are to be assembled – although verbal labels ('coat front', 'bikini top back', etc.) provide an indication, and the page does also include a photograph of the finished garment. This photograph, however, would have to be seen as a separate analytical structure, with higher naturalistic modality than the pattern itself. The magazine uses the same strategy as the social studies textbook: one picture to entice you, another to give you a more objective analysis of the Carrier.

Especially when the Carrier is abstract, there may not be a single principle for the way in which Possessive Attributes should be assembled. The Carrier cannot be visualized in an assembled state, and any arrangement of the Possessive Attributes is therefore possible: an unstructured analytical process is like a more or less unordered list. This can be seen, for instance, in advertisements which display all the parts that make up the engine of a car, or the full range of products manufactured by an advertiser, in order to impress the viewer with their sheer abundance.

2 Temporal analytical processes

The examples we have discussed so far represent the things they represent as objects. They focus on spatiality. But there is also the category of the *time line*, a process which seems to occupy an intermediate position between the narrative and the analytical. Time lines involve the temporal dimension, and this suggests narrative. Yet they are not vectorial, and, rather than representing history as a gradual unfolding of events, they analyse it into successive stages with fixed and stable characteristics, stages which can then be treated as though they were things. For instance, we interpret a diagram like figure 3.17 as analytical, as 'saying': 'the evolution of humankind *consists* of the "Ape" stage, the "Apeman" stage, the "Australopithecus" stage (etc.)', with 'the evolution of humankind' as Carrier, and the stages as Possessive Attributes.

The essential characteristic of temporal analytical processes is that they are realized by time lines: the participants (sometimes whole structures, 'scenes') are arranged on an actual or imaginary line, usually horizontal, sometimes vertical. The time line may be *topographical*, drawn to scale, or *topological*, assembling the participants in the right sequence, but not drawing the time intervals 'to scale', as in figure 3.17.

Time lines need not be straight, and they may involve all kinds of geometrical

Fig 3.17 Evolution (from a Swedish history textbook)

The handwritten timeline reads:

1970 – Born 26 February, Athens, Greece
1 –
2 – My sister Mary born, 24 May
3 –
4 – We came to Australia to live in Sydney
5 – Started primary school
6 – My brother George born, 30 November
7 – Got our first dog, Blacky
8 – Bad car accident. I was in hospital for six weeks
9 – Started music lessons
1980 – Had operation on my hip
1 – Grandmother died
2 – Started high school
3 – Went back to Greece for six weeks
4 –

Fig. 1.4 A personal history timeline.

△ **Fig 3.18 A personal history timeline**

day and
years. C
million
years or
As yo
appeare
the en
words,
million

CHECK
1 How
2 What
earth?
3 Can y
4 What
5 Which
Where d
6 Which

THINK
1 Use a
to find o
a micro
b reptile
c mamr
Draw a
group.
2 One c
out what
— which
and so c
when thi
ago.
Think ab
happene
right ord
born. Th
The time
about ho

Conti

A conti
there ai

symbolism. Figure 3.19, taken from a Swedish junior highschool history textbook, is a particularly interesting example. Here time does not progress linearly, but takes turns, goes downhill, moves towards the viewer, and changes colour, from a crystalline blue to a drab brown (the colour code employed by the series of four books of which the book containing this illustration is part, has blue as the colour of history and brown as the colour of social studies). The result is a rather ethnocentric and patriarchal story which could be said to reveal, behind the surface of Sweden's modern and egalitarian welfare state, a deep longing for the primitive uncertain life of the nomadic hunter. When 'Man' first appeared on the horizon of time, so this story goes, he was a hunter and a maker of tools. He then acquired a wife, but she, the woman of 'homo erectus' was not yet 'erectus' herself, and, where her man fixed his gaze upon the future, she looked back towards the past. Then 'Man' invented fire – a male achievement, for woman is not shown to be part of it, not even as an admiring onlooker. Next, he began to cover his body and begot a child. But at this point, the point where history takes a backward turn, a curious inversion occurred. It was now he who crouched and she who was 'erectus', he who looked

⬧   Fig 3.19 Evolution (Ohman, 1989)

backwards and she who fixed her gaze upon a future which, however, was no longer there, as time had already turned backwards. But all was not lost. The union of the two provided a very 'erect', very male, and very Nordic 'homo sapiens' as the outcome of evolution, as 'our' ancestor, here placed in the centre of the composition and close to the viewer. This story about Swedish identity is told by visual means only, and it illustrates a text which is told, not as Swedish history, but as a history of the world. The twisting and turning of the time line in figure 3.19 does of course give it a dynamic quality and reminds us of the helix in figure 2.26. The categories of visual grammar do not have clearcut edges, and specific representations can merge two or more structures, for instance the narrative and the analytical, as in this example.

3 Exhaustive and inclusive analytical processes

(Spatial) structured analytical processes can be *exhaustive*, that is, they can exhaustively represent the Possessive Attributes of a Carrier, so that all of the Carrier is accounted for, all of its space taken up by Possessive Attributes. To put it in another way, in an exhaustive analytical structure there is assembly: the Possessive Attributes are joined together to make up a complex shape. Structured analytical processes can also be *inclusive*, that is, they can show us only some of the Possessive Attributes of a Carrier, leaving much of the Carrier unaccounted for, as blank space not taken up by Possessive Attributes. The circles on the left and right of Schramm's third communication model (figure 2.24) form exhaustive analytical structures, embedded in the larger narrative structure: the 'Sender' and the 'Receiver' are here analysed as being made up out of the same three components ('Encoder', 'Interpreter' and 'Decoder'), assembled in different ways, and every part of the space of the circles is covered by Possessive Attributes. The point is not, of course, that the analysis *is* in fact exhaustive. 'Senders' and 'Receivers' may well have other components beside these three. The point is that the analysis is presented *as though* it is exhaustive, as though the Carriers have these major components and no others. Just as we have to assume that a map showing the states of Australia shows us *all* the states of Australia, and a picture of the outfit of an Antarctic explorer, *all* the parts of this outfit, so we have to assume that this diagram shows us all the major components of the 'Sender' and the 'Receiver'. Of course, 'encoding', 'interpreting' and 'decoding' might be seen as activities rather than as components. However, Schramm has *represented* them here as though they were parts of a machine, as though 'Senders' and 'Receivers' *have* these elements, or *consist of* these elements. As so often in diagrams, doings have been turned into things, spatialized and objectified.

In inclusive analytical structures, the Possessive Attributes do not exhaustively divide up the space of the Carrier. They are contained *within* the Carrier, and so take up part of its space, but not all: other parts are left blank, unanalysed. This structure also entails the possibility of *partial inclusion* and *exclusion*. In figure 3.20 A and B are Possessive Attributes of the Carrier formed by the largest circle, C is a *Partial Possessive Attribute* (in part belonging to the Carrier, in part outside it), and D is excluded, hence not a Possessive Attribute. In other words, where exhaustive structures are formed by the welding together of Possessive Attributes, inclusive structures are formed by the full or partial overlapping of the participants. And the structure is *recursive*: a Possessive Attribute can become the Carrier of other Possessive Attributes, as in the case with B in the example above: it is a Possessive Attribute with respect to the larger circle, but a Carrier with respect to E. We can see this structure at work in Riley and Riley's communication model (figure 2.5). It does not tell us that 'over-all social systems' exhaustively consist of two 'larger social structures' and 'larger social structures' of two

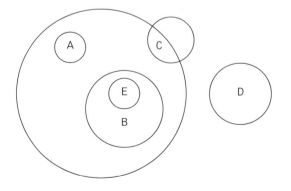

⬤ Fig 3.20 Inclusive analytical structures

and not more than two 'primary groups', but that 'over-all social systems' contain (beside the many other things they may also contain) at least two 'larger social structures', and that 'larger social structures' contain at least two 'primary groups'. Individuals such as 'C' and 'R' are partial Possessive Attributes of the Carrier/Attribute 'larger social structure' and fully Possessive Attributes of the Carrier 'over-all social system'. To give a gloss on this structure: according to Riley and Riley, individuals cannot escape the 'over-all social system', but they can, at least in part, free themselves from the constraints of 'larger social structures'.

Many maps have a similar structure. A map of a state or nation which shows cities and towns, for instance, is not read as meaning that every city and every town has been included, or that the state or nation contains no Possessive Attributes other than cities and towns. It is read as meaning that these are some (the major) cities and towns of that state or nation, or rather, that these are the cities and towns of interest and relevance to you, the reader of this particular map. Inclusive structures are here embedded within exhaustive structures: the map as a whole may be primarily concerned with the boundaries that exhaustively divide the Carrier into Possessive Attributes (Europe into nations, Australia into states, etc.), but these Possessive Attributes themselves are Carriers in embedded inclusive structures with Possessive Attributes such as major cities, rivers, lakes, etc.

4 Conjoined and compounded exhaustive structures

In *conjoined* exhaustive structures, Possessive Attributes are either *connected*, by a line lacking a feature of directionality, or *disengaged*, by a layout of the Possessive Attributes

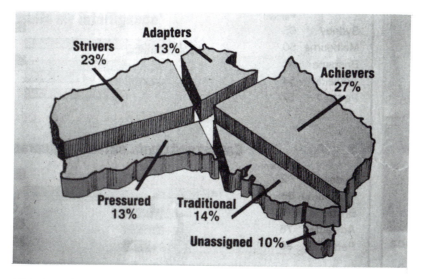

Fig 3.21 Australia: the segments (*The Bulletin*, 10 January 1989)

which separates them, yet clearly shows how they fit together. The latter is the case, for instance, of the 'pie chart' in figure 3.21, where the disengagement of the Possessive Attributes acquires symbolic value, showing, literally and figuratively, the rifts that divide the nation. The former is the case in the communication model on top of figure 2.6, where all the participants are connected by lines. Such connecting lines may be purely abstract connectors, as in figure 2.6, or have a feature of *conductivity*.

connector ——————————————— conductor ═══════════════

⬤ **Fig 3.22 Connectors and conductors**

Conductors are connectors that also represent a Possessive Attribute, a physical entity, for instance wiring, a pipeline, a road, a railway track (see e.g. figure 3.8, where the conductors are however, vectorialized), and they may also be abstract, as in some communication models. Realized by a double line, conductors indicate a *potential* for dynamic interaction between the Possessive Attributes they connect. As such, they are both participant and process, connected element and connector, compounded and conjoining.

In compounded structures the Possessive Attributes are welded together, while at the same time retaining their distinct identities. This is as much the case in a pie chart such as that shown in figure 3.23, as in a technical drawing, for instance the drawing of a machine for crushing ore, in figure 3.24.

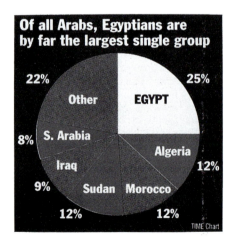

⬤ **Fig 3.23 Arabs (*Time Magazine*, 25 February 1991)**

Fig. 4—Fourth stage crusher—"Gyradisc"

Hydraulic clamp

Feed distributor

Hydraulic rams

Upper and lower liners

Spring-loaded safety release

Lubrication system

Fig 3.24 Fourth-stage crusher (Merritt, 1984)

5 Topographical and topological processes

When analytical structures are *topographical* they are read as accurately representing the physical spatial relations and the relative location of the Possessive Attributes. All of the types of structured analytical processes we have discussed so far may be topographical: we read the picture of the ore crusher in figure 3.24 as accurately scaling down the dimensions and relative location of the parts of the machine, just as we read topographical maps as accurately scaling down, for example, the dimensions of a lake, and its distance from other Possessive Attributes (mountains, rivers) and from the boundaries of the Carrier.

When analytical structures are *topological*, they are read as accurately representing the logical relations between participants, the way in which participants are connected to each other (whether they have common boundaries, or are partially or wholly included in each other, in which sequence they are connected, etc.) but not the actual physical size of the participants or their distance from each other, or, in the case of inclusive structures, from the boundaries of the Carrier. An electrical circuit diagram, for instance, is topological (figure 3.25). It does not signify, say, that lamps a and b are 'above' and 'at the right of' the battery, and it does not accurately scale down the distance between the battery and a lamp a, or between the two lamps. But it does signify that they are connected in this particular sequence, just as figure 3.17 signifies that 'Ape', 'Apeman', 'Australopithecus', etc. made their first appearance in history in the order shown. Pictures of electronic

⬤ Fig 3.25 **Electric circuit diagram (Hill, 1980)**

circuits, on the other hand, are topographical: they accurately scale up the dimensions of the pieces of circuitry they represent (see figure 3.26).

Maps, too, may either be topographical, or topological, as, for instance, in maps of urban transport systems. The digital networks we discussed in the previous section are also topological diagrams, abstract maps, as they are based on adjacency, col-*location*. In other words, abstract diagrams, too, can be either topological or topographical. Schramm's communication model (figure 2.6), for instance, is topological. It does not tell us that the 'Source' is on the left, or to the west, of the 'Encoder', it tells us only that the participants are connected in this sequence. This is not to say that the placement of the 'Source' to the left of the 'Encoder' is not significant, only that its significance derives, not from the ideational, but from the textual structure of the diagram (see chapter 6). Halliday's diagram of the 'nature of linguistic structures and their relations to other fields of scholarship' (1978: 10), on the other hand, is an intricate piece of abstract topography (see figure 3.27). The diagram uses distance to indicate how close the various kinds of language study are from what is here seen as the central and most important form of language study, the study of 'language as system'. It uses distance in a figurative, yet finely calibrated, way: 'phonetics', for example, is closer to 'language as system' than the study of dialects and registers. And it uses relative size in the same way: the study of language takes up a much greater area than all the other 'fields of scholarship' together. As in

⬤ Fig 3.26 **Electronic circuit (*Electronics and Music Maker*, June 1984)**

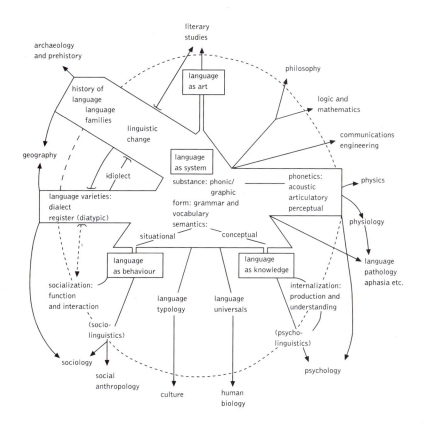

⬯ **Fig 3.27 The nature of linguistic structure (Halliday, 1978)**

medieval maps, the cartographer's 'home town' is both exaggerated in size and represented internally more accurately and with more detail than the surrounding 'countryside'.

6 Dimensional and quantitative topography

Like topographical visuals, charts are drawn to scale. The scale, however, is based, not on the physical dimensions of the participants, but on the quantity or frequency of aggregates of participants that are taken to be identical. Pie charts, for instance (see e.g. figure 3.21), divide a Carrier (the population of Australia) into components, Possessive Attributes, that are in fact *aggregates* of participants analysed as being the same in some respect, and it tells us, not that 'Achievers' are found next to, and to the south-east of, 'Adapters', but that the *number* of 'Achievers' stands to the number of 'Adapters' as the *size* of the Possessive Attribute labelled 'Achievers' stands to the size of the Possessive Attribute labelled 'Adapters': quantity is translated into relative size – although it is of

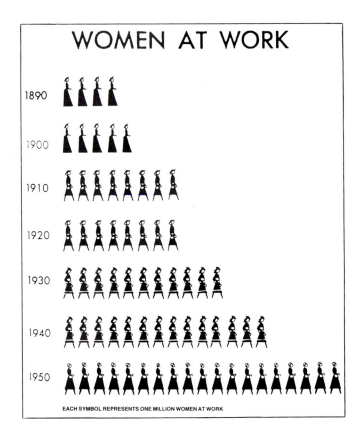

Fig 3.28 Women at work (Modley and Lowenstein, 1952)

course also possible to represent quantity with quantity, as in figure 3.28, a now perhaps rather old-fashioned example which uses Otto von Neurath's 'picture language' Isotype (see e.g. Lupton, 1989).

Pie charts and bar charts (see figure 3.30) are *one-dimensional*: they show us one (abstract) Carrier (in the case of figure 3.21, the concrete Carrier 'Australia' is a metonym for the abstract Carrier 'the population of Australia') and its Possessive Attributes. Their structure is quite similar to that of stack diagrams (see figure 3.7). They are exhaustive, compounded analytical structures. The difference lies only in their peculiar kind of abstraction and peculiar kind of topographical accuracy, both of which are *quantitative*.

7 Spatio-temporal analytical structures

Two-dimensional charts create a conjunction between a *set* of such (exhaustive, compounded, quantitatively abstract and topographical) analytical structures and a time

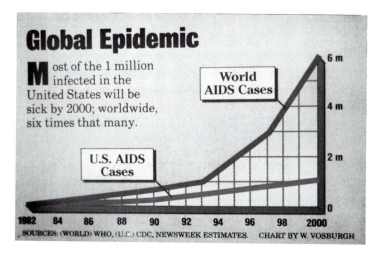

Fig 3.29 Global epidemic (*The Bulletin*, 26 June 1990)

line, for the sake of comparative analysis along an ordered time scale. In the case of line graphs this can result in the quasi-vectorial, quasi-narrative structure typified by temperature charts, profit charts, company growth charts, etc. (see figure 3.29). In other words, the substitution of a line for discrete bars creates something like a dynamic process (transcodable as 'change', 'grow', 'decrease', etc.), and backgrounds or even erases the analytical structures that underlie the graph, so that the graph no longer says 'In 1988 the Carrier ("incidence of AIDS") consisted of 500,000 Possessive Attributes

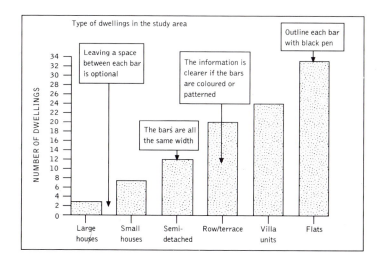

Fig 3.30 Types of dwelling (Bindon and Williams, 1988)

("AIDS cases") *and* in 1990 the Carrier consisted of 800,000 Possessive Attributes *and...* (etc.)', but 'The Actor ("the epidemic") acts ("spreads rapidly").' To complicate matters one-dimensional structures can be represented as though they were two-dimensional, and so produce a sense of progress or decline, depending on the order in which the Possessive Attributes are plotted along the horizontal axis – an order not given by relations of conjoinedness or compoundness, or of inclusion or exclusion, but solely by quantity. The bar chart in figure 3.30 can easily be (mis)taken as saying, not that more people live in flats than in large houses, but that people, as time progresses, increasingly live in flats.

Something quite similar can happen in language. Hodge and Kress (1978, 1993) drew attention to the effects of the transformation of nominalization, which turns clauses (reports of events) such as *people learned* into nominals (names of objects) such as *people's learning* which may then become actors in new events (*the new learning spread*). Martin *et al.* (1988) have described this process in history textbooks. They comment that such transformations favour the 'anthropomorphic metaphor of birth, growth and death' (p. 157) and allow historians to analyse history in successive periods in which similar things go on. In other words, despite their apparent status as active, dynamic processes, these structures still serve to establish stable, conceptual orders.

This dynamization of two-dimensional analytical processes cannot occur when the arrangement is vertical (see figure 3.31). The Possessive Attributes then remain discrete, and the graphs as a whole suggest a stable order rather than a dynamic process. This is borne out, for instance, by the fact that one cannot 'fill in' the space of the Carrier.

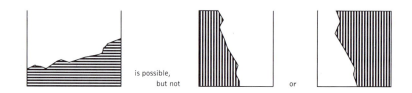

is possible, but not   or

● Fig 3.31 Dynamization of analytical processes

It is our impression that there has been, in Western cultures, a shift from a focus on the vertical to a focus on the horizontal, a change from a concern with 'What is the state of affairs?' and 'Where are we?' to 'Where are we going?' and 'Have we progressed or are we in decline?' This is borne out also by the fact that scripts which were traditionally written top–down are now beginning to be written from left to right.

In figure 3.32 we summarize the distinctions introduced in this section. Note that the superscript 'I' means 'if' and the superscript 'T' 'then'. In other words: if there is a topographical time line then the topography must be quantitative.

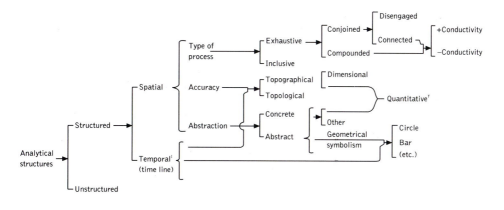

⬤ **Fig 3.32 Analytic image structures**

REALIZATIONS

Unstructured analytical process

An unordered set of participants ('Possessive Attributes') is interpreted as the set of parts of a whole which itself is not represented.

Temporal analytical process

A set of participants ('Possessive Attributes') is ordered linearly on a (horizontal or vertical) time line and interpreted as the set of successive stages of a temporally unfolding process.

Exhaustive analytical process

A participant ('Carrier') is depicted as made up of a number of parts ('Possessive Attributes') and the structure is interpreted as showing all the parts from which the whole is made up.

Dimensional topographical accuracy

The Carrier and the Possessive Attributes of an analytical process are drawn to scale.

Quantitative topographical accuracy

The size of the Possessive Attributes in an analytical process accurately represents the number or some other

	quantitative attribute of the Possessive Attributes.
Topological accuracy	The Carrier and the Possessive Attributes of an analytical process are not drawn to scale, but the way they are interconnected is drawn accurately.
Abstraction	The participants in an analytical process may be concrete.

SYMBOLIC PROCESSES

Symbolic processes are about what a participant *means* or *is*. Either there are two participants – the participant whose meaning or identity is established in the relation, the *Carrier*, and the participant which represents the meaning or identity itself, *the Symbolic Attribute* – or there is only one participant, the *Carrier*, and in that case the symbolic meaning is established in another way, to be described below. The former type of process we will call *Symbolic Attributive*, the latter *Symbolic Suggestive*.

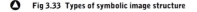

O   **Fig 3.33 Types of symbolic image structure**

Art historians have charted the formal pictorial characteristics which can realize the Symbolic Attribute relation (see especially Hermeren, 1969). Symbolic Attributes are objects with one or more of the following characteristics. (1) They are made salient in the representation in one way or another, for instance by being placed in the foreground, through exaggerated size, through being especially well lit, through being represented in especially fine detail or sharp focus, or through their conspicuous colour or tone. (2) They are pointed at by means of a gesture which cannot be interpreted as an action other than the action of 'pointing out the symbolic attribute to the viewer' – here we can include also the arrows which can connect visual realizations of participants with verbal realizations of the same participant, or vice versa, as in figure 2.4, for these also establish a relation of identity through 'pointing'. (3) They look out of place in the whole. (4) They are conventionally associated with symbolic values. Such conventional symbols were very common in the Middle Ages and the Renaissance: see, for instance, figure 3.34, where the apple, looking somewhat out of place in St Jerome's study, symbolizes the Fall,

Temptation, Original Sin, and so brings these immediately to mind for the viewer of the painting.

In figure 3.35 the Symbolic Attribute is formed by the portrait of the artist Brett Whiteley on the wall, and it becomes a Symbolic Attribute because of the non-naturalistic and highly conspicuous way in which it is lit. The photo was published shortly after the artist's death, and confers on Whiteley's daughter the symbolic values associated with her father, whose public image was that of an artist living a life of romantic excess.

The scientist depicted in figure 3.36 is clearly not doing anything with or to the fungi which are displayed in the foreground and of which he is holding one in his right hand. His position in relation to the fungi seems contrived and posed. Again, the fungi are the Attributes that establish his identity as an expert on fungi. The flowers in figure 3.37 are also a Symbolic Attribute. Their placement, near the foot of the bed, is impractical and contrived. They are not an ordinary part of the setting. They are there to say, 'this woman is (like) a flower'.

Human participants in Symbolic Attributive processes usually pose for the viewer, rather than being shown as involved in some action. This does not mean that they are necessarily portrayed front-on and eye level, or that they necessarily look at the viewer, even though all of these will often be the case. It means that they take up a posture which cannot be interpreted as narrative: they just sit or stand there, for no reason other than to display themselves to the viewer.

Fig 3.34 *St Jerome in his Study* **(Jan van Eyck, 1434) (from Hermeren, 1969)**

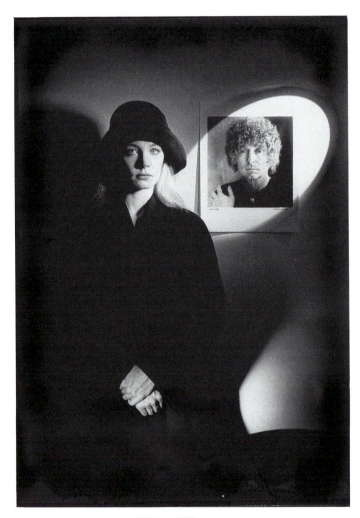

Fig 3.35 Arkie Whiteley (*Sydney Morning Herald*, 20 June 1992)

Symbolic Suggestive Processes have only one participant, the Carrier. They cannot be interpreted as analytical, because in this kind of image detail tends to be de-emphasized in favour of what could be called 'mood' or 'atmosphere'. This can be realized in a number of ways: the colours may all blend together, into a hazy blue, for instance, or a soft golden glow; the focus may be soft; or the lighting may be extreme, either in the way it reduces or in the way it increases contrast, rendering the participants as outlines or silhouettes. It is this which lends Symbolic Suggestive pictures their genericity, their quality of depicting not a specific moment but a generalized essence. The *way in which* the blurring of detail occurs then lends symbolic value to the Carrier – a soft golden glow, for instance, would confer on the Carrier all the values associated with softness, and with gold. As a

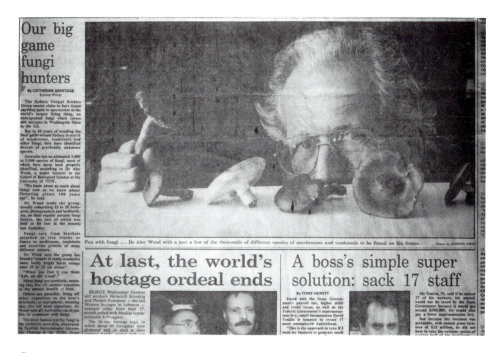

○ **Fig 3.36 Fun with fungi (*Sydney Morning Herald*, 18 June 1992)**

○ **Fig 3.37 Sheer Magic advertisement (*Women's Weekly*, December 1987)**

○ **Fig 3.38 Oil drilling in the Sahara (Oakley, 1985)**

result Symbolic Suggestive processes represent meaning and identity as coming from within, as deriving from qualities of the Carrier themselves, whereas Symbolic Attributive processes represent meaning and identity as being conferred to the Carrier.

Figure 3.38 shows an oil drilling installation in the Sahara desert. The de-emphasizing of detail, and hence the 'mood' of the picture, results from the extreme lighting conditions in which the setting sun plays the role of a low backlight. In this way the oil drilling installation becomes a symbol for the disappearance of the old Bedouin lifestyle. The accompanying text in fact ends with a quote from a Bedouin, lamenting the demise of traditional ways of life – followed by the photo.

Expressionist landscapes (e.g. Nolde's *Autumn Evening*, see colour plate 1) also diminish the detail of the representation, in favour of overall colour effects evolving a strong mood, and imbuing the Carrier ('autumn evening') with symbolic meanings.

EMBEDDING

Sentences can be simple (containing only one clause/process) or complex (containing several clauses, each with their own process, co-ordinated with or subordinated to each other). Pictures, too, can be simple or complex. We have already discussed how in figure 2.1 the relation between the Aborigines and the fire constitutes a second, minor, transactional process, subordinated to the 'major' process which is constituted by the relation between the British and the Aborigines; and how participants such as the British or the landscape can themselves be read as analytical structures, with a Carrier (e.g. the landscape) and Possessive Attributes (e.g. rocks and trees). Which of these structures are major and which are minor is, in visuals, determined by the relative size and relative conspicuousness of the elements. The cover of the book from which we took 'Aboriginal tools and British guns' provides an example of this kind of complexity (figure 3.39). We can recognize four different processes in this picture:

(1) A classificational process in which the five children are Subordinates of the class of 'young Australians', in what we have called a Covert Taxonomy. They are shown against a neutral background and arranged in a symmetrical fashion, in a circle which is closed (and reiterated) by the globe. (We will discuss the meaning of circularity more fully in chapter 6.)
(2) A number of analytical processes in which each child is Carrier in relation to a number of (prototypical, 'essential') Possessive Attributes (skin colour, colour and kind of hair, colour of eyes, items of clothing) — attributes which create visual concepts of their different ethnicities.

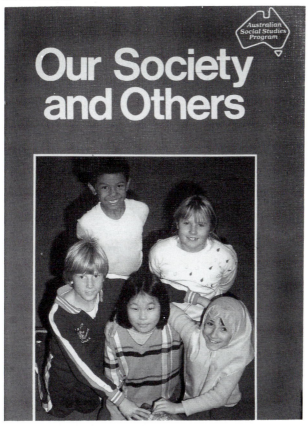

Fig 3.39 Our society and others (Oakley, 1985)

(3) A symbolic attributive process in which the globe is a conventional symbol with strong associations. It is placed in the foreground of the picture, and two of the children touch it with a gesture which cannot easily be interpreted as an action other than one that draws the viewer's attention to the globe. The children are thus shown to be part of the world, a microcosm of the world in Australia.

(4) Transactional processes in which three of the children have put their arms round other children. The boy on the left would seem to be the major Actor here, while the two girls are Goal with respect to his action. The two girls, who have their arms round each other, on the other hand, relate in a more reciprocal way. They are what we have called Interactors.

From this multiple analysis we can see that the picture (even when we disregard the interactive and compositional structures which are also present, and which will be discussed in the next three chapters) forms a powerful, multidimensional structure.

Turning to the relation between these processes, we might say that because of its sheer size and conspicuousness, the circular arrangement of the children is dominant, while the analytical processes are embedded in it: five children are co-classified, and each of them can be further analysed in terms of Possessive Attributes. In other words, the major message is that these children belong to the same category, despite the difference in gender and ethnicity; the minor message is that they are, nevertheless, different. As far as the transactional and symbolic processes are concerned, we would argue that the white lines on the boy's tracksuit form strong and dominant vectors.

Perhaps the transactional process of which this boy is Actor and the symbolic process of which he is Carrier weigh as heavily in the scale as the classificational process, and also form major processes. The transactional processes of which the girls in the foreground are both Actor and Goal, and the symbolic process of which the girl on the right is the Carrier, however, are considerably less conspicuous and might be interpreted as minor processes. In other words, as Actors of the gesture of solidarity, and as Carriers of the symbolic value of 'representing the world', the 'ethnic' girls have, in this representation, a much less significant role to play than the white Australian boy in his tracksuit.

CONCEPTUAL STRUCTURES IN LANGUAGE

The 'relational' and 'existential' processes in language form the equivalent of the conceptual processes in visual communication (see Halliday, 1985: 112ff.). Like conceptual images, they represent the world in terms of more or less permanent states of affairs or general truths, rather than in terms of actions or mental processes. There are two main categories of relational process, the *Attributive* and the *Identifying* process. The meaning of an Attributive process clause can be schematically described as 'a is an attribute of x'. The attribute 'a' is then simply called *Attribute*, and the participant whose attribute it is, is the *Carrier* – we have borrowed these terms in our analysis of images. In *Some people are racist*, for instance, *some people* is Carrier, *are* is the Relational (Attributive) process, and *racist* is the Attribute. Attributive processes can be *Intensive*, that is, they can be about what a Carrier *is*, as in the example just given; they can be *Circumstantial*, that is, they can be about 'where' or 'when' or 'what with' a Carrier is (e.g. in *Their home was in Ho Chi Minh City*, *their home* is Carrier, *was* an Attributive (Circumstantial) Relational process, and *in Ho Chi Minh City* an Attribute); and they can be *Possessive*, that is, they can be about what a Carrier *has* (e.g. in *I didn't own a thing in the world*, *I* is Carrier, *own* the Attributive (Possessive) Relational process, and *a thing in the world*, the Attribute).

The meaning of an *Identifying Relational process* clause can be schematically described as 'a is the identity of x'. The identity 'a' is then termed the *Value* and the participant 'x' whose identity it is, is called the *Token*. In *Rev. Peter Nyangingu is the Minister of the Uniting Church at Ernabella*, *Rev. Peter Nyangingu* is Token, *is* is the Identifying Relational process, and *the Minister of the Uniting Church at Ernabella* is the Value. The Value, then, tends to be a 'status' or 'function' or 'meaning' which serves to identify the Token, and the Token is the name or some description of the holder of the status, or of the occupant of the function, or of the sign which has the meaning. Picture captions are often identifying clauses, with a reference to the picture as Token and the meaning of the Picture as Value (for instance, *This is oyster farming in Palm Island*). Identifying and Attributive clauses can be distinguished from each other by means of the reversibility test: in Identifying clauses the order of the participants can be reversed (e.g. *The Minister of the Uniting Church at Ernabella is Rev. Peter Nyangingu* is just as acceptable as *Rev. Peter Nyangingu is the Minister of the Uniting Church at Ernabella*), in Attributive clauses, this is not the case (*Racist are some people* is much more unusual than *Some people are racist*).

Existential clauses simply state that 'something exists' or 'something happens'. They have only one participant, the *Existent*, that is, the participant whose existence the structure affirms. Existents may either be *Events* (e.g. in *It is terrible weather*) or *Entities* (e.g. in *There was a public library*). The presence of a 'dummy subject' (*there* or referentless *it*) is the principal identifying characteristic of existential clauses (see Halliday, 1985: 130).

This brief overview shows that there are some points of contact between the way conceptualizations are realized in language and in images. Classificational and Analytical structures, for instance, are akin to, respectively, Intensive and Possessive Attributive clauses, Symbolic Attributive structures can be seen as akin to Identifying clauses, and there is perhaps also some affinity between Symbolic Suggestive structures and Existential clauses. But the differences are greater than the similarities, and especially in the area of Classificational and Analytical images, the visual semiotic has a range of structural devices which have no equivalent in language: the difference between visual conceptualization and linguistic conceptualization is evidently quite large. All the more important to have a vocabulary for expressing what can be done and is done with each in concrete texts that combine the two semiotics, texts such as 'The Overland' (figure 3.40), a school project by an eight-year-old boy. Looking first at the words, the structure of the verbal text on the left page is Possessive Attribute throughout. There is a Carrier ('The Overland'), and there are six Possessive Attributes ('five first class carriages', 'three second class carriages', 'two dining car's, 'two engines' and 'one club car', 'one motor rail cart'). The process itself is elided.

The picture, too, is concerned with the relation of parts to a whole. It has all the hallmarks of an exhaustive, structured analytical process: the picture is front-on and eye level, there is no Setting, and the different Possessive Attributes (signs, windows, wheels, suspension and rails) are shown clearly, but without unnecessary detail: it is relatively 'abstract'. The relation between picture and text is not one of illustration. The picture does not duplicate the text, it does not represent visually what has already been represented linguistically. Nor is there a relation of 'anchorage' (Barthes, 1977) in which the text elaborates the information given in the picture without providing new information. It is true that both text and picture are about part–whole relations but this does not mean they duplicate each other because in the text the Carrier is the *train as a whole*, whereas in the picture the Carrier is *one of the carriages of the train*. The child has taken a topic, the

Fig 3.40 'The overland'

Overland Express, and treated it verbally and visually in such a way that each part of the text supplements the other part.

Let us analyse the second page. The words are as follows:

It goes from ADELAIDE to Melbourne rail Australian National root.

Here we have first of all a non-transactional action, with an Actor ('it') and an Action ('goes'), as well as two Circumstances of place ('from Adelaide' and 'to Melbourne'). There follows an identification of the route, with the Token and the Process elided ('rail Australian National root'): the child objectifies the action 'going', turns it into a thing, a 'route', by means of an identifying relational process in which the 'root' is Value. Finally the route is described in more detail, through a visual analytical process in which the relevant section of Australia is the Carrier, and Adelaide, Melbourne and the 'route' the Possessive Attributes, in a process which uses many of the structural devices of the analytical visual to show precisely how the Possessive Attributes are spatially related, how they 'fit together'.

'My Adventure' (figure 3.41) is another school project, written by a child from the same school and year as the author of 'The Overland'. Most of the verbal processes are transactional and non-transactional actions in which the narrator is Actor: he walks, finds a cave, finds some nails, and so on. He is not describing something but telling a story, narrating a particular event:

Not long ago I went for a journey down to the beach. I walked all along the beach until I found a cave. That cave was big. Then there was some wood but I couldn't make a raft without nails. Just then I found some nails in the cave. I said to myself 'Somebody must have been here'. So I got a piece of wood and started making the raft. I used a piece of wood for a. . . .

Still, there is also a conceptual element. In this part of the story the writer is preoccupied with the materials needed for building a raft. There is a hidden attributive process, something like 'the materials for a raft are wood and nails', but it is transformed into the story of the finding of these materials (which emerge mysteriously in a big cave). As in the story that opens the book of Genesis, which is also a narrative concerned with conceptualizing the elements that make up a whole, the world, the writer alternates actional and transactional processes ('I found some nails') with more conceptual existential processes ('then there was some wood').

The verbal text stops abruptly, in the middle of the Circumstance of Purpose, and it is continued, not on the following page, but by the picture, which shows what these materials were used for: the parts of a raft. It is an Unstructured Analytical process, with the sail, and the raft itself (already complete with mast and rudder) as Possessive Attributes. These are, in the child's conceptualization, the parts from which a raft is made. However, there is also a strong narrative element in this picture: it has a Setting (the shoreline, the cave) and it does not use the frontal, eye-level perspective typical of most

⬢ **Fig 3.41 'My adventure'**

analytical images (and already successfully used by the author of 'The Overland') but a high and oblique angle. In both the picture and the words the writer blends the conceptual and the narrative, or rather, narrativizes the conceptual. In the verbal text he does this through conjunctions ('then', 'just then', etc.), through the use of the past tense and through the use of transactional and non-transactional Action processes with the narrator as a (first-person) Actor. In the picture he does it through the use of a Setting and a narrative perspective. Finally, the words and the picture again complement each other. The picture does not illustrate the story but continues it.

It is clear, we hope, that children actively experiment with the representational resources of word and image, and with the ways in which they can be combined. Their drawings are not just illustrations of a verbal text, not just 'creative embellishment'; they are part of a 'multimodally' conceived text, a semiotic interplay in which each mode, the verbal and the visual, is given a defined and equal role to play.

4 Representation and interaction: designing the position of the viewer

In the previous chapter we have discussed visual resources for the representation of interactions and conceptual relations between the people, places and things depicted in images. But visual communication also has resources for constituting and maintaining another kind of interaction, the interaction between the producer and the viewer of the image. Another way of saying this is that images involve two kinds of participants, *represented participants* (the people, the places and things depicted in images), and *interactive participants* (the people who communicate with each other *through* images, the producers and viewers of images), and three kinds of relations: (1) relations between represented participants; (2) relations between interactive and represented participants (the interactive participants' attitudes towards the represented participants); and (3) relations between interactive participants (the things interactive participants *do* to or for each other through images).

Interactive participants are therefore real people who produce and make sense of images in the context of social institutions which, to different degrees and in different ways, regulate what may be 'said' with images, and how it should be said, and how images should be interpreted. In some cases the interaction is direct and immediate. Producer and viewer know each other and are involved in face-to-face interaction, as when we make photographs of each other to keep in wallets or pin on pinboards, or draw maps to give each other directions, or diagrams to explain ideas to each other. But in many cases there is no immediate and direct involvement. The producer is absent for the viewer, and the viewer is absent for the producer. Think of photographs in magazines. Who is the producer? The photographer who took the shot? The assistant who processed and printed it? The agency who selected and distributed it? The picture editor who chose it? The layout artist who cropped it and determined its size and position on the page? Most viewers will not only never meet all these contributors to the production process face to face, but also have only a hazy, and perhaps distorted and glamourized idea of the production processes behind the image. All they have is the picture itself, as it appears in the magazine. And producers, similarly, can never really know their vast and absent audiences, and must, instead, create a mental image of 'the' viewers and 'the' way viewers make sense of their pictures. In everyday face-to-face communication it is easy enough to distinguish interactive participants from represented participants: there is always an image-producer and a viewer (who, depending on the situation, may swap roles with the producer, add to the scribbled floorplan or diagram, for instance, and then there are the represented participants (for instance, the people on the quick sketch of the dinner table arrangement, or the landmarks on the hand-drawn map), and these may, of course, include the producer and/or the viewer themselves. Producer and viewer are physically present. The participants they represent need not be. But when there is a disjunction between the context of production and the context of reception, the producer is not physically present, and the viewer is alone with the image and cannot reciprocate – an illuminating exception is the case of the 'defacement' of billboard advertisements, when graffiti artists 'respond' to the initial 'turn' or statement of the image.

Something similar occurs in writing. Writers, too, are not usually physically present when their words are read, and must address their readers in the guise of represented participants, even when they write in the first person. Readers, too, are alone with the written word, and cannot usually become writers in turn. Literary theorists (e.g. Booth, 1961; Chatman, 1978) have addressed this problem by distinguishing between 'real' and 'implied' authors, and between 'real' and 'implied' readers. The 'implied author' is a disembodied voice, or even 'a set of implicit norms rather than a speaker or a voice' (Rimmon-Kenan, 1983: 87): 'he, or better, *it* has no voice, no direct means of communicating, but instructs us silently, through the design of the whole, with all the voices, by all the means it has chosen to let us learn' (Chatman, 1978: 148). The 'implied reader', 'preferred reading position', etc., similarly, is 'an image of a certain competence brought to the text and a structuring of such competence within the text' (Rimmon-Kenan, 1983: 118): the text selects a 'model reader' through its 'choice of a specific linguistic code, a certain literary style' and by presupposing 'a specific encyclopedic competence' on the part of the reader (Eco, 1979: 7). This we can know. Of this we have evidence in the text itself. Real authors and real readers we cannot ultimately know. This bracketing out of real authors and real readers carries the risk of forgetting that texts, literary and artistic texts as much as mass media texts, are produced in the context of real social institutions, in order to play a very real role in social life – in order to do certain things to or for their readers, and in order to communicate attitudes towards aspects of social life and towards people who participate in them, whether authors and readers are consciously aware of this or not. Producers, if they want to see their work disseminated, must work within more or less rigidly defined conventions, and adhere to the more or less rigidly defined values and beliefs of the social institution within which their work is produced and circulated. Readers will at least recognize these communicative intentions and these values and attitudes for what they are, even if they do not ultimately accept them as their own values and beliefs. They can 'recognize the substance of what is meant while refusing the speaker's interpretations and assessments' (Scannell, 1994: 11).

However important and real this disjunction between the context of production and the context of reception, the two do have elements in common: the image itself, and a knowledge of the communicative resources that allow its articulation and understanding, a knowledge of the way social interactions and social relations can be encoded in images. It is often said that the knowledge of the producer and the knowledge of the viewer differ in a fundamental respect: the former is active, allowing the 'sending' as well as the 'receiving' of 'messages'; the latter is passive, allowing only the 'receiving' of 'messages'. Producers are able to 'write' as well as 'read', viewers are able only to 'read'. Up to a point this is true, at least in the sense that the production of images is still a specialized activity, so that producers 'write' more fluently and eloquently, and more frequently, than viewers. But we hope our attempts to make that knowledge explicit will show that the interactive meanings are visually encoded in ways that rest on competencies shared by producers and viewers. The articulation and understanding of social meanings in images derives from the visual articulation of social meanings in face-to-face interaction, the spatial positions allocated to different kinds of social actors in interaction (whether they are seated or standing, side by side or facing each other frontally, etc.). In this sense the interactive dimension of images is the 'writing' of what is usually called 'non-verbal communication', a 'language' shared by producers and viewers alike.

The disjunction between the context of production and the context of reception has yet another effect: it causes social relations to be *represented rather than enacted*. Because the producers are absent from the place where the actual communicative transaction is completed, from the locus of reception, they cannot say 'I' other than through a substitute 'I'. Even when the viewer receives an image of the 'real author' or a contributor to the production process, the presenter in a television programme, the painter in a self-portrait, the owner of the company (or the worker in the centuries-old distillery) in an advertisement, that image is only an image, a double of the 'real author', a representation, detached from his or her actual body. And the 'real authors' may also speak in the guise of someone else, of a 'character', as when, instead of the owner of a company, it is Uncle Sam, or a larger than life walking and talking teddy bear, who addresses us in an advertisement. This dimension of representation is another one which has been studied extensively in literary theory (e.g. Genette, 1972). The relation between producer and viewer, too, is represented rather than enacted. In face-to-face communication we must respond to a friendly smile with a friendly smile, to an arrogant stare with a deferential lowering of the eyes, and such obligations cannot easily be avoided without appearing impolite, unfriendly or impudent. When images confront us with friendly smiles or arrogant stares, we are not obliged to respond, even though we do recognize how we are addressed. The relation is only represented. We are *imaginarily* rather than really put in the position of the friend, the customer, the lay person who must defer to the expert. And whether or not we identify with that position will depend on other factors – on our real relation to the producer or the institution he or she represents, and on our real relation to the others who form part of the context of reception. All the same, whether or not we identify with the way we are addressed, we do understand how we are addressed, because we do understand the way images represent social interactions and social relations. It is the business of this chapter to try and make those understandings explicit.

THE IMAGE ACT AND THE GAZE

Figure 4.1 displays the page from which the picture of the Antarctic explorer (figure 2.4) was taken. On the left we see photographs from which the Australian Antarctic explorer Sir Douglas Mawson looks directly at the viewer. The somewhat schematic drawing of a 'generalized' explorer is figure 2.4, and this explorer does not look at the viewer. The photos and the drawing serve different communicative functions: the photos (especially the close-up) seek above all to bring about an imaginary relation between the represented

Sir Douglas Mawson

One of the most famous of these Antarctic explorers was the Australian, Douglas Mawson.

Douglas Mawson was a scientist—a geologist. He wanted to find minerals and to claim some of this large continent for Australia. He first went to Antarctica as a member of the British Antarctic Expedition, led by Sir Ernest Shackleton, in 1907-1909. During this expedition, Mawson became one of the first men to climb Mount Erebus, a volcano and one of Antarctica's highest mountains. Mawson was so impressed by what he saw on his first journey that he made up his mind to go back again, as soon as he could. He wanted to discover more about this large, unexplored land.

Only two years later, Mawson was back in Antarctica with his own party of explorers. This time he was the leader.

Look at the clothes worn by explorers to Antarctica.

Mawson's second journey to Antarctica has been described as one of the greatest tales of human courage ever told. To find out why, read the story yourself or ask your teacher to tell you the story.

Journey into the unknown

Mawson's party set up their base camp at Commonwealth Bay, on the Antarctic coast south of Australia. They built a small hut on the narrow, stony beach, surrounded by cliffs of ice 80 metres high.

20

Unfortunately, as they soon found out, this was not a good place for a camp as hurricanes blew for almost eight months of the year. Mawson's men often measured wind speeds of 300 kilometres an hour—the strongest winds ever recorded on Earth. Fierce winds picked up rocks from the beach and threw them at the walls of the hut, making so much noise that the men inside the hut found it almost impossible to talk to each other. Mawson called Commonwealth Bay "The Home of the Blizzard".

When there was finally a break in the weather, Mawson divided his men into five small parties. Each party set out in a different direction to explore the land around the base camp.

Mawson set off on 10 November taking two men with him. They were Dr Xavier Mertz, a Swiss scientist and mountaineer, and an Englishman, Belgrave Ninnis. Their journey was to be the longest—they were to explore the coast as far as possible to the west of Commonwealth Bay.

Mawson's party took with them three dog sledges loaded with almost a thousand kilograms of food, fuel, clothing and shelter. To pull these heavily laden sledges, they took seventeen Greenland husky dogs. These dogs were bred for such harsh conditions and heavy work by the Eskimos of the frozen lands around the North Pole.

21

Fig 4.1 Antarctic explorer (Oakley, 1985)

explorer and the children for whom the book is written, a relation perhaps of admiration for, and identification with, a national hero. And this means also that the producer of the images (the institution of educational publishing) addresses the children in the voice of the national hero and makes that national hero an 'educational' voice. The drawing, on the other hand, seeks, first of all, to be read as a piece of objective, factual information, and in this way aims to set into motion the actual process of learning.

There is, then, a fundamental difference between pictures from which represented participants look directly at the viewer's eyes, and pictures in which this is not the case. When represented participants look at the viewer, vectors, formed by participants' eyelines, connect the participants with the viewer. Contact is established, even if it is only on an imaginary level. In addition there may be a further vector, formed by a gesture in the same direction, as in figure 4.2.

This visual configuration has two related functions. In the first place it creates a visual form of direct address. It acknowledges the viewers explicitly, addressing them with a visual 'you'. In the second place it constitutes an 'image act'. The producer uses the image to *do* something to the viewer. It is for this reason that we have called this kind of image a 'demand': the participant's gaze (and the gesture, if present) demands something from the viewer, demands that the viewer enter into some kind of imaginary relation with him or her. Exactly what kind of relation is then signified by other means, for instance by the facial expression of the represented participants. They may smile, in which case the viewer

○　**Fig 4.2 Recruitment poster (Alfred Leete, 1914) (Imperial War Museum)**

is asked to enter into a relation of social affinity with them; they may stare at the viewer with cold disdain, in which case the viewer is asked to relate to them, perhaps, as an inferior relates to a superior; they may seductively pout at the viewer, in which case the viewer is asked to desire them. The same applies to gestures. A hand can point at the viewer, in a visual 'Hey, you there, I mean you', or invite the viewer to come closer, or hold the viewer at bay with a defensive gesture, as if to say: stay away from me. In each case the image wants something from the viewers – wants them to do something (come closer, stay at a distance) or to form a pseudo-social bond of a particular kind with the represented participant. And in doing this, images define to some extent who the viewer is (e.g. male, inferior to the represented participant, etc.), and in that way exclude other viewers.

In the history of art, this look was a significant innovation. Although in Italian painting small figures among the bystanders of the Crucifixion and the other biblical scenes can be seen to look at the viewer from the fourteenth century onwards, the 'demand' picture comes into its own in the fifteenth century. According to Panofsky (1953: 190), it originated in self-portraits, and Jan van Eyck was the first to use it in *Man in a Red Turban* (1433), which is regarded by most art historians as a self-portrait.

> In 1433 Jan van Eyck made one of the great discoveries in portraiture. In the portrait of a 'Man in a Red Turban', completed in October 21 of that year, the glance of the sitter is turned out of the picture and sharply focussed on the beholder with an air of skepticism intensified by the expression of the thin mouth with its slightly compressed corners. For the first time the sitter seeks to establish direct contact with the spectator.... We feel observed and scrutinized by a wakeful intelligence.
>
> (Panofsky, 1953: 198)

Others trace it back further. According to Belting (1990) 'the suggestion of reciprocity between the viewer and the person depicted in the image' had a devotional purpose. By the thirteenth century, monks in their cells 'had before their eyes images of the Virgin and her crucified son, so that while reading, praying and sleeping, they could look upon them and *be looked upon* with the eyes of compassion' (p. 57, our italics).

Represented participants who look at the viewer are usually human (or animal), but not always: the headlights of a car can be drawn as eyes looking at the viewer, for instance, and on the screen of one automatic bank teller, a creature whose combined head and body has the box-like shape of a machine, smiles at the viewer, holding out his hand in an inviting gesture, thus 'demanding' a friendly relation between the machine and its user (figure 2.22). The point is, whether they are human or not, by being represented as looking at the viewer, they are represented *as* human, anthropomorphized to some degree.

Other pictures address us indirectly. Here the viewer is not object, but subject of the look, and the represented participant is the object of the viewer's dispassionate scrutiny. No contact is made. The viewer's role is that of an invisible onlooker. All images which do not contain human or quasi-human participants looking directly at the viewer are of this kind. For this reason we have called this kind of image an 'offer' – it 'offers' the represented participants to the viewer as items of information, objects of contemplation, impersonally, as though they were specimens in a display case.

It is always interesting to study which kinds of represented participants are, in a given context, depicted as demanding an imaginary social response of some kind from the viewer, and which are not. In the Australian primary school social studies textbook *Our Society and Others*, for instance, immigrant families smile at the viewer. However, the human participants in pictures from these immigrants' countries of origin do *not* look at the viewer, not even in close-up portraits, as, for instance, in the portrait of an Italian grandmother who stayed behind. In the chapter on Aborigines, by contrast, hardly any of the Aboriginal participants look at the viewer. The Aboriginal poet Oodgeroo Noonuccal, referred to in the book as Kath Walker, and depicted in close-up in the last illustration of that chapter, is the only exception (see figure 4.4 below). Her expression, her make-up, her hair style and dress hardly distinguish her from non-Aboriginal women of her age. At most her skin is somewhat darker, but even that is not very pronounced in the

Fig 4.3 *Man in a Red Turban* (Jan van Eyck, 1433) (from Panofsky, 1953)

black-and-white shot. Other Aboriginal people in the chapter are much more clearly depicted as 'other', and even if they do, occasionally, look directly at the viewer, they do so from a long distance, which greatly diminishes the impact of their look, or are figures in the background, looking blankly and more or less accidentally in the direction of the camera. Aboriginal people, in this primary school textbook, are depicted as objects of contemplation, not as subjects for the pupil to enter into an imaginary social relation with. Immigrants, by contrast, at least once they are in Australia, are portrayed as people with whom the pupils should engage more directly, and in a friendly way, as equals.

The choice between 'offer' and 'demand', which must be made whenever people are depicted, is not only used to suggest different relations with different 'others', to make viewers engage with some and remain detached from others; it can also characterize pictorial genres. In some contexts, for instance television newsreading and the posed magazine photograph, the 'demand' picture is preferred: these contexts require a sense of connection between the viewers and the authority figures, celebrities and role models they depict. In other contexts, for example feature film and television drama and scientific illustration, the 'offer' is preferred: here a real or imaginary barrier is erected between the represented participants and the viewers, a sense of disengagement, in which the viewer must have the illusion that the represented participants do not know they are being looked at, and in which the represented participants must pretend that they are not being watched. And what in one context is accepted convention may in another be a startling mistake or an innovative experiment. Film theorists (e.g. Allen, 1977; Wollen, 1982) have hailed the look at the camera as a daring, Brechtian, 'self-reflexive' style figure, but in television newsreading the look at the camera is commonplace and, we would think, not exactly 'self-reflexive' – at least for the presenters: an interviewee who looks at the camera in a television news programme breaks the rules in an unacceptable way. Not everyone may address the viewer directly. Some may only be looked *at*, others may themselves be the bearers of the look. There is an issue of communicative power or 'entitlement' (Sacks, 1992) involved in this, not only in pictures, but also in everyday face-to-face communication, for instance in interactions between men and women:

> As he answers the girl's last statement he begins talking and reaches the point where normally he would look away, but instead he is still staring at her. This makes her uncomfortable, because she is forced either to lock eyes with him, or to look away from him while *he* is talking. If he continues to talk and stare while she deflects her eyes, it puts her into the 'shy' category, which she resents. If she boldly locks eyes with him, he has forced her into a 'lover's gaze', which she also resents.
>
> (Morris, 1977: 76)

Diagrams, maps and charts are most often found in contexts that offer the kind of knowledge which, in our culture, is most highly valued – objective, dispassionate knowledge, ostensibly free of emotive involvement and subjectivity. Hence the 'demand' is rare in these visual genres. But there are contexts in which the two forms of address are combined. School textbooks, for instance, may construct a progression from 'demand' to 'offer' pictures, and this not only in the course of a chapter, as in the chapter on Antarctic exploration, but also in the course of a whole book or series of books, and indeed, in the course of education as a whole: illustrations that serve to involve students emotively in the subject matter gradually drop out as higher levels of education are reached. In senior highschool textbooks we find 'demand' pictures at most in the cartoons which, in almost apologetic fashion, seek to alleviate the seriousness of the text from time to time, as in a cartoon in a geography textbook (Bindon and Williams, 1988) where a girl looks despondently at the viewer, with the words 'What does hypothesis mean?' in a dialogue balloon emanating from her mouth. In the context of education, the 'demand' picture plays an ambivalent role. On the one hand, it is not a highly valued form, but a form deemed suitable only for beginners, a form one grows out of as one climbs the educational ladder; on the other hand, it plays an indispensable role in educational strategy: objective knowledge must, apparently, be built upon a foundation of emotive involvement, of identification with celebratory mythologies, for instance. This foundation must then, gradually, be repressed, for if it is not repressed, the knowledge built on it cannot be seen to be objective. Outside the sphere of education, the value of the 'demand' picture will depend on the assumed educational level of the reader. When, for instance, the mass media (or automatic teller machines) begins to use 'demand' pictures, those educated in the linguistic and visual genres of objective knowledge and impersonal address may feel patronized, 'addressed below their class'. Those not so educated (or those who contest the value of such an education) may feel that communication has become more effective (and more fun) than was the case in the era of more formal and impersonal public communication.

The meanings conveyed by 'demands' and 'offers' can be related to the grammatical system of person. As we have seen, 'demand' pictures address the viewer directly, realizing a visual 'you'. But this is not matched by a visual 'I'. The 'I' is absent in pictures, or rather, objectified, hiding behind a he/she/they. The 'demand' picture therefore recalls more the language of, for instance, advertisements and instructions, where 'you's' abound but 'I's' are rare, than say, of the language of personal letters where 'I's' and 'you's' are likely to be equally common. 'Real producers' cannot refer to themselves directly. They must speak impersonally, as in bureaucratic and scientific language, where 'I's' are also repressed. The public, on the other hand, is addressed directly. And yet, as we have seen, the distinction between 'offers' and 'demands' derives historically from attempts of Renaissance painters to find ways of saying 'I', in the self-portraits which expressed their new found self-confidence and status of independent artists rather than humble craftsmen.

The concepts of 'offer' and 'demand', however, also have a more direct equivalent in language, and we have in fact taken them from Halliday's description of four basic speech acts (or 'speech functions' as he calls them in his *Introduction to Functional Grammar*, 1985). Each of these speech acts, says Halliday, has its 'expected' and its 'discretionary' (alternative) social response, and each is realized by a specific syntactic arrangement. Thus speech acts can (1) 'offer information', that is, form a statement, in which case the response sought is 'agreement', although the statement may of course be contradicted; they can (2) 'offer goods-and-services' (e.g. *Would you like a drink?*) in which case the expected response is 'acceptance', although the offer may also be rejected; they can (3) 'demand information', that is, form a question, in which case the expected response is an answer, although the listener may also disclaim the question, for instance by saying *I don't know* or *I can't tell you that*; and (4), they can 'demand goods-and-services', that is, constitute some kind of command, in which case the expected response is for the listener to undertake what he or she has been asked to do, although listeners may of course also refuse to do so.

These speech acts are realized by what linguists call the 'mood system'. 'Mood' is a clause element which consists of the subject, together with the finite element of the verbal group. The subject can be recognized because it is the element that would be 'picked up' in the tag question (e.g. in *Women cannot live by diamonds alone*, the subject would be *women* – the tag question would be *Can they?*). The finite element can be recognized because it is one of a small number of verbal operators or 'auxiliaries' which serve to express tense (operators that indicate past tense such as *did, was, had, used to*; and operators that indicate future tense, such as *will, shall, would, should*) and to express modality (operators that express low probability, such as *can, may, could, might*; operators that express 'median' probability, such as *will, would, should*, and operators that express high probability, such as *must, ought to, need, has to, had to*). 'Polarity' (the opposition between 'it is the case' and 'it is not the case') is also part of the finite element of the verbal group, expressed by *not* in the case of negative polarity and unmarked in the case of positive polarity. The finite element and the lexical verb may be 'fused' (e.g. *loves* is said to fuse *does* and *love* – the relevant verbal operator would appear if a tag were added as in *He loves you, doesn't he?*).

Three of the four speech acts listed above are realized by permutations of the subject and the finite. The 'offer of information' is realized by the indicative mood, in which the finite element follows the subject, as in the following example taking from *Vogue* (the part of the clause that does not belong to the 'mood' element Halliday calls the 'residue'):

Women cannot live by diamonds alone

Subject Finite Residue

The question is realized by the interrogative mood, which either has the subject following the finite, in the case of 'polar' question (the kind of question to which one can just answer 'yes' or 'no'), or in the case of a 'wh-question' (a question beginning with a wh-word like *who, what*, etc.) a wh-subject followed by the finite, or the finite element followed by the subject:

Can women live by diamonds alone?

Finite Subject Residue

Who could live by diamonds alone?

Subject Finite Residue

What   could women live by?

Residue Finite Subject Residue

The imperative mood, which realizes the command, has no subject, and, when polarity is positive, no finite either:

Don't   live by diamonds alone

Finite Residue

Live by diamonds alone

Residue

The speech act of 'offering goods-and-services' is not realized by a permutation of subject and finite. It can be realized by idioms (e.g. *Here you are*) or questions, in conjunction with specific mental process verbs (e.g. *Do you want a drink?*) or commands (*Have a drink*) and, indeed, in various other ways.

There are many subtypes of these four basic kinds of speech act. They are realized through specific combinations of additional linguistic features. A 'prediction', for example, is an 'offer of information' with future tense and either second- or third-person subject, or first-person subject with a 'non-volitional' verb (e.g. *You will live by diamonds alone*, or *I will die young*). A 'promise' is an 'offer of information' with future tense, a first-person subject and a volitional verb (e.g. *I will buy you diamonds*). It would take us too far to discuss these in detail. The point to remember is that in language there are a few 'core' types and a very large number of further types which are constructed out of the core types. The same is true in the case of images. A visual 'invitation' is a 'demand' picture with a beckoning hand and a smiling expression, a visual 'summons' a 'demand' picture with a beckoning hand and an unsmiling expression, a visual 'warning' a 'demand' picture with a raised forefinger and a stern expression, and so on.

Despite these similarities, it would seem that images do not realize all four of the primary speech acts. When images 'offer', they primarily offer information. Of course, an image, say an advertising image, may show someone offering something to the viewer, and this offer may in fact be a real offer, which can be obtained by writing to an address specified in the advertisement. But if there is such an 'offer of goods-and-services' in images, it must take the form of an 'offer of information'. It must be represented. It cannot be enacted directly.

When images 'demand', they demand, one could say, the 'goods-and-services' that realize a particular social relation. Of course, an image could show a gesture of puzzlement, a 'silent' question, but the example is somewhat contrived and would need verbal reinforcement, or reinforcement by a conventional visual sign, for instance a question mark. There is no 'image act' for every 'linguistic act'. But this need not be so forever. What can be 'said' and 'done' with images (and with language) does not derive from intrinsic and universal characteristics of these modes of communication. It is quite possible to extend the semantic reach and use of images into domains which formerly were the exclusive province of language, as is already done, on a small scale, in places where people are unlikely to have any given language in common, for example international airports.

SIZE OF FRAME AND SOCIAL DISTANCE

There is a second dimension to the interactive meanings of images, related to the 'size of frame', to the choice between close-up, medium shot and long shot, and so on. Just as image-producers, in depicting human or quasi-human participants, must choose to make them look at the viewer or not, so they must also, and at the same time, choose to depict them as close to or far away from the viewer – and this applies to the depiction of objects also. And like the choice between the 'offer' and the 'demand', the choice of distance can suggest different relations between represented participants and viewers. In handbooks about film and television production size of frame is invariably defined in relation to the human body. Even though distance is, strictly speaking, a continuum, the 'language of film and television' has imposed a set of distinct cut-off points on this continuum, in the same way as languages impose cut-off points on the continuum of vowels we can produce. Thus the close shot (or 'close-up') shows head and shoulders of the subject, and the very close shot ('extreme close-up', 'big close-up') anything less than that. The medium close shot cuts off the subject approximately at the waist, the medium shot approximately at the knees. The medium long shot shows the full figure. In the long shot the human figure occupies about half the height of the frame, and the very long shot is anything 'wider' than that. Stylistic variants are possible, but they are always seen and talked about in terms of this system, as when film and television people talk of 'tight close shots' or 'tight framing', or about the amount of 'headroom' in a picture (i.e. space between the top of the head and the upper frame line).

In everyday interaction, social relations determine the distance (literally and figuratively) we keep from one another. Edward Hall (e.g. 1966: 110–20) has shown that we carry with us a set of invisible boundaries beyond which we allow only certain kinds of people to come. The location of these invisible boundaries is determined by configurations of sensory potentialities – by whether or not a certain distance allows us to smell or touch the other person, for instance, and by how much of the other person we can see with our peripheral (60°) vision. 'Close personal distance' is the distance at which 'one can hold or grasp the other person' and therefore also the distance between people who have an intimate relation with each other. Non-intimates cannot come this close, and if they do so, it will be experienced as an act of aggression. 'Far personal distance' is the distance that 'extends from a point that is just outside easy touching distance by one person to a point where two people can touch fingers if they both extend their arms', the distance at which 'subjects of personal interests and involvements are discussed'. 'Close social distance' begins just outside this range and is the distance at which 'impersonal business occurs'. 'Far social distance' is 'the distance to which people move when somebody says "Stand away so I can look at you"' – 'business and social interaction conducted at this distance has a more formal and impersonal character than in the close phase'. 'Public distance', finally, is anything further than that, 'the distance between people who are and are to remain strangers'. These judgements apply, of course, within a particular culture, and Hall cites many examples of the misunderstandings which can arise from intercultural differences in the interpretation of distance.

With these differences correspond different fields of vision. At intimate distance, says Hall (1964), we see the face or head only. At close personal distance we take in the head and the shoulders. At far personal distance we see the other person from the waist up. At close social distance we see the whole figure. At far social distance we see the whole figure 'with space around it'. And at public distance we can see the torso of at least four or five people. It is clear that these fields of vision correspond closely to the traditional definitions of size of frame in film and television, in other words, that the visual system of size of frame derives from the 'proxemics', as Hall calls it, of everyday face-to-face interaction. Hall is aware of this and in fact acknowledges the influence of the work of Grosser, a portrait painter, on his ideas. According to Grosser (quoted in Hall, 1966: 71–2), at a distance of more than 13 feet, people are seen 'as having little connection with ourselves', and hence 'the painter can look at his model as if he were a tree in a landscape or an apple in a still life'. Four to eight feet, on the other hand, is the 'portrait distance':

> the painter is near enough so that his eyes have no trouble in understanding the sitter's solid forms, yet he is far enough away so that the foreshortening of the forms presents no real problem. Here at the normal distance of social intimacy and easy conversation, the sitter's soul begins to appear. . . . Nearer than three feet, within touching distance, the soul is far too much in evidence for any sort of disinterested observation.

The distances people keep, then, depend on their social relation – whether this is the more permanent kind of social relation on which Hall mainly concentrates (the distinction between intimates, friends, acquaintances, strangers, etc.) or the kind of social relation that lasts for the duration of a social interaction and is determined by the context (someone in the audience of a speech given by an acquaintance or relative would nevertheless stay at public distance, the distance of the 'stranger'). But these distances also, and at the same time, determine how much of the other person is in our field of vision – just as does the framing of a person in a portrait or film shot.

Like the 'demand' picture, the close-up came to the fore in the Renaissance. Ringbom (1965) argues that it has its origin in devotional pictures, where it served to provide 'the "near-ness" so dear to the God-seeking devout' (p. 48). In Italian and Dutch paintings of the early sixteenth century it acquired a 'dramatic' function, allowing 'the subtlest of emotional relationships with a minimum of dramatic scenery' (*ibid.*).

The people we see in images are for the most part strangers. It is true that we see some of them (politicians, film and television stars, sports heroes, etc.) a good deal more than others, but this kind of familiarity does not of itself determine whether they will be shown in close shot or medium shot or long shot. The relation between the human participants represented in images and the viewer is once again an imaginary relation. People are portrayed *as though* they are friends, or *as though* they are strangers. Images allow us to imaginarily come as close to public figures as if they were our friends and neighbours – or to look at people like ourselves as strangers, 'others'. In the primary school social studies textbook from which we have quoted several examples, three Aboriginal boys are shown in long shot, occupying only about a quarter of the height of the 'portrait' format frame. The caption reads 'These people live at Redfern, a suburb of Sydney.' They are shown impersonally, as strangers with whom we do not need to become acquaintances, as 'trees in a landscape'. Although they do look at the viewer, they do so from such a distance that it barely affects us. Indeed, they are so small that we can hardly distinguish their facial features. 'Their soul does not yet begin to appear', to coin Grosser's words. The caption, significantly, gives them no name; in fact, where the more friendly 'boys' could have been, the quite formal 'people' has been used.

The portrait of the Aboriginal poet Oodgeroo Noonuccal (figure 4.4), already mentioned in the previous section of this chapter, is a tight close shot. *She* is depicted in a personal way. If this was all we could see of her in reality, we would be close enough to touch her. As mentioned, the section in which the photo occurs concludes a chapter on Aborigines in which no other Aborigine smiles at the viewer in this way. One of her poems is quoted: 'Dark and white upon common ground/ In club and office and social round/ Yours the feel of a friendly land/ The grip of the hand' (Oakley *et al.*, 1985: 164). But Noonuccal's message is not borne out by the way 'dark and white' are portrayed in the chapter.

Patterns of distance can become conventional in visual genres. In current affairs

○ **Fig 4.4 Oodgeroo Noonuccal (Oakley, 1985)**

television, for example, 'voices' of different status are habitually framed differently: the camera 'moves in for bigger close-ups of subjects who are revealing their feelings, whereas the set-up for the "expert" is usually the same as that for the interviewer – the breast pocket shot'. Both kinds of 'statused participants' tend to be 'nominated' (their names appear on the screen in superimposed captions) and 'have their contributions framed and summed up' (Brunsdon and Morley, 1978: 65). In other words, distance is used to signify respect for authorities of various kinds, on television as in face-to-face interaction.

In diagrams the human figure is almost always shown in medium long or long shot – objectively, 'as if he were a tree in a landscape'. The pictures in figure 4.5 illustrated a front-page newspaper story about a murder case in Sydney. The diagrams show exactly what happened, from an objectifying and impersonal distance (and from a high angle). The close-up photos accompany testimonies by former patients of the victim, but are represented as also 'friends' of us readers of the *Sydney Morning Herald*, and therefore as people whose relation with the victim we should identify with. As in the chapter on Antarctic exploration, the personal and the impersonal, the emotive and the detached, are combined.

So far we have discussed social distance in relation to human represented participants, but unlike the system of 'offer' and 'demand', the system of social distance can apply also to the representation of objects and of the environment. As size of frame is traditionally

HIS PATIENTS

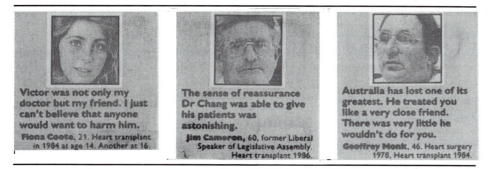

⬙ Fig 4.5 The murder of Dr Chang (*Sydney Morning Herald*, 5 July 1991)

defined in terms of specific sections of the human body, beginning students of film and television are often at a loss as to which terms to use for describing shots of objects and landscapes. The scale of seven sizes of frame seems too fine-grained. There are no clearcut equivalents for the shoulder, the waist, the knees. And objects come in many different shapes and sizes. We would nevertheless suggest that at least three significant distances can be distinguished, and that there are correspondences between these distances and our everyday experience of objects and of the environment, in other words, that size of frame can also suggest social relations between the viewer and objects, buildings and landscapes. At close distance, we would suggest, the object is shown as if the viewer is engaged with it – as if he or she is using the machine, reading the book or the map, preparing or eating the food. Unless the object is very small, it is shown only in part, and often the picture includes the user's hand, or a tool, for instance a knife scraping the soft margarine in an advertisement. Film and television 'cutaways' ('overshoulders') of objects, in which the objects shown are integrated into an action through the editing, use this distance. At middle distance, the object is shown in full, but without much space around it. It is represented as within the viewer's reach, but not as actually used. This type of picture is common in advertising: the advertised product is shown in full, but from a fairly close range, and a steep angle, as if the viewer stands just in front of the table on which it is displayed. At long distance there is an invisible barrier between the viewer and the object. The object is there for our contemplation only, out of reach, as if on display in a shop window or museum exhibit. This can be seen in science textbooks, and also, at times, in advertisements for luxury items, such as perfume bottles and expensive cars. It should be remembered, of course, that print advertisements are often photographic composites, and so may lack frames around the objects they represent. In that case our sense of distance may be derived from other factors, such as the amount of detail we can discern, or our angle of vision.

The same kind of distinctions can be made with respect to representations of buildings and landscapes. We can see a building from the distance of someone about to enter it, in which case we will not see the whole of the building, as is, again, often the case in film shots in which the building is related to some action. We can also see it from the distance of someone who has just identified it as his or her destination, and is surveying it for a moment, before moving towards it. In that case the frame will include only the building and leave out the surrounding environment. Or we can see it, so to speak, from behind the gates that keep the public at a respectful distance from the palace, or the fortress, or the nuclear reactor, and in that case the representation will include also the space around the building. Landscapes, too, can be seen from within; from a kind of middle distance, with a foreground object suggesting, perhaps, that the viewer is imaginarily located within the landscape, but stopping for a moment, as if to take stock of what is ahead; or from a long distance, from the air, perhaps, or from a 'look-out' position, a place not itself in the landscape, but affording an overview of it, as, for instance, in many of the photographic illustrations in geography textbooks.

The English language, finally, can also realize social distance, through the combination of a large number of choices which, taken together, make up choices in formality of style (see Joos, 1967). Intimate language is a kind of personal language, spoken perhaps only by the members of a couple or family, or by a group of school friends. The speakers of such a 'language of intimates' often have special names for each other, names which outsiders do not get to use. And the language itself is minimally articulated: a half-word is enough to understand each other. Facial expressions, eye contact, intonation, voice quality, etc. carry most of the meaning, and people who are in an intimate relation with each other become finely attuned to the reading of meanings conveyed in this way. 'Personal' language is casual, with a good deal of colloquialism and slang. Non-verbal expression still carries much of the meaning but not so much that 'half-a-word is enough'. In 'social' language speech is still formal, but will tend to steer clear of all too easy-going colloquialisms, and retain a hint of formality. And there is, in this kind of situation, less sharing of information and assumptions. The language needs to be more articulate, more verbally explicit, so that non-verbal expression is no longer as important as in intimate and personal style. Public language, finally, is the language used in more or less formal address. Here language becomes monologic: listeners no longer participate as they do in the other styles of speech. Speech is no longer improvised, but thought out in advance, perhaps even fully or partially written out. Intonation and other forms of non-verbal expression become as formal, as much subjected to control as syntax and word usage. Speech must be fully explicit, meanings fully articulated verbally. Colloquialisms are out of place and a more formal vocabulary must be employed. Writers can of course use these styles to address us *as* friends or even intimates, even when we are not, just as pictures can give us close-ups of people who, in reality, are and will remain strangers to us – think of the colloquial, chummy informality with which we are addressed in many advertisements.

PERSPECTIVE AND THE SUBJECTIVE IMAGE

There is yet another way in which images bring about relations between represented participants and the viewer: perspective. Producing an image involves not only the choice between 'offer' and 'demand' and the selection of a certain size of frame, but also, and at the same time, the selection of an angle, a 'point of view', and this implies the possibility of expressing subjective attitudes towards represented participants, human or otherwise. By saying 'subjective attitudes', we do not mean that these attitudes are always individual and unique. We will see that they are often socially determined attitudes. But they are always encoded as though they were subjective, individual and unique. The system of perspective which realizes 'attitude' was developed in the Renaissance, a period in which individuality and subjectivity became important social values, and it developed precisely to allow images to become informed by subjective points of view. Paradoxically, while these were the meanings encoded, perspective rests on an impersonal, geometric foundation, a construction which is a quasi-mechanical way of 'recording' images of reality. Socially determined viewpoints could, in this way, be naturalized, and presented as 'studies of nature', faithful copies of empirical reality. Only recently has it become possible again to see that perspective is also 'a daring abstraction' (Hauser, 1962: 69), and to discuss its semiotic effects, for instance in film theory (e.g. Comolli, 1971).

Pre-Renaissance forms, frescoes on the wall of a church nave, for example, or mosaics in the domed roof of a church, did not have perspective to position the viewer. Viewers of such works were positioned, not by the internal structure of the work, but by the structure of its environments, both the immediate environment of the church, its proximity to the altar for instance, and the wider social environments. In other words, the syntax of the object depended for its completion, its closure, not on a particular relation with the viewer but on a particular relation with its surroundings, and the point of view was the position the viewer actually took up in relation to the image: 'The world in the picture was experienced as a direct continuation of the observer's own space' (Arnheim, 1974: 274). As a result, the viewer had a certain freedom in relation to the object, a degree of what, today, we would call 'interactive use' of the text, albeit in the context of a highly constrained social order. From the Renaissance onwards, visual composition became dominated by the system of perspective, with its single, centralized viewpoint. The work became an autonomous object, detached from its surroundings, movable, produced for an impersonal market, rather than for specific locations. A frame began to separate the represented world from the physical space in which the image was viewed: at the time perspective was developed, pictures began to be framed precisely to create this division, to mark off the image from its environment, and turn it into a kind of 'window on the world'. At the same time images became more dependent on the viewer for their completion, their closure, and viewers became more distanced from the concrete social order in which the world had formerly been embedded: they now had to learn to internalize the social order. This yielded greater freedom with respect to the immediate, concrete social context, but diminished freedom in relation to the work. A parallel can be made with the developments which, more or less simultaneously, took place in music (see Shepherd, 1977). In medieval modes, based as they were on the pentatonic, any note of the scale could stand in only intervallic relation to any other note. Hence any note could provide a sense of resolution, of closure. In the new diatonic music a strict hierarchy was established between the fundamentals, so that any melody, whatever the harmonic progressions it traversed, had to return, ultimately, to the same predetermined note, the 'tonic', in the key of which the piece was scripted. The notes in music thus relate to the key centre in the same fixed way in which viewers relate to the perspectival centre of the visual work.

There are then, since the Renaissance, two kinds of images in Western cultures: subjective and objective images, images *with* (central) perspective (and hence with a 'built-in' point of view) and images *without* (central) perspective (and hence without a 'built-in' point of view). In subjective images the viewer can see what there is to see only from a particular point of view. In objective images, the image reveals everything there is to know (or that the image produced has judged to be so) about the represented participants, even if, to do so, it is necessary to violate the laws of naturalistic depiction, or, indeed, the laws of nature. The history of art has many striking examples of this, for example the sculptures of winged bulls and lions which flanked the doors of Assyrian temples: from the side these had four moving legs, and from the front two stationary legs, five altogether, so as to provide, from every side, a view from which no essential parts were missing. Modern technical drawings may still show what we know about the participants they represent, what is objectively there, rather than what we would see if we were looking at them in reality, rather than what is subjectively there. If we were, in reality, to see the front of the cube in figure 4.6 the way we know it 'objectively' is (a square), we would not at the same time be able to see the top and the side. It is an impossible picture (or, a possible picture of a highly irregular hexahedron, rather than a cube) from the point of view of what we can see in reality. Yet in many contexts (for instance, assembly instructions for a piece of furniture) an 'objective' picture like this is entirely acceptable. Objective images, then, disregard the viewer. They say, as it were: 'I am this way, regardless of who or where or when you are.'

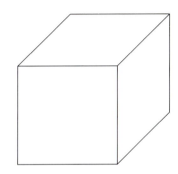

◯ Fig 4.6 Frontal-isometric cube

The point of view of the subjective, perspectival image has been selected for the viewer. As a result there is a kind of symmetry between the way the image-producer relates to the represented participants, and the way the viewer must, willy-nilly, also relate to them. The point of view is imposed, not only on the represented participants, but also on the viewer, and the viewer's 'subjectivity' is therefore subjective in the original sense of the word, the sense of 'being subjected to something or someone'. In a short essay on Chinese art, Bertolt Brecht has commented on this:

> As we know, the Chinese do not use the art of perspective. They do not like to see everything from a single point of view. Chinese composition thus lacks the compulsion to which we have become altogether accustomed ... and rejects the subjugation of the observer.
>
> (Brecht, 1967: 278–9)

The system of perspective is fundamentally naturalistic. It developed in a period in which the world of nature was no longer seen as manifesting a divine order (which was also, and at the same time, a social order), but as an autonomous and ultimately meaningless order whose laws also governed the conduct of people. It was explicitly grounded in the new scientific spirit, legitimized by the authority of scientific observation and the physical laws of nature. The new music, similarly, was constructed as congruent, not with a (divine and) social order, but with the physical laws of sound.

In the late nineteenth century, after centuries of hegemony, both systems came into crisis, in the high arts (Cubism, twelve-tone music) as well as in the popular arts. Film, for example, still uses perspectival images, but, in a near-Cubist fashion, provides multiple and constantly shifting viewpoints in its editing. Modern television, especially in programmes not based on the model of film, such as news programmes, has gone a step further, and challenges perspective also within the image. A newsreader may have, behind him or her, on the left a verbal text, on the right a chromakeyed moving picture on the wall (a wall which is in fact a kind of two-dimensional screen on which to project a 'layout', and in front of which to position the newsreader). Modern magazine layouts form another category of visual works which are no longer based solely on the compositional principles of perspective. Of course, they still contain many perspectival images but these have been subordinated to a structure that can no longer be said to be perspectival. Two examples may illustrate this.

The advertisement for Special Mild cigarettes (figure 4.7) is still predominantly naturalistic. There is a superimposed verbal text, but it has been made to blend in as much as possible with the background using a slighty darker blue against a background of blue

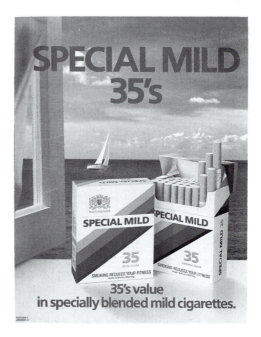

Fig 4.7 Special Mild advertisement (*Women's Weekly*, December 1987)

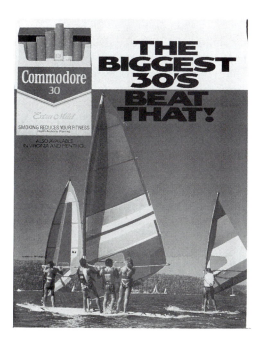

◯ Fig 4.8 Commodore advertisement (*Women's Weekly*, November 1987)

sky, and repeating this colour in the more unobtrusive space at the bottom of the page. The packets of cigarettes are exaggerated in size, but they are placed at an angle, to create an impression of depth. Semantic hierarchy is established, not just by the relative visual salience of the represented participants, but also by the perspectival system of foreground and background. This creates a special relation in which the viewer is, so to speak, positioned behind the window, in the space of the owner of the house, and hence also of the smoker of the cigarettes. Even though slightly transgressed in the direction of Surrealism, the composition is grounded in the natural. What we observe here could also be observed in reality: there could be a window opening out on the ocean in this way, with two packets of cigarettes on the window sill. This cannot be said of the Commodore advertisement (figure 4.8). In this advertisement, the viewer, rather than being positioned in the natural world, is confronted with a world which openly presents itself as a semiotic construct, mixing perspectival and non-perspectival elements in such a way as to give the appearance of a continuum of forms from the representational to the significational, while the advertisement as a whole remains non-naturalistic: the cigarettes in this advertisement cannot be said to be 'above' the boat in the same way as the cigarettes in the Special Mild advertisement can be said to be 'in front of' the boat. The two advertisements thus exemplify a shift from the dominance of nature to the dominance of signification, and from the dominance of the perceptual to the dominance of the conceptual – in a way very similar to that which we observed in chapter 1, when we compared *Baby's First Book* to Dick Bruna's *On My Walk* and *On The Farm*.

INVOLVEMENT AND THE HORIZONTAL ANGLE

When we prolong the converging parallels formed by the walls of the houses in figure 4.9, they come together in two vanishing points. Both points are located outside the vertical boundaries of the image, as shown in figure 4.10. These vanishing points allow us to reconstruct what we can see even without the aid of geometrical projection: the scene has been photographed from an oblique angle. The photographer has not situated her/himself in front of the Aborigines, but has photographed them from the side.

Figure 4.10 shows how the position from which the photo was taken can be reconstructed by dropping lines from the vanishing points in such a way that they meet to form a 90° angle on the line drawn through the closest corner of the cottages. Figure 4.11 shows the scene from above. The line (ab) represents the frontal plane of the subject of the photograph: the line formed by the front of the cottages, which, as it happens, is also the line along which the Aborigines are lined up. The line (cd) represents the frontal plane of the photographer (and hence of the viewer). Had these two lines been parallel to one another, the horizontal angle would have been frontal, in other words, the photographer

⬥ Fig 4.9 Aborigines (Oakley, 1985)

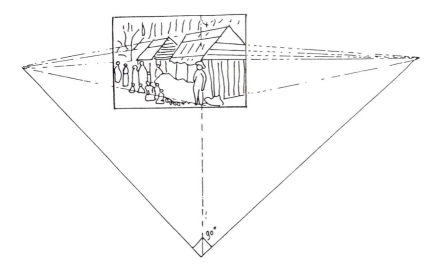

○ **Fig 4.10 Schematic drawing: vanishing points of 'Aborigines' (figure 4.9)**

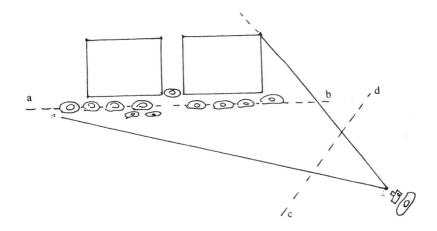

○ **Fig 4.11 Schematic drawing: top view of 'Aborigines' (figure 4.9)**

would have been positioned in front of the Aborigines and their cottages, facing them. Instead, the two lines diverge: the angle is oblique. The photographer has not aligned her/himself with the subject, not faced the Aborigines, but viewed them 'from the sidelines'.

Horizontal angle, then, is a function of the relation between the frontal plane of the image-producer and the frontal plane of the represented participants. The two can either be parallel, aligned with one another, or form an angle, diverge from one another.

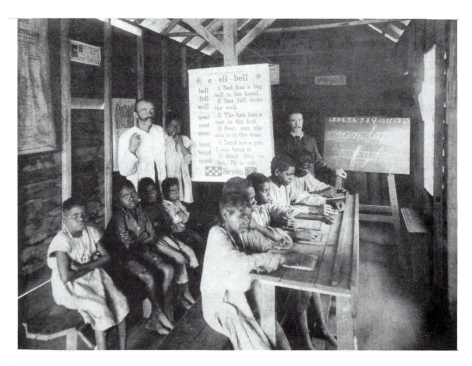

Fig 4.12 Aboriginal children at school (Oakley, 1985)

Fig 4.13 Schematic drawing: vanishing point of 'Aboriginal children at school' (figure 4.12)

The image can have either a frontal or an oblique point of view. It should be noted that this is not strictly an either/or distinction. There are degrees of obliqueness, and we will, in fact, speak of a frontal angle so long as the vanishing point(s) still fall(s) within the vertical boundaries of the image (they may fall outside the horizontal boundaries).

Figure 4.12 has a frontal angle. As shown in figure 4.13, there is only one major vanishing point, and it lies inside the vertical boundaries of the image. Figure 4.14 shows how the frontal plane of the photographer (line ab) and the frontal plane of the represented participants (line cd) run parallel – that is, *if one only considers one set of represented participants*, the teachers, the blackboard and the reading chart. The frontal plane of the Aboriginal children (line ef) makes an angle of 90° with the frontal plane of the teachers and with the frontal plane of the photographer. The Aboriginal children have been photographed from a very oblique angle!

The difference between the oblique and the frontal angle is the difference between detachment and involvement. The horizontal angle encodes whether or not the image-producer (and hence, willy-nilly, the viewer) is 'involved' with the represented participants or not. The frontal angle says, as it were: 'what you see here is part of our world, something we are involved with.' The oblique angle says: 'what you see here is *not* part of our world; it is *their* world, something *we* are not involved with.' The producers of these two photographs have, perhaps unconsciously, aligned themselves with the white teachers and their teaching tools, but *not* with the Aborigines. The teachers are shown as 'part of our world', the Aborigines as 'other'. And as viewers we have no choice but to see these represented participants as they have been depicted. We are addressed as viewers for whom 'involvement' takes these particular values. In reality, they might not – we might be Aboriginal viewers, for example. It is one thing for the viewer to be limited by what the photograph shows (and to understand what this means, for example exclusion, in the case of an Aboriginal viewer); it is another thing to actually identify with the viewpoint encoded in the photo. We can accept or reject, but either way we first need to understand what is meant.

The primary school social studies textbook *Our Society and Others* provides a further illustration. A shot of the NSW Parliament House in Sydney is frontal, and taken from

◢ Fig 4.14 Schematic drawing: top view of 'Aboriginal children at school' (figure 4.12)

a low angle. A shot of the church is taken from an oblique and somewhat higher angle. The former illustrates a section about Sydney in the chapter 'What is a City?'; the latter a section about a Maori family in the chapter on immigrants. Religion is depicted as something which, in the context of primary school social studies, does not belong to 'our society' – the book contains statements like 'The British believed in one God' (note the past tense) and questions like 'Do you think a church or a cemetery is like a sacred site?' It fosters a detached, outsider's attitude towards the Christian religion.

In the depiction of humans (and animals) 'involvement' and 'detachment' can interact with 'demand' and 'offer' in complex ways. The body of a represented participant may be angled away from the plane of the viewer, while his or her head and/or gaze may be turned towards it (see e.g. figure 4.24 below) – or vice versa. The result is a double message: 'although I am not part of your world, I nevertheless make contact with you, from my own, different world'; or 'although this person is part of our world, someone like you and me, we nevertheless offer his or her image to you as an object for dispassionate reflection.' The latter is the case, for example, in an illustration from a Dutch junior highschool geography textbook (Bols *et al.*, 1986: 21). In a section entitled 'De Derde Wereld in onze straat' ('The Third World in our street'), two pictures are shown side by side. On the left we see three older women, their headscarves an emblem of their status as immigrants. They are photographed from an oblique angle, hence as 'not part of our world' and in long shot, hence as 'others', 'strangers'. On the right we see, left in the foreground, a blonde girl, clearly meant to be taken as Dutch, with a black friend, who has his arm around her. The angle is a good deal more frontal than that of the shot of the three women, and the shot is a close-up: she is shown as like 'us', Dutch highschool students, and from 'close personal' distance. But she does not make contact with the viewers. She does not invite the viewers to identify with her, and with her relationship to a black man. Instead, the viewer is invited to contemplate her relationship detachedly, to ponder the fact that some people like 'us' have relationships with black people, but not, it is implicitly suggested, 'we' viewers ourselves. She is a phenomenon to be observed, not a person addressing the viewer.

Equally complex and ambivalent is the back view. One of the authors, at age 21, photographed his parents in a snow-covered park, just outside Brussels (figure 4.15), and, perhaps more importantly, it was this picture he chose to pin on the pinboard of his student room in Amsterdam, rather than one of the other, more frontal pictures he had taken on the same day. At the time, his feelings for his parents were complex. Deep attachment mixed with only half-understood desire to distance himself from the world in which he was brought up. Perhaps the picture crystallized these confused emotions for him. On the one hand, it showed his parents turning their back on him, walking away from him (a reversal, of course, of the actual situation); on the other hand, it showed this gesture of 'turning one's back', in a sense, 'frontally', in a maximally 'confronting' way. But to expose one's back to someone is also to make oneself vulnerable, and this implies a measure of trust, despite the abandonment which the gesture also signifies. Perhaps the picture reminded him of a passage from a Dutch novel he liked at the time:

Through the window he sees them walk away. 'How much I love that man', he thinks, and how impossible he has made it for me to express that. . . . His mother has linked arms with him. With hesitant steps she walks beside him on the frozen pavement. He keeps looking at them until they turn the corner, near the tall feathered poplars.

(Wolkers, 1965: 61)

How is 'involvement' realized in language? Perhaps the system of possessive pronouns comes closest to realizing the kinds of meanings we have discussed here. But the two systems, the visual system of horizontal angle and the linguistic system of possessive pronouns, differ in many ways. Involvement, as we have seen, is always plural, a matter of 'mine' and 'his/her/its'; a matter of distinguishing between what belongs to 'us' and what to 'them'. And while in language one cannot easily have *degrees* of 'ourness' and 'theirness', in images such gradation is an intrinsic part of the system of involvement. Finally, there is no 'yours' in the system of horizontal angle. The visual 'you-relation' is, as we have seen, realized by the system of 'offer' and 'demand'. Perspective puts a barrier

△ **Fig 4.15 Photograph of author's parents, 1968**

between the viewer and the represented participants, even in the case of a frontal angle: the viewer looks *at* the represented participants and has an attitude towards them, but does not imaginarily engage with them.

POWER AND VERTICAL ANGLE

Textbooks of film appreciation never fail to mention camera height as an important means of expression in cinematography. A high angle, it is said, makes the subject look small and insignificant, a low angle makes it look imposing and awesome: 'Low angles generally give an impression of superiority, exaltation and triumph . . . high angles tend to diminish the individual, to flatten him morally by reducing him to ground level, to render him as caught in an insurmountable determinism' (Martin, 1968: 37–8). But this leaves the viewer out of the picture. We would rather say it in a somewhat different way: if a represented participant is seen from a high angle, then the relation between the interactive participants (the producer of the image, and hence also the viewer) and the represented participants is depicted as one in which the interactive participant has power over the represented participant – the represented participant is seen from the point of view of power. If the represented participant is seen from a low angle, then the relation between the interactive and represented participants is depicted as one in which the represented participant has power over the interactive participant. If, finally, the picture is at eye level, then the point of view is one of equality and there is no power difference involved.

This is, again, a matter of degree. A represented participant can tower high above us or look down on us ever so slightly. In many of the illustrations in school textbooks we look down rather steeply on people – workers in the hall; children in a school yard. In such books the social world lies at the feet of the viewer, so to speak: knowledge is power. The models in magazine advertisements and features, and newsworthy people and celebrities in magazine articles, on the other hand, generally look down on the viewer: these models are depicted as exercising symbolic power over us. It is different, again, with pictures of the products advertised in the advertisements: these are usually photographed from a high angle, depicted as within reach, and at the command of the viewer.

How is power realized in language? Here we need, again, to remember the difference between face-to-face communication and mediated communication. In the classroom, for example, power will manifest itself first of all in the relation between teacher and pupil. This, as Cate Poynton has shown (1985: ch. 6), is in the main realized through the *difference* between the linguistic forms that may be used by the teachers and the linguistic forms that may be used by the pupils; in other words, through a lack of reciprocity between the choices available to each party in the interaction. The teacher may use first names in addressing the pupils; the pupils may not use first names in addressing teachers. The teacher may use imperatives to 'demand goods-and-services'; the pupils would have to use polite forms, for instance questions. This lack of reciprocity has its effect on every level of language: phonology, grammar, vocabulary, discourse, and on ideational, inter-personal, as well as textual meanings. If there is, in face-to-face communication, any question of power relation between represented participants and the pupils, then this results from the power relation between the teacher and the pupils.

To some extent this is the case in writing also, and not just because in writing, as in mediated communication generally, the absence of the writer causes, from the start, a fundamental lack of reciprocity (you cannot talk back to the writer), but also because the writer and the reader are often unequal in a number of other ways. The reader may be addressed directly, by means of the second-person pronoun *you*, while the writer hides behind impersonal forms. Mental processes may be attributed to the reader while the writer's mental processes are never referred to. Imperatives may be used, as modulated processes predicated of the reader (*you can, you should, you need*, etc.), while such forms are not used of the writer. Here are some examples of texts in which power is encoded in this way, the first from a Revlon advertisement, the second from *Our Society and Others*:

> Wrinkles. They don't start where you think they do. They start underneath your skin. That's why Anti-Aging Daily Moisturizer goes beyond mere surface treatment.

> When you study places and people you need to have a way of keeping the information you collect. One way of doing this is to take *notes* from the books which you read. You cannot write down all the things you read as this would mean writing out the whole book. Notes are a short way of recording the most important information.

In the first text the writer does not directly refer to him/herself, but writes as an impersonal authority, in terms of relational processes ('They start underneath your skin'). The reader is referred to directly ('you'), and the writer not only knows what the reader thinks ('where you think they do'), but also that the reader's thoughts are misguided: the authority of the writer is firmly based on the reader's ignorance. In the second text, too, the writer does not directly refer to him/herself, but writes impersonally, in terms of relational processes ('Notes are a short way of recording the most important information'), while the reader is addressed directly ('you'). The processes with which the reader is associated are modulated in various ways ('you need', 'you cannot'). In both cases the lack of reciprocity which realizes power is encoded in the text itself.

But this omniscient knowledge of the reader's mind, this direct postulation of what the reader needs (must do, should think, will feel, and so on) and this lack of reciprocity between the writer and the reader or the speaker and hearer, cannot be realized in the same way in images. In images, the power of an image-producer must, as it were, be transferred onto one or more represented participants – the power of the advertiser on the model, the power of the producer of the textbook on the ordinary people represented in the textbook. The nearest equivalent in speech would be the use of evaluative adjectives. We might, for example, transcode a picture in which we look down on factory workers or refugees as 'the *humble* workers' or 'the *downtrodden* refugees'. In the issue of *The Australian Women's Weekly* from which we have taken some of our examples, this kind of transcoding occurs a number of times. The magazine contains photographs of a bejewelled Queen Elizabeth and of the actor Michael Douglas

– both taken from a low angle. On the cover the relevant articles are announced by the following lines: 'DAZZLING – The Queen's jewels'; 'FASCINATING – Michael Douglas' "Fatal Attraction"'. But this, of course, makes what is in fact an attitude towards the represented participants into a characteristic of the represented participants: it objectifies the attitude.

NARRATIVIZATION OF THE SUBJECTIVE IMAGE

In many cases there is no immediately apparent motivation for point of view (and for size of frame). The angle may be high and frontal, and so convey power over and involvement with the represented participants, but the precise nature of the relation of power and involvement is not given. Thus a high-angle picture of workers in a factory could be said to be taken from the viewpoint of a supervisor in an elevated office, with a window overlooking the factory, but this remains a metaphor. We do not see the office in the picture. Other possibilities might also serve to make concrete the relation of power and involvement. In other cases the (imaginary) viewer intrudes in the picture to a greater or lesser degree. In advertising pictures this is often done by including the hands of the imaginary viewer in the foreground of the picture. These hands can tell us a lot about the viewer. They can be male or female, groomed in different ways; they can wear driving

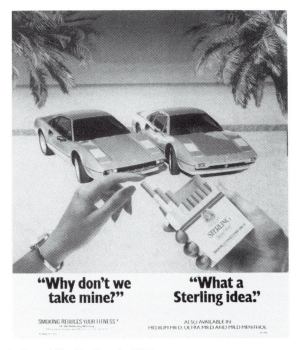

Fig 4.16 Sterling advertisement (*New Idea*, November 1987)

gloves, expensive rings, and so on. Figure 4.16 uses this device to show that the viewpoint is that of a couple.

In films the sequencing of images can fulfil this function. The shot of the factory, showing the workers from a high angle, can be preceded by a low-angle shot of the elevated office, with a supervisor behind the window looking down at the workers. In such cases the text narrativizes the point of view and imposes a fictional viewer between the represented and the interactive participants. But even when their origins are not shown, viewpoints can always be related to concrete situations. One can, and perhaps should, always ask 'Who could see this scene in this way?' 'Where would one have to be to see this scene in this way, and what sort of person would one have to be to occupy that space?'

OBJECTIVE IMAGES

Scientific and technical pictures, such as diagrams, maps and charts, usually encode an objective attitude. This tends to be done in one of two ways: by a directly frontal or perpendicular top–down angle. Such angles do suggest viewer positions, but special and privileged ones, which neutralize the distortions that usually come with perspective, because they neutralize perspective itself. To illustrate this with a simple example, when a cube is drawn perspectivally, its sides are not of equal length, and the degree of distortion depends on the angle, on the encoded viewer position. The cube does not look 'as we know it is', with all its sides of equal length, but 'as we see it', from a particular position. But from directly in front the third dimension disappears, and the cube appears flat, with all its sides of equal length. From above, exactly the same effect occurs. Perspective and its attitudinizing effect have been neutralized:

▲ Fig 4.17 Cube seen from an angle, frontally and from above

Frontal and top–down angles, however are not objective in entirely the same way. The frontal angle is the angle of maximum involvement. It is orientated towards action. The pictures of the Antarctic explorer (figure 2.4) could be transcoded as 'These are the clothes you should wear and this is the way you should wear them if you want to explore the Antarctic.' The frontal angle is the angle of 'this is how it works', 'this is how you use it', 'this is how you do it' (see figure 4.18). The top–down angle, on the other hand, is the angle of maximum power. It is orientated towards 'theoretical', objective knowledge. It contemplates the world from a god-like point of view, puts it at your feet, rather than within reach of your hands. Abstract diagrams can sometimes be read in both ways. A

⬤   **Fig 4.18 Thermometer (Hill, 1980)**

communication model, for instance (e.g. figure 2.2) can be read as a map ('top–down', a schema, a 'theory of communication': 'this is what communication looks like, from the point of view of a disinterested observer'), or as a frontal view, a blueprint, a 'practical manual of communication' ('this is what you do when you communicate') – and this is perhaps one of the sources of its social power.

A third objective viewpoint, the cross-section, and the 'X-ray' view, should also be considered: its objectivity derives from the fact that it does not stop at appearances, but probes beyond the surface, to deeper, more hidden levels. In our culture it is almost exclusively used in diagrams, although one can sometimes also observe experiments with it in children's drawings.

Not all diagrams, maps and charts, however, are completely objective. The vertical angle of the Gulf War map in figure 4.19, is high, but not completely top–down, and its horizontal angle is oblique, causing us to look at the theatre of war from the sidelines, in a relatively detached way. In books about science for young children we find similar angles (see e.g. figure 5.15), their obliqueness perhaps suggesting that they are not (or not yet quite) meant as 'how to do it' pictures.

Elements of perspective may also be added to graphs and cross-sections, and in all cases a sense of reality, of physical existence, is given to abstract, two-dimensional visuals. Having first been abstracted from the concrete, three-dimensional world of people, places and things, they are now restored to it, but in a transformed way, as new, human-made kinds of things and places. Thus we can see, for instance in lavishly produced annual company reports, three-dimensional bar graphs, looking like skyscrapers or monoliths, against a background of clean and smooth hills in flat, primary colour. In figure 4.20 graphs become a setting for action: tourists move through the abstractly represented, but nevertheless three-dimensional, world of the international tourist business, just as may

ALLIED ACTION AS GROUND WAR NEARS

Four allied Army helicopters attack complex of 15 Iraqi bunkers somewhere north of the Saudi border. Up to 500 Iraqis surrendered and were taken south in US transport helicopters

US Hercules transport planes drop 15,000lb 'daisy cutter' bombs on Faylakah Island in preparation for possible ground offensive

Force of US infantry, armour and artillery meet large Iraqi force on border destroying 5 tanks, 20 artillery and taking 7 POWs. One US serviceman killed and two armoured vehicles lost

Reports of allied forays with tanks crossing fortified border positions to attack Iraqi targets

US planes destroy 28 tanks, 26 other vehicles, three artillery pieces and three ammunition dumps

Fig 4.19 Gulf War map (*Sydney Morning Herald*, 22 January 1991)

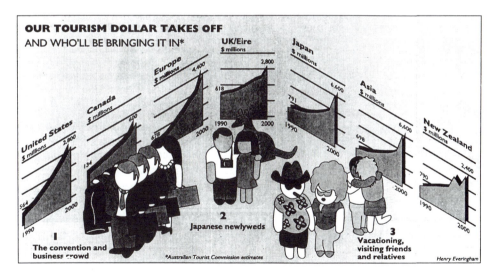

Fig 4.20 An increase in tourism (*Sydney Morning Herald*, 23 January 1991)

also be the case in television news graphics, where a further sense of reality may be given to such pictures by means of animation.

The addition of perspective adds nothing to the representational meaning of these diagrams, maps and charts; but it does add attitudinal meanings. In all these examples the angle is high, *explicitly* attitudinalizing the objective stance of the god-like top–down view, and often narrativizing it as the view from the satellite, that modern tool of the production of visual knowledge and symbol of informational power. The horizontal angle, on the other hand, may vary: with the 'increase in tourism' we are directly involved; the events of the Gulf War (figure 4.19), on the other hand, we watch 'from the sidelines', as bystanders. This process of attitudinalization happens, not so much in the contexts where this new visual knowledge is produced and this new informational power exercised, but in the contexts in which it is disseminated in popularized form, and celebrated: here conceptual and schematic images are dressed up in the clothes of visual reality, and literally and figuratively 'animated'.

To conclude this section we add some notes on different, less 'subjective' kinds of perspective. If, in central perspective, the kind of perspective we have been discussing so far, something is seen from the front and at eye level, the sides, top and bottom will be hidden from view. A cube would appear as in drawing 1 of figure 4.21. If the same cube

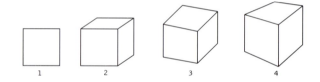

1   2   3   4

⬤ **Fig 4.21** (1) Cube seen from the front; (2) cube in frontal-isometric perspective; (3) cube in angular-isometric perspective; (4) cube seen from an angle in central perspective

is seen from an oblique angle, one of the sides will come into view, but the other will remain hidden. If the angle is high, so that we look down on the cube, the top will also come into view, as in drawing 4 of figure 4.21. But in this case the front will no longer be a square. It will be distorted. The horizontal parallels in an image in central perspective converge towards one or more vanishing points – and so do the vertical parallels, although this is often less obvious, as vertical distances are not so great, and as vertical distortion is often 'corrected' in drawings and paintings.

Drawing 2 in figure 4.21, on the other hand, is an example of 'frontal-isometric' perspective. Here the front of the cube is not distorted, yet we can see the side and the top. And the horizontal parallels do not converge towards a vanishing point. Frontal-isometric perspective is based on the 'objective' dimensions of the represented participants, on what we know these dimensions to be, rather than on how they *appear* to us. For this reason frontal-isometric perspective is used in technical drawings, where it is important to be able to measure the dimensions of the represented objects from the drawing. In frontal-iso-metric perspective, then, there is not as yet a choice between involvement and detachment.

⬤   Fig 4.22 Detail from a fourteenth-century Spanish nativity (from Arnheim, 1974)

It is the analogy in visual terms of the 'impersonality' characteristic of scientific language.

The perspective used in drawing 3 of figure 4.21 is called angular-isometric perspective. Here the front *is* distorted, the square no longer represented as a square. But the horizontal and vertical parallels do not converge. There is no end to space in this kind of perspective – it stretches on indefinitely. Angular-isometric perspective was used, for example, in eighteenth-century Japanese woodcuts – Japanese artists of this period always chose an oblique point of view, as well as a relatively high angle. They looked at the world without a sense of involvement, from a detached point of view, from a meditative distance.

This brief survey does not exhaust the possibilities. In medieval art 'inverted perspective' was sometimes used (see figure 4.22). This allows both sides of an object to be seen and causes the perspectival vectors to diverge rather than converge. It can often be found in children's drawings (young children also tend to draw the world as they know it to be, rather than as they see it) and, in recent times, has been taken up by painters such as Picasso and Braque, who looked for more objective ways of representing the world, regarding the simple viewpoint of central perspective as one-sided and restrictive, and viewing reality as multifaceted, a complex whole of often incompatible and mutually clashing viewpoints. In this way, as Arnheim notes (1974: 132), 'they make the contradictions of which Marxists speak visual'.

A SUMMARY

Figure 4.23 summarizes the main kinds of interactive meaning we have discussed in this chapter. It should be remembered that these are 'simultaneous systems' (as indicated by the curly brackets): any image must either be a 'demand' or an 'offer' *and* select a certain size of frame *and* select a certain attitude. In the next few sections we will discuss some examples at greater length, to show how the systems of 'contact', 'social distance' and 'attitude' interact to create more complex and subtle relations between represented and interactive participants.

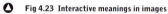

◆ **Fig 4.23 Interactive meanings in images**

REALIZATIONS

Demand	gaze at the viewer
Offer	absence of gaze at the viewer
Intimate/personal	close shot
Social	medium shot
Impersonal	long shot
Involvement	frontal angle
Detachment	oblique angle
Viewer power	high angle
Equality	eye level angle
Represented participant power	low angle

TWO PORTRAITS AND TWO CHILDREN'S DRAWINGS

Rembrandt's famous *Self-portrait with Saskia* dates from 1634. John Berger (1972: 111) calls it 'an advertisement of the sitter's good fortune, prestige and wealth', and he adds, 'like all such advertisements it is heartless'. Yet, from the point of view of the interactive meanings we have discussed in this chapter, the painting is perhaps a little more complex than Berger's remarks suggest. On the one hand, it is a 'demand' picture – Rembrandt and Saskia smile at the viewer, Rembrandt perhaps a little more effusively and invitingly than Saskia: he even raises his glass in a gesture directed at the viewer. On the other hand, he has shown himself and Saskia from behind, and from what Hall would call 'close social' distance, with Saskia a little further away from the viewer than Rembrandt – her head is considerably smaller than Rembrandt's even though she is sitting on his lap and should therefore, strictly speaking, be closer to the viewer than Rembrandt (the angle at which

Fig 4.24 *Self-portrait with Saskia* (Rembrandt, 1634) (Pinakotek, Dresden)

her head is turned to acknowledge the viewer also seems unnatural). Is Rembrandt distancing himself (and Saskia even more) from the viewer, excluding the viewer from involvement and intimacy with his new-found (and Saskia's already established) social status, thus contradicting the invitation? Perhaps, but the portrait is also a self-portrait. Rembrandt, the miller's son, now married into a wealthy and respectable family and living in grand style, also distances *himself* from his new self (and to some extent from Saskia), as if he cannot feel fully involved and intimate with his new environment. As a self-portrait the picture may be self-congratulatory and smug, 'heartless', but it also betrays a degree of alienation, positioning the represented Rembrandt in a complex and contradictory social class position, between the world of his origins, which is also the point of view of the picture, and the world of Saskia into which he has moved. This, we think, makes it a little less smug, and a little more touching than Berger gave it credit for.

Figure 4.25 shows a later self-portrait, painted in 1661. By this time, Saskia has died

⬥ Fig 4.25 *Self-portrait* (Rembrandt, 1661) (Kunsthistorisches Museum, Vienna)

and Rembrandt has gone bankrupt. He now lives with his former housekeeper, Hendrickje, in a more downmarket neighbourhood, and in much reduced circumstances. In this portrait he is able to come face to face with himself, to confront himself (and the viewer) squarely and intimately with himself 'He is an old man now. All has gone, except a sense of the question of existence, of existence as a question' (Berger, 1972: 112).

The picture on the cover of 'My Adventure', the story by an eight-year-old boy which we have already featured in the previous chapter, constitutes a 'demand': the little boy is looking at us, and smiling. He seeks our recognition. He wants to be acknowledged. On the other hand, the angle is oblique, and high, and the boy is shown from a great distance. Not only does the writer of this story show himself in the role of being shipwrecked, he also shows himself as 'other' (the oblique angle), as someone over whom the viewer has power (the high angle) and as socially distant, a 'stranger' (the long shot). In other words, he uses the interactive resources of the subjective image (quite precociously, we feel) to show himself as small, insignificant and alienated, yet demanding recognition from the viewer. At the same time the act of drawing himself like this affords him, as the producer of the image, some power over that image of himself, an outlet for his feelings. In support of this interpretation it can be noted that the boy does not exactly play a heroic role in the story. After creating the raft, and just as the raft 'started to be good fun', everything goes wrong for him: he loses his money and never finds it again, the raft collapses and is

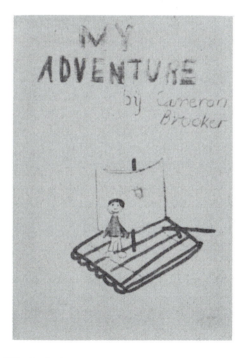

Fig 4.26 **Cover illustration of 'My adventure'**

lost irretrievably, and the hero has to walk all the way home, wet and cold. It is an unhappy ending for a hero unable to control the unpleasant events that happen to him.

Figure 4.27 is the front cover of a 'story' on sailing boats by a child from the same class as the author of 'My Adventure'. Its subject is similar: people on a boat. But the systems of 'image act', 'social distance' and 'attitude' take on very different values. The characters do not look at us: the picture is an 'offer'. The angle is frontal and eye level, and the two figures in the boat are neither particularly distant, nor particularly close. There is no setting, no texture, no colour, no light and shade. The sailing boat is drawn with geometrical accuracy. But for the two figures, simply drawn, and more or less identical, except for their size (a father and son?), this could be a technical drawing. As such it suits the objective, generic, title, 'Sailing Boats', just as the cover illustration of 'My Adventure' suits that story's subjective, specific title. In most of the illustrations inside the essay, no human figures are seen, as though the child already understands that the 'learning' of technical matters should be preceded by a 'human element' to attract non-initiates to the subject.

Clearly, children actively experiment both with the interactive resources of language and with the interactive resources of visual communication. They are active sign-makers. And the different ways in which these two children represent boats show two different subjectivities at work.

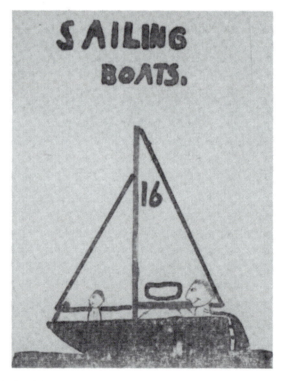

Fig 4.27 Cover illustration of 'Sailing boats'

5 Modality:
designing models of reality

MODALITY AND A SOCIAL THEORY OF THE REAL

One of the crucial issues in communication is the question of the reliability of messages. Is what we see or hear true, factual, real, or is it a lie, a fiction, something outside reality? To some extent the form of the message itself suggests an answer. We routinely attach more credibility to some kinds of messages than to others. We 'know', for instance, that photographs do not lie; and a 'report', we know, is more reliable than a 'story'. More generally, and with particular relevance to the visual, we regard our sense of sight as more reliable than our sense of hearing, 'I saw it with my own eyes' as more reliable evidence than 'I heard it with my own ears.'

Unfortunately, we also know that while the camera does not lie, or not much, at any rate, those who use it and its images can and do. The questions of truth and reality remain insecure, subject to doubt and uncertainty, and, even more significantly, to contestation and struggle. Yet, as members of a society, we have to be able to make decisions on the basis of the information we receive, produce and exchange. And in so far as we are prepared to act, we have to trust some of the information we receive, and do so, to quite some extent, on the basis of modality markers in the message itself, on the basis of textual cues for what can be regarded as credible and what should be treated with circumspection. These modality markers have been established by the groups within which we interact as relatively reliable guides to the truth or factuality of messages, and they have developed out of the central values, beliefs and social needs of that group.

In this chapter we will discuss these modality cues. As throughout the book, we take them to be motivated signs – signs which have arisen out of the interest of social groups who interact within the structures of power that define social life, and also interact *across* the systems produced by various groups within a society. As we have discussed in the Introduction, the relation between the signifiers and signifieds of motivated signs is, in principle, one of transparency. Sign-makers choose what they regard as apt, plausible means for expressing the meanings they wish to express. We are therefore focusing on the range of signs from which such choices can be made – some of them specialized modality markers, others part of a much wider and more general range of means of expressing meanings of truth and falsehood, fact and fiction, certainty and doubt, credibility and unreliability.

A social semiotic theory of truth cannot claim to establish the absolute truth or untruth of representations. It can only show whether a given 'proposition' (visual, verbal or otherwise) is represented *as* true or not. From the point of view of social semiotics, truth is a construct of semiosis, and as such the truth of a particular social group, arising from the values and beliefs of that group. As long as the message forms an apt expression of these beliefs, communication proceeds in an unremarkable, 'felicitous' fashion. This does mean, however, that our theory of modality has to account for a complex situation: people not only communicate and affirm as true the values and beliefs of *their* group. They also communicate and accord degrees of truth or untruth to the values and beliefs of other groups.

The term 'modality' comes from linguistics and refers to the truth value or credibility of (linguistically realized) statements about the world. The grammar of modality focuses on such modality markers as the auxiliary verbs which accord specific degrees of modality to statements, verbs like *may, will* and *must* (cf. the difference between *He may come* and *He will come*) and their related adjectives (e.g. *possible, probable, certain*) and adverbs (see Halliday, 1985: 85–9). But modality is not only conveyed through these fairly clearcut linguistic systems (see Kress and Hodge, 1993: 127). Take this example, from *Our Society and Others* (Oakley *et al.*, 1985). Clearly, it not only contains statements such as 'Aboriginal people had no religion' and 'the whole land was a cathedral', but also indications of the truth value of these statements:

> Governor Phillip, the settlers, and the convicts could find no churches or cathedrals or works of art like those of Britain. Perhaps this made them think that Aboriginal people had no religion. In fact, the Aborigines had very complicated religious beliefs. These had been passed down from one generation to the next through Dreamtime stories for thousands of years. For the Aborigines the whole land was a cathedral. Their art was joined to their religion. Much of their art had been kept safely for thousands of years.
>
> (Oakley *et al.*, 1985: 142)

The statement 'Aboriginal people had no religion' is given low modality. The writers distance themselves from it by attributing it to 'Governor Phillip, the settlers, and the convicts', by formulating it as a subjective idea ('this made them *think* that . . .') and by using the past tense (after all, what was true in the past need not be true in the present). The writers' own statements (e.g. 'the Aboriginals had very complicated religious beliefs') are not qualified in this way; they are formulated as objective facts ('In *fact*, the Aborigines had . . .') and not attributed (it is curious, however, that they are not extended to the present time!). The statements that embody the 'beliefs' of the Aborigines, finally, are given lower modality. They are explicitly attributed to the Aborigines and therefore not subscribed to by the writers, and they are qualified by terms like 'story', 'dream' and 'belief', terms which, in our culture, signify low modality and are contrasted with high-modality terms such as 'reality', 'fact' and 'truth'.

The example shows that modality is 'interpersonal' rather than 'ideational'. It does not express absolute truths or falsehoods; it *produces* shared truths aligning readers or listeners with some statements and distancing them from others. It serves to create an imaginary 'we'. It says, as it were, these are the things 'we' consider true, and these are the things 'we' distance ourselves from, for instance: 'we' have no religion, but the Aborigines do, and although this religion is true for 'them', it is not true for 'us'. Nevertheless, as (for 'us') art and religion are not 'joined', 'we' can appreciate Aboriginal religion as 'art', as beautiful 'stories' and 'dreams' (art, in our culture, has lower modality than, for instance, science – hence the greater licence given to artists). We call the 'we' the text attempts to produce 'imaginary' because many of the children who are made to read the book may in fact 'have religion'. However, we realize that the social groupings discursively instituted in this way may be very real and may have very real effects on children's lives.

The concept of modality is equally essential in accounts of visual communication. Visuals can represent people, places and things as though they are real, as though they actually exist in this way, or as though they do not – as though they are imaginings, fantasies, caricatures, etc. And, here too, modality judgements are social, dependent on what is considered real (or true, or sacred) in the social group for which the representation is primarily intended. Consider, for instance, the 'speech circuit' diagram from de Saussure's famous *Course in General Linguistics* (1974 [1916]), shown in figure 5.1. It depicts two humans, 'A' and 'B', and a process, circular and continuous, described as the 'unlocking of sound-images in the brain', followed by the 'transmitting of an impulse corresponding to the image to the organs used in producing sounds', followed by the 'travelling of the sound waves from the mouth of A to the ear of B' (*ibid.*: 11–12). In another version (figure 5.2) de Saussure schematizes the diagram even further, making it look almost like an electrical circuit.

The photograph in figure 5.3 also represents the speech process, or rather part of it, since we see only 'A' speaking, and only 'B' 'unlocking sound-images in his brain'. It is a scene from Robert Aldridge's movie *The Big Knife* (1955), with Rod Steiger and Jack Palance.

The three representations of the speech process differ in a number of ways. First, while the photograph restricts itself to representing what would normally be visible to the naked eye, the diagrams do not: they make visible what is normally invisible (mental processes, 'sound-images in the brain') and they do show what can normally only be heard ('sound waves'). To do so they take recourse to abstract graphic elements (dotted and continuous lines, arrows) and to language. Second, while the photograph presents us with a moment frozen in time, the diagrams depict a process that takes a certain amount of time to unfold: one utterance of 'A' as well as one utterance of 'B', at the very least. Third, while the photograph depicts 'A' and 'B' in great detail, showing strands of hair, wrinkles,

A   B

⬥ **Fig 5.1 Speech circuit (de Saussure, 1974 [1916])**

Audition   Phonation

c = concept
s = sound-image

Phonation   Audition

⬓ **Fig 5.2 Schematized speech circuit (de Saussure, 1974 [1916])**

⬓ **Fig 5.3 Rod Steiger and Jack Palance in *The Big Knife* (Aldridge, 1955)**

glimmers of light in Steiger's dark glasses, the diagrams reduce the two to schematic profiles, or even circles, minimal geometric shapes, abstract elements. And while the photograph shows depth, modelling caused by the play of light and shade, and a setting, a background, the diagrams omit all of these. They are abstract and schematic where the photograph is concrete and detailed; conventionalized and coded where the photograph presents itself as a naturalistic, unmediated, uncoded representation of reality.

Does this mean that diagrams are less 'real' than photographs, and hence lower in modality, and that photography is more true than diagrammatic representation? Not necessarily. To the viewers for whom de Saussure's diagrams are intended, they may in fact be *more* real than the photograph, in the sense that they reveal a truth which represents more adequately what the speech process is *really* like.

Reality is in the eye of the beholder; or rather, what is regarded as real depends on how reality is defined by a particular social group. From the point of view of naturalism reality is defined on the basis of how much correspondence there is between the visual representation of an object and what we normally see of that object with the naked eye (or, in practice, on the capacity of 35mm photography to resolve detail and render tonal or colour differentiation: images, including photographs, can be experienced as 'hyper-real', as showing 'too much detail', 'too much depth', 'too much colour' to be true). Scientific realism, on the other hand, defines reality on the basis of what things are like *generically* or *regularly*. It regards surface detail and individual difference as ephemeral, and does not stop at what can be observed with the naked eye. It probes beyond the visual appearance of things. In other words, reality may be in the eye of the beholder, but the eye has had a cultural training, and is located in a social setting and a history, for instance in the community of linguists, or of semioticians in de Saussure's day, a community which saw reality in that form, in terms of abstractions and deeper regularities. A 'realism' is produced by a particular group, as an effect of the complex of practices which define and constitute that group. In that sense, a particular kind of realism is itself a motivated sign, in which the values, beliefs and interests of that group find their expression.

As the examples suggest, definitions of reality are also bound up with technologies of representation and reproduction. For us, now, as commonsense viewers, everyday members of society at large, the defining technology is that of 35mm colour photography. And the relatively recent change from the dominance of black and white to the dominance of colour in many domains of visual communication shows how quickly these histories develop, and how closely they are related to technological change.

Each realism has its naturalism, that is, a realism is a definition of what counts as real, a set of criteria for the real, and it will find its expression in the 'right', the best, the (most) 'natural' form of representing that kind of reality, be it a photograph or a diagram. This is not to say that all realisms are equal. Although different realisms exist side by side in our society, the dominant standard by which we judge visual realism and hence visual modality, remains for the moment, naturalism as conventionally understood, 'photo-realism'. In other words, the dominant criterion for what is real and what is not is based on the appearance of things, on how much correspondence there is between what we can 'normally' see of an object, in a concrete and specific setting, and what we can see of it in a visual representation – again, at least in theory, for in effect it is based on currently dominant conventions and technologies of visual representation. We judge an image real when, for instance, its colours are approximately as saturated as those in 35mm photographs. When they are more saturated, we judge them exaggerated, 'more than real', excessive. When they are less saturated we judge them 'less than real', 'ethereal', for instance, or 'ghostly'. And the same can be said about other aspects of representation, the rendition of detail, the representation of depth, and so on. Pictures which have the perspective, the degree of detail, the kind of colour rendition, etc. of 35mm colour photography taken with a standard lens have the highest modality, and are seen, as 'naturalistic'. As detail, sharpness, colour, etc. are reduced or amplified, as the perspective flattens or deepens, so modality decreases.

Like many other advertisements, the advertisement in colour plate 2 is a composite text. It shows a picture of the product (the jar of instant coffee), with a verbal caption, and a picture which visualizes the pleasure the product will afford. This picture, showing two lovers sharing an intimate moment, uses soft focus and soft colours, tending towards the same golden-brown hue, and so deliberately lowering modality, representing 'what using the product will be like' as fantasy or promise, as 'what might be', rather than as reality, as 'what is'. The picture of the product itself, however, is in sharper focus and uses more saturated and differentiated colours: the product is given higher modality, higher reality value, than the promise of bliss attached to it, and the advertisement as a whole therefore accords varying degrees of 'credibility' to the different representations it contains, just like the text on 'Aboriginal religion'. The lower modality of the photo of the romantic scene, however, is not a matter of the scene itself being improbable or fantastic (although that, too, often happens in advertising photographs). Probable as well as improbable events may have high or low modality. Just as in language one can say *There certainly are ghosts* (high modality) and *I believe ghosts may exist* (low modality), so in pictures one may have realistic and not-so-realistic depictions of ghosts.

What is the difference between these uses of colour? We would put it this way: the more that is taken away, abstracted from the colours of the representation, the more colour is *reduced*, the lower the modality. There is a continuum which runs from full colour saturation to the absence of colour, black and white, in which only the brightness values of the colours, their 'darkness' or 'lightness', remains. There is also a continuum which runs from full colour differentiation to a 'reduced palette' and eventually monochrome. For example, eighteenth-century landscape painting (e.g. Claude Lorrain) was often restricted to various shades of brown for the foreground and to desaturated, silvery blues for the distance. This is not the only way in which abstraction from 'naturalistic' colour is possible. The colour of many objects is not even. Pale skin for instance, may vary in redness, may have the blue veins showing through, and so on, and such differences may either be rendered or abstracted from. In other words, colour may be idealized to a greater or lesser degree – a scale which runs from naturalistic photography via the choice of different values of a colour for the representation of light and shade, to the flat, unmodulated colour used by children in their drawings, or, for example, in the work of painters such as Matisse. Matisse was not a child, of course, when he produced the paintings we now admire. His unmodulated colours expressed a different view of what counts as real, as do the unmodulated colours in children's drawings – we will comment on this in more detail later. From the point of view of naturalism, however, modality is decreased in such images. The continuum from modulated to flat colour is at the same time a continuum from high to low modality. And in both cases the rule applies: the greater the abstraction (away from saturation, differentiation and modulation) the lower the modality.

It should be stressed that what we are talking about is not abstraction from what we actually see, from 'the real world'. The literature of other ages and cultures attests to the fact that people have marvelled at the 'lifelikeness' of works which, by our standards, are far from 'naturalistic'. What we are talking about at this point is abstraction relative to the standards of contemporary naturalistic representation.

MODALITY MARKERS

So far we have discussed the role of colour as a marker of naturalistic modality, in terms of three scales:

(1) *Colour saturation*, a scale running from full colour saturation to the absence of colour, that is to black and white.

(2) *Colour differentiation*, a scale running from a maximally diversified range of colours to monochrome.

(3) *Colour modulation*, a scale running from fully modulated colour, with, for example, the use of many different shades of red, to plain, unmodulated colour.

At the one end of these scales the particular dimension of colour is maximally reduced. At the other end it is most fully articulated, used to its maximum potential. Each point of the scale has a certain modality value in terms of the naturalistic standard. However, the point of highest modality does not coincide with either extreme of the scale: naturalistic modality increases as articulation increases, but at a certain point it reaches its highest value and thereafter it decreases again. Naturalistic modality scales could therefore be represented as in the following example:

Black and white / Maximum colour saturation
Lowest modality / Highest modality / Low(er) modality

● **Fig 5.4 Modality scale for colour saturation**

We will now discuss the other key markers of visual modality on which we already touched in our discussion of figure 5.3.

(4) *Contextualization*, a scale running from the absence of background to the most fully articulated and detailed background.

Within the naturalistic coding orientation, the absence of setting lowers modality. By being 'decontextualized', shown in a void, represented participants become generic, a 'typical example', rather than particular, and connected with a particular location and a specific moment in time. The scale of 'contextualization' runs from 'full contextualization' to 'plain, unmodulated background'. One step away from 'full contextualization' we find settings which are out of focus to a greater or lesser degree, or which lose detail through overexposure, resulting in a kind of ethereal brightness, or underexposure, resulting in muddy darkness, or through the loss of visual detail in the depiction. Further decontextualization can be achieved through ellipsis: a few 'props' suffice to suggest a setting, or a small, irregularly shaped patch of green under the feet of a figure with a few lines suggesting grass, indicates the setting, while the rest of the paper is left blank. Or perhaps the background may merely show an irregular pattern of light and shade, or a field of unmodulated colour, or black, or white.

Again, the most fully articulated background does not have the highest naturalistic modality. The limitations imposed by the resolution of standard 35mm photographic emulsions and by the depth of field of standard lenses normally cause the background to be less articulated than the foreground. When the background is sharper and more defined than this, a somewhat artificial, 'more than real' impression will result, as, for instance in older Hollywood movies shot in a studio with back projection (a close-up of an actor in a car, in front of a rear window behind which we see the receding landscape in sharp focus), or in much Surrealist painting, such as in the work of Salvador Dalí.

(5) *Representation*, a scale running from maximum abstraction to maximum representation of pictorial detail.

An image may show every detail of the represented participants: the individual strands of hair, the pores in the skin, the creases in the clothes, the individual leaves of the tree, and so on, or it may abstract from detail to a greater or lesser degree. Again, there is a point beyond which a further increase of detail becomes 'hyper-real' and hence lower in modality from the point of view of 'photographic' naturalism. Similarly, in discussing decontextualization, above, we have pointed out that reduced representation of detail may form one of the ways in which the modality of backgrounds, of what is 'distant', is lower than the modality of the foreground (there is a parallel here with the lower modality of the past tense in language).

In photography it is not only sharpness of focus, but also exposure which can reduce detail. In artwork a variety of techniques could be ranked on a scale from maximum to minimum detail. Texture can become stylized, rendered by lines which trace the folds in the clothes, for example, and these lines may be many and fine, as in detailed engravings, or few and coarse, as in quick and ready styles of drawing. In medical drawings, for example, texture may become entirely conventional: dots to indicate the texture of one layer of skin, short, curved lines to indicate the texture of another. Texture can also be omitted altogether: the participant is then represented merely by the lines that trace its contour. Beyond this, the contour may be simplified to different degrees: a head may become a circle, the eyes two dots, the mouth a short, straight line. Diagrams and geometrical art take abstraction even further and reduce the shape of things to a small vocabulary of abstract forms, as in the paintings of Mondriaan, or in figure 5.2, de Saussure's schematized 'speech circuit' diagram.

(6) *Depth*, a scale running from the absence of depth to maximally deep perspective.

By the criteria of standard naturalism, central perspective has highest modality, followed by angular-isometric perspective, followed by frontal-isometric perspective, followed by depth created by overlapping only. Again, perspective can become 'more than real', as when strong convergence of vertical lines is shown, or a 'fish eye' perspective is used.

(7) *Illumination*, a scale running from the fullest representation of the play of light and shade to its absence.

Naturalistic depictions represent participants as they are affected by a particular source of illumination. Less naturalistic images, on the other hand, may abstract from illumination, and show shadows only in so far as they are required to model the volume, especially of round objects. They have 'shading' rather than shadow. Or they use shading to indicate receding areas and highlights to indicate protruding areas, often in ways which have no explanation in terms of the logic of illumination. This can be done to different degrees: with a fully modulated darkening of the areas of shadow; with just two degrees of brightness, one for the 'lit' areas and one for those in shadow; with more or less dense hatching or dotting of the shaded areas, and so on. At the extreme end of the scale, light and shade are abstracted from altogether, and line rather than shading is used to indicate receding contours.

(8) *Brightness*, a scale running from a maximum number of different degrees of brightness to just two degrees: black and white, or dark grey and lighter grey, or two brightness values of the same colour.

Brightness values can also contrast to a greater or lesser degree: in one picture the difference between the darkest and the lightest area may be very great (deep blacks, bright whites), in another the difference may be minimal, so that a misty, hazy effect is created. The paintings of Rembrandt are interesting from this point of view, in part because his use of illumination and brightness is so often invoked as a paradigm example of naturalism, and in part because of the way his subtle divergences from naturalism often acquire ideational functions, in a broadly allegorical sense. We will discuss this in chapter 6.

The ability of photography to render black and white is limited, as is its ability to differentiate brightness values. Again, a contrast range and a range of brightness values which exceeds this ability may be experienced as 'more than real' and hence as being of lower modality.

It follows from our discussion that modality is realized by a complex interplay of visual cues. The same image may be 'abstract' in one or several markers and 'naturalistic' in others. Impressionist paintings, for example, often have a narrow brightness range, and abstract from light and shadow, but they have a highly naturalistic approach to colour. Yet, from this diversity of cues an overall assessment of modality is derived by the viewer.

From all this it might seem that the realization of modality in images is much more complex and finely graded than the realization of modality in language. Yet language, too, allows complex combinations of different modality cues. Take, for instance, the sentence *I absolutely don't think he could possibly have done it.* Is this 'low', 'middle' or 'high' modality? How does one 'compute' these various modality cues into one 'degree of credibility'? Frequently there are even contradictions: *It is probably definitely true that . . .* And in language, too, the value of modality cues depends on context. In academic writing, for example, qualifications such as *It may well be the case . . .* or *It is quite possible that . . .* (both low modality, strictly speaking), serve in fact to increase the credibility of the text, as indicators of the care with which the writer's judgements were made, and hence of the reliability of these judgements.

CODING ORIENTATION

So far we have described the value of modality markers in terms of the naturalistic criteria for 'what counts as real'. We have hypothesized that the ability of modern colour photography to render detail, brightness, colour, etc. constitutes for our culture today a kind of standard for visual modality. When this standard is exceeded, an image becomes 'more than real' – an effect which can be achieved not only in art (and is often the favoured modality in Surrealism), but also by means of the special techniques, materials and equipment of studio photography. A certain standard of photographic naturalism, dependent on the state of photographic technology and on current photographic practices (and hence ever evolving, and even at this time beginning to be superseded by standards drawing on electronically produced images) has become the yardstick for what is perceived as 'real' in images, even when these images are not photographs. Underpinning this is the belief in the objectivity of photographic vision, a belief in photography as capable of capturing reality as it is, unadulterated by human interpretation. Behind this, in turn, is the primacy which is accorded to visual perception in our culture generally. Seeing has, in our culture, become synonymous with understanding. We 'look' at a problem. We 'see' the point. We adopt a 'viewpoint'. We 'focus' on an issue. We 'see things in perspective'. The world 'as we see it' (rather than 'as we know it', and certainly not 'as we hear it' or 'as we feel it') has become the measure for what is 'real' and 'true'.

So visual modality rests on culturally and historically determined standards of what is real and what is not, and not on the objective correspondence of the visual image to a reality defined in some ways independently of it. At the moment holograms are probably still seen by most people as 'more than real'. In the images we are most used to, the absence of the third dimension, the flatness of the picture, does not function as an indicator of low modality, just as the absence of perspective in cultures whose art does not employ it does not function as an indicator of low modality for members of those cultures.

As we have already discussed in relation to de Saussure's 'speech circuit', however, even within our own culture the same standards for what is 'real' and what is not do not apply in every context. In technological contexts, a different concept of reality underlies visual modality, a concept we could call 'Galilean reality'. In the early seventeenth century Galileo wrote:

> I do not find myself absolutely compelled to apprehend [objects] as necessarily accompanied by such conditions as that they must be white or red, bitter or sweet, sonorous or silent, smelling sweetly or disagreeably.... I think that these tastes, smells, colours etc. with regard to the object in which they appear to reside are nothing more than mere names.... I do not believe that there exists anything in external bodies for exciting tastes, smells, sounds, etc., except size, shape, quantity and motion.
>
> (quoted in Mumford, 1936: 48)

Here 'real' means 'what can be known by means of the methods of science', that is by means of counting, weighing and measuring. By this standard of what is real, a technical line drawing, without colour or texture, without light or shade, and without perspective, can have higher modality than a photograph. Everyday commonsense naturalism and realism no longer merge here. The realism (and hence the 'naturalism') of scientific–technical images is of a different kind, based, in the end, on the questions 'Can we use it?', 'Can we measure the real dimensions from it?', 'Can we find out from it how to set up the experiment?' and so on. Whatever does not contribute to this purpose merely adds a dimension of 'illusionism' to the picture, and dilutes 'Galilean realism' with commonsense 'naturalism'. The latter, of course, is sometimes done for the purpose of communicating scientific ideas or technological complexities to a public of non-initiates. In his book *Writing Biology* (1990) Greg Myers compares the reporting of the 'same' research findings in specialist and popular journals such as *Scientific American*, and visual representations in the latter tend to be lavish, full-colour and 'hyper-real', while in the former sparse line drawings are the only form of visual image. Furthermore, we have to be aware that there are competing theories of reality in today's science, despite the fact that for many practical purposes Galilean reality remains of overriding importance. Alternative theories might lead to different standards for high and low modality.

In other contexts the 'hyper-real' does not have the decreased modality it has in 'photographic' naturalism. Magazine photos of food are one example. A different principle for what counts as real operates here, the converse of Galilean reality: the more a picture can create an illusion of touch and taste and smell, the higher its modality. In such images everything is done to appeal to 'sensory' qualities: reality here is constituted precisely by those sensations which Galileo branded as illusions: texture, colour, 'feel'. It is here that the affective values of colours come into their own, for example. The emotive value of colour is sometimes seen as a general characteristic of colour. But in scientific–technological contexts, colour may be conventional (more or less arbitrary 'colour codes' to facilitate the reading of complex diagrams), and in naturalism colours are there 'because they are there in reality'. From the point of view of the 'sensory' definition of reality, on the other hand, colours are there to be experienced sensually and emotively – it is for this reason that people enjoy the highly saturated and unmodulated colours of, say, Matisse, or that children enjoy the highly saturated and unmodulated colours of their plastic toys. Within naturalism these colours are 'less than real', but within a realism that takes subjective emotions and sensations as the criterion for what is real and true, they have the highest modality.

There is, finally, a third area in which the standard of 'photographic' naturalism does not apply, the area of 'abstract realism' – both in science (e.g. the 'speech circuit' diagram in figures 5.1 and 5.2) and in abstract art. Higher education in our society is, to quite some extent, an education in detachment, abstraction and decontextualization (and against naturalism), and this results in an attitude which does not equate the appearance of things with reality, but looks for a deeper truth 'behind appearances'. Just as academically trained persons may accord greater truth to abstract expository writing than to stories about concrete, individual events and people, so they may also place higher value on visual representations which reduce events and people to the 'typical', and extract from them the 'essential qualities'.

While our ideas here are drawn to a large extent from the theoretical work of Jurgen Habermas (especially his *Theory of Communicative Action*, 1984), and to some extent from that of Bourdieu (1986), we will use Bernstein's term 'coding orientation' (1981) for these different reality principles. Coding orientations are sets of abstract principles which inform the way in which texts are coded by specific social groups, or within specific institutional contexts. We distinguish the following:

(1) *Technological coding orientations*, which have, as their dominant principle, the 'effectiveness' of the visual representation as a 'blueprint'. Whenever colour, for example, is useless for the scientific or technological purpose of the image, it has, in this context, low modality.

(2) *Sensory coding orientations*, which are used in contexts in which the pleasure principle is allowed to be the dominant: certain kinds of art, advertising, fashion, cooking, interior decoration, and so on. Here colour is a source of pleasure and affective meanings, and consequently it conveys high modality: vibrant reds, soothing blues, and so on – a whole psychology of colour has evolved to support this.

(3) *Abstract coding orientations*, which are used by sociocultural elites – in 'high' art, in academic and scientific contexts, and so on. In such contexts modality is higher the more an image reduces the individual to the general, and the concrete to its essential qualities. The ability to produce and/or read texts grounded in this coding orientation is a mark of social distinction, of being an 'educated person' or a 'serious artist'.

(4) The commonsense *naturalistic coding orientation*, which remains, for the time being, the dominant one in our society. It is the one coding orientation all members of the culture share when they are being addressed as 'members of our culture', regardless

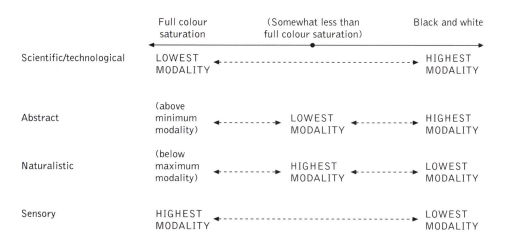

○ **Fig 5.5 Modality values of colour saturation in four coding orientations**

of how much education or scientific–technological training they have received. Individuals with special education or group allegiance may draw on non-naturalistic coding orientations in certain contexts, but they are likely to revert to the naturalistic coding orientation when they are 'just being themselves'. They may, for example, use the abstract coding orientation when visiting a gallery, and the naturalistic coding orientation when watching television or reading a magazine. For those without such education, however, abstract and technological images will never have high modality and always remain 'unreal'. Today, however, naturalism is coming into crisis, as a result of new ways of thinking and new image technologies. In this context the role of some or all of the non-naturalistic coding orientations is likely to become of increasing importance.

The diagram in figure 5.5 shows how the same colour continuum, running from 'no abstraction' to 'full abstraction' (abstraction always being a matter of degree) can have different modality values, according to the four coding orientations. It is drawn here for colour saturation, but it could also have been drawn for any of the other modality markers we discussed in the previous section.

MODALITY IN MODERN ART

The issue of modality becomes particularly complex in modern art, because it has, to a large extent, been the project of modern art to redefine reality, and to do so in contradistinction to photographic naturalism. In this section we will attempt to discuss a few of the issues, beginning with some Australian examples.

The picture in colour plate 3 shows William Dobell's portrait of Joshua Smith, a painting which won the annual Australian Archibald Prize competition for portrait painting in 1943. It was the first modern painting to do so. All previous winners had been conventional 'academic' portraitists, staying well within the bounds of naturalistic depiction. After Dobell had been awarded the Prize, a number of conservative painters took the trustees of the Prize to court for giving it to a painting which, they argued, was not eligible, as it was not a portrait but a caricature. The prosecutor, Garfield Barwick, interrogated Dobell about every detail of the painting, asking him whether he had faithfully represented the ears, the neck, the arms, and so on. The painter, in exasperation, answered: 'Yes, within the limits of art.' From a naturalistic point of view, the painting does of course have comparatively low modality, both in the direction of 'less than real' and in the direction of 'more than real'. Colour differentiation is greatly reduced, to a palette of orange, yellow and brown. The representation of detail, on the other hand, is amplified, exaggerated, 'more than real'. From a naturalistic point of view, the prosecutor was right. But he applied a criterion which was no longer valid in the context of modern art, a way of matching modality values to the scales of colour differentiation, representation and so on which, in the history of modern art, had been successfully contested decades earlier. In modern art, the truth of painting no longer lies in being faithful to appearances, but in being faithful to something else, for example to some modern abstract truth, in the case of this rather 'expressionist' painting, to 'the spirit of the man', and 'the essence of what he looks like', as Dobell himself formulated it during the trial.

Attempts to alter definitions of reality are always likely to produce scandal, and therefore resisted. Whether in the trials of Lawrence's novel or Dobell's painting, the issues are far larger and more far-reaching than aesthetics or artistic convention. Changes in the definition of reality have profound cultural and social effects, and this helps to explain extreme reactions such as the proscription of 'entartete Kunst' or the burning of books.

Despite the trial, future winners of the Archibald Prize would, without exception, be modern artists rather than conventional portrait painters. The picture shown in colour plate 4, a portrait of the writer Patrick White by Louis Kahan, is one of them. It shows a different modality configuration, a different set of abstractions and amplifications. Unlike Dobell, Kahan does not deviate from the naturalistic representation of detail: if one disregards the strangely unseeing eyes, White's features are rendered with naturalistic faithfulness. But texture is amplified: the figure of White seems to have been carved out of some porous, chalky rock, and the rendition of its surface is so detailed that one can almost feel its cold, wet touch – a 'sensory' orientation, but in the direction of displeasure rather than pleasure. Colour, on the other hand, is greatly reduced: in what is at once a pun on White's name and a symbolic gesture, White is drained of all colour. Thus Kahan depicts him as cold, hard, almost repulsive to the touch, and the expression of this 'truth' has taken precedence over the faithful rendering of outward appearances, indeed, has become possible only by means of these 'deviations' from the naturalistic standard. The visual pun reminds us that modality is always related to the values, meanings and beliefs of a particular

Fig 5.6 *Card-players* (Theo van Doesburg, 1916–17) (Doesburg Archive, The Hague)

Fig 5.7 *Composition 9* (abstract version of *Card-players*) (Theo van Doesburg, 1917) (from Jaffé, 1986)

group, in this case an 'ordering' of the figure of Patrick White within the system of Australian high culture, and of Australian society generally.

Our second example pertains to the geometric abstractionism of the 1920s. When European painters, after studying visible reality for centuries, began to conceive of it as made up of abstract, geometrical elements (circles, cones, squares, triangles) reality was redefined as a configuration of basic elements, just as had already happened, for instance, in physics. Within this new definition of reality, painters at first still sought to produce recognizable representations, as shown in figure 5.6. Mondriaan, who tried to paint trees in this way, complained that it was difficult to represent trees as arrangements of

○ **Fig 5.8** *Colour Project for the Schröder Residence* (Gerrit Rietveld, 1923–4) (Catalogue 81, Stedelijk Museum, Amsterdam)

rectangular shapes. But soon these painters went a step further and abandoned the attempt to reconcile the visible surface appearance of things with their geometric inner structure (see figure 5.7). From here it was only one step to, for instance, Gerrit Rietveld's *Colour Project for the Schröder Residence* (1923–4).

Rietveld's work (figure 5.8) is no longer a reduced, abstract representation of reality, but a design for a new reality, yet to be constructed. Of course, blueprints and plans had existed alongside visual representation long before the 1920s, but in separate domains. In this century, however, they became intertwined. Art became intertwined with design, just as science had already become intertwined with technology. The boundaries between representing reality and constructing reality became blurred. And when real things were produced from designs such as these, the processes of abstraction could come full circle and yield 'naturalistic' images again (figure 5.9).

In the work of Ryman, a contemporary American artist, abstraction is perhaps taken to its limit. Many of his paintings are, at least at first glance, white surfaces. Everything is reduced, everything abstracted. There is no colour, no line, no background. And, in terms of our earlier chapters, there is neither representation of action or of social constructs, nor yet any indication of textuality, of composition. This truly is the degree zero of representation.

But if reduction and abstraction serve to reveal otherwise hidden, inner truths, the same might be said about Ryman's paintings. Indeed, like so many other non-naturalistic

⬣   Fig 5.9 Photograph of the Schröder residence ('Rietveld House') (from Brown, 1958)

artists, he sees his work as realistic, and calls his paintings 'realistic paintings': they aspire to present the reality and the truth of the *process* of representation and the process of perception, and thereby perhaps also of the social and cultural world.

There is, however, another, much less abstract feature of Ryman's painting: his concern with texture. His work shows a constant preoccupation with the materials of representation, and with the materiality of the processes of representation. Some of the paintings leave a patch of the canvas uncovered and only thinly cover the rest. Others display a variety of brush-strokes or, by contrast, completely de-emphasize the way in which the paint is applied, resulting in totally flat, presumably sprayed surfaces. Again others emphasize the frame, or the means by which frames are attached to walls, or the flatness of the painting, by rotating it through 90 degrees, and so foregrounding its two-dimensionality.

In other words, there is a strong representational concern in these paintings, but it is a concern with representing the process of representation. Does this suggest low modality, given the enormous distance from everyday naturalism? Or does it suggest the highest modality, in which the negation of representation forms an ultimate truth, or in which the highest modality is accorded to the representation which does not represent but simply is?

As before, our answer is one which refers to the social. Whether a representation is judged credible or not is not necessarily a matter of absolute truth. What one social group considers credible may not be considered credible by another. This is why we see modality as interactive, rather than ideational, as social, rather than as a matter of some independently given value. Modality both realizes and produces social affinity, through aligning the viewer (or reader, or listener) with certain forms of representation, namely those with which the artist (or speaker, or writer) aligns himself or herself, and not with others. Modality realizes what 'we' consider true or untrue, real or not real. In this lies some of the power of art. To the extent that people are drawn into this 'we', new values, new modes of thinking and perceiving can establish themselves. And when enough people are drawn in, the organs of popular(-izing) culture, such as advertising, will quickly move in to amplify the new forms, and move them into the mainstream of culture.

MODALITY CONFIGURATIONS

The examples in the previous section show that the modality values in art can be complex. A painting can reduce naturalism in the way it treats colour, amplify it in the way it treats texture, and yet represent its subject in a naturalistic way, as in plate 4. It can be abstract in respect of one modality marker, naturalistic in respect of another and sensory in respect of yet another, and this allows a multiplicity of possible modality configurations, and hence a multiplicity of ways in which artists can relate to the reality they are depicting, and 'define' reality in general. In many other kinds of images, too, 'modality markers' do not move *en bloc* in a particular direction across the scales, say from the abstract to the sensory, but behave in relatively independent ways. Most glossy magazine food photo-graphs, for instance, are highly sensory in their depiction of the food. The colours are intense. The texture of the food is shown in sharp detail. Lighting enhances the fresh droplets of water on a bunch of grapes, or the viscosity of a sauce, or the glazing of the ham and the cherries in a pie. But the surrounding objects tend to have lower modality. The weave of the tablecloth, on which the food is displayed, for instance, may be only just be visible and often the setting is absent altogether, with the food shown against a black background. In other words, such pictures are not only sensory, they are also abstract. The 'sensorily' depicted food is taken out of its context, idealized and essentialized. And this shows that each of the modality choices in such a modality configuration is expressive of specific meanings, which then come together in the whole.

From our inventory of modality markers we could construct 'modality prints' (borrowing the metaphor of 'voice print', 'DNA print', etc.) to characterize the modality

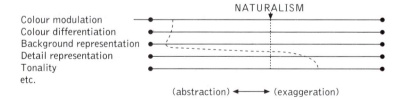

NATURALISM

Colour modulation
Colour differentiation
Background representation
Detail representation
Tonality
etc.

(abstraction) ◄———► (exaggeration)

◐   Fig 5.10 Modality configuration

configurations, and show which modality markers are reduced, made 'less than real', and which are amplified, made 'more than real' – and this *either* in relation to an anchoring point of commonsense high naturalistic modality (as one might do for an audience of 'lay' people at an art exhibition, taking the representational function of art as a commonsense point of departure) *or* in relation to an anchoring point situated in some other realism. Figure 5.10 is an attempt to show what we have in mind.

Such modality configurations would describe what, in a specific genre or a specific work, is regarded as real, as adequate to reality. And it would also demonstrate that images are polyphonic, weaving together choices from different signifying systems, different representational modes, into one texture. In this view, a term such as 'painting' is an artificial construct which brings together and treats as a homogeneous unit what is in reality a complex configuration of different voices, different representational modes. (In the same way it can be said that 'grammar' is an artifice of theory, describing widely different representational modes – phonic substance, intonation, lexis, syntax, etc.) And it is of course from here that the interesting questions can be asked: are there, or could there be, social and historical explanations for these modality configurations?

A few examples may help clarify our argument. The first is a painting by Roderic O'Conor called *Yellow Landscape*. As the title suggests, it shows a summer landscape, with undulating hills rising from or behind a coastline, covered with a mixture of woods and fields (colour plate 5). The painting is naturalistic in some respects: the degree of detail, the articulation of the background, the perspective, the naturalistic palette of colours, the degree of colour saturation. In other respects, however, it is less naturalistic, and tends towards the abstract: the marked texture of the thick striped patterns, the irregular strong *bands* of colour which replace a more naturalistic mixing and distributing of colour, the distribution of light and shade, and the colour modulation and differentiation. These more abstract features give the painting an intellectual, analytical dimension: the foregrounding and separating of the component colours constitutes an intellectual analysis of perception and of light which usurps, so to speak, the space of naturalistic colour modulation and differentiation. On the other hand, the strong colours, no longer harnessed to naturalistic depiction, become now available as signifiers in their own right, and as expressive of emotive, 'sensory' meanings. Thus the painting, within a naturalistic frame, uses visual analysis to open up a space for the pure expression of emotive and subjective meanings.

Our second example comes from a science textbook for the upper years of primary school, produced in Australia (figure 5.11). This is a scientific–technical picture for children. As such it forms a compromise between the naturalistic and the technological coding orientation, perhaps because a 'pure' technological picture would have been regarded by the writer as beyond the understanding of young children. On the one hand, it is a drawing and not a photograph and it lacks a Setting; on the other hand, it uses perspective (angular–isometric), colour (idealized, flat colour), and it shows at least something of light and shade (though in a rather simple and, in part, inconsistent way), and of texture (the grain of the wood, the texture of the head of the nail, the creases in the piece of cloth). The producer of this image perhaps operates with the assumption that children are familiar with the naturalistic coding orientation (that is, 'where they come

Fig 5.11 Compass (Jennings, 1986)

from') and have to be inducted into the technological coding orientation (that is, the progression into disciplinary knowledge). The image captures this transitional phase.

Diagrams, maps and charts for lay readers may be 'naturalized' in similar ways. Newspaper diagrams and maps, for instance, may be drawn in perspective (see the Gulf War map in figure 4.19). Magazines may add colour and pictorialize pie charts and the bars of bar graphs (e.g. figure 3.21 and figure 6.6, where the humanized pie chart even throws a shadow). In company brochures or annual reports the bars of bar graphs may become three-dimensional and rise, like featureless skyscrapers from a clean landscape of undulating hills in strong, flat colour. This shows that modality is a system of social deixis which 'addresses' a particular kind of viewer, or a particular social/cultural group, and provides through its system of modality markers an image of the cultural, conceptual and cognitive position of the addressee. At the same time it shows the transition across and between such groups, and in doing so, demonstrates the social aspect of modality. Most crucially, it shows how modality is motivated, in the close matching of modality and the modal address (location) of specific (and assumed) aspects of the viewer's subjectivity.

Figure 5.12 shows a drawing by Newton, illustrating the set-up for one of his colour experiments. Figure 5.13 is a modern scientific illustration showing the set-up for an experiment by Stratton which caused him to see himself stretched out in space as indicated in the drawing. To modern eyes, Newton's drawing has not yet advanced very far in the direction of high technological modality: he uses (inverted) perspective, and shows the

Fig 5.12 Drawing by Newton (Bodleian Library)

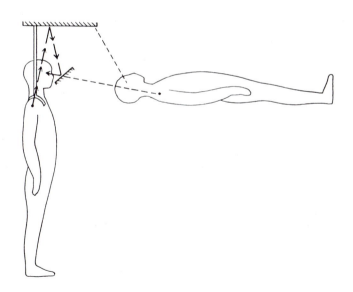

Fig 5.13 Drawing of Stratton's experiment (Gregory, 1990)

Setting. The modern drawing, by contrast, leaves out the setting and simplifies the forms, concentrating on the relation between them, rather than on the representation of the experimenter and the mirrors.

As Halliday has shown (Halliday and Martin, 1993: 54–68), Newton's writing did not yet have the objective, impersonal stance and the lexical density of modern scientific writing. At the same time he made some decisive moves towards developing the grammatical resources that would become characteristic of scientific writing. Clearly the same can be said of his scientific drawings. And that shows that, however great the differences between the verbal and the visual grammar, they derive from similar concerns and orientations.

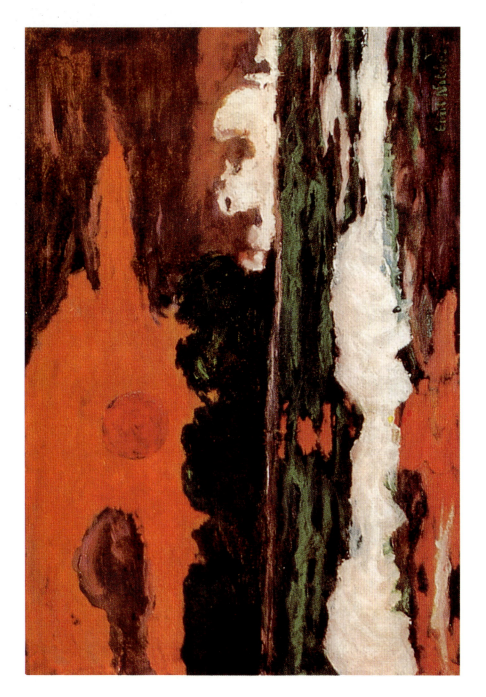

Plate 1 *Tropical Sun* (Emil Nolde, 1914)

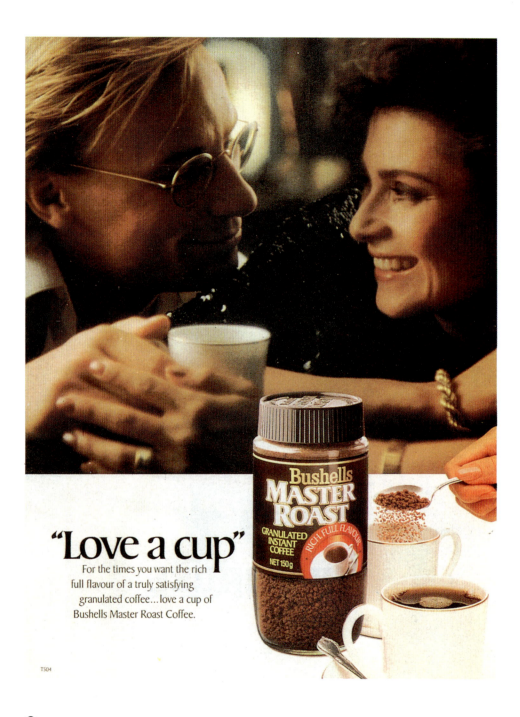

Plate 2 Bushells advertisement (*Women's Weekly*, 1987)

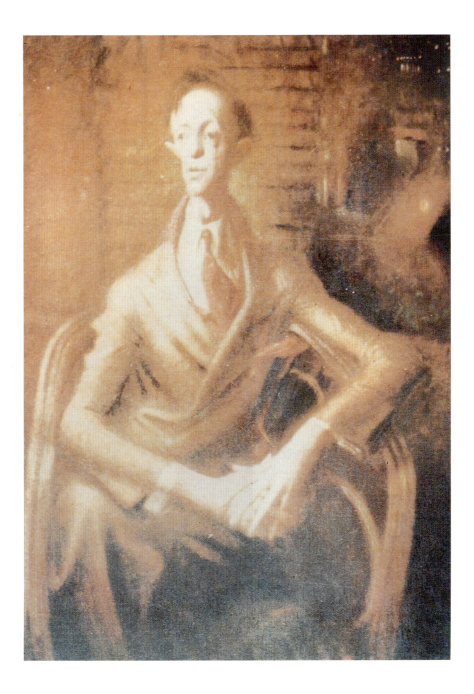

Plate 3 *Joshua Smith* (William Dobell, 1943) (Art Gallery of New South Wales)

Plate 4 *Patrick White* (Louis Kahan, 1963) (Art Gallery of New South Wales)

A Wieviele Kinder auslän-
discher Eltern sind in eurer
Schule?
Fragt sie, seit wann ihre Eltern in
Deutschland sind, was sie arbei-
ten, warum sie hierher kamen, ob
sie bleiben wollen und warum.

Stellt im Atlas fest, woher ausländische Arbeiter kommen, woher
Flüchtlinge. Laßt euch erzählen,
wie es dort aussieht. Lest in Erd-
kundebüchern oder Reiseführern
nach. Achtet dabei besonders auf
die Arbeits- und Lebenssituation.

H Im Sekretariat eurer Schule
gibt es Zahlen über ausländische
Schüler.

Vorschläge zum Gespräch:
○ Gibt es Probleme mit auslän-
dischen Schülerinnen und Schü-
lern?
○ Welche Lösungsmöglichkeiten
seht ihr?
○ Was denken ausländische
Schüler über die Bundesrepublik?
○ Was denken deutsche Schüler
über Ausländer?

A Stellt euch vor, daß an
einem Tage alle ausländischen
Arbeiter die Bundesrepublik ver-
lassen müßten. Bildet Gruppen
und überlegt, was z.B.
○ Bauunternehmer,
○ Kinder der Arbeiter,
○ Gaststättenbesitzer,
○ die Arbeiter selbst,
○ Leiter von Krankenhäusern,
○ Leiter von Reinigungsfirmen für
Probleme hätten, tun müßten . . .
Tragt die Ergebnisse zusammen
und besprecht sie.

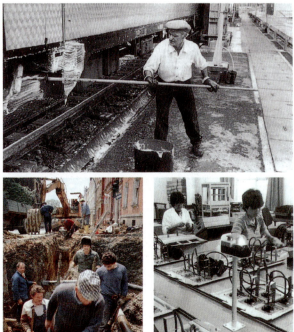

⬤ Plate 6 Vertical triptych (Nitzschke, 1990)

Plate 7 *Cossacks* (Wassily Kandinsky) (Tate Gallery)

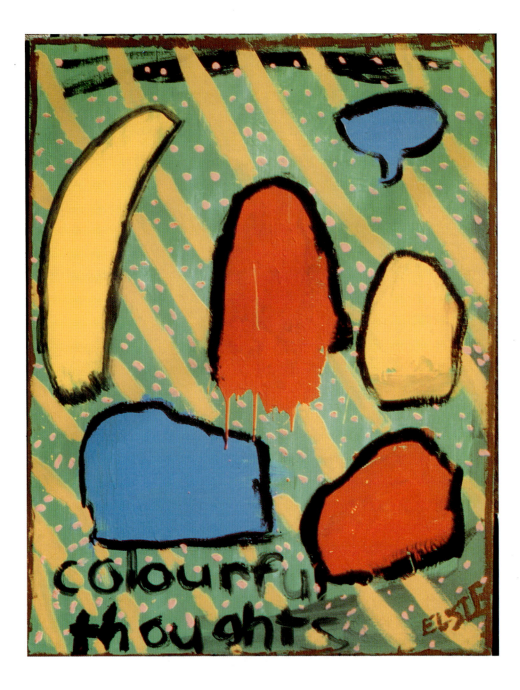

Plate 8 *Colourful Thoughts*

6 The meaning of composition

COMPOSITION AND THE MULTIMODAL TEXT

In previous chapters we have considered the way images represent the relations between the people, places and the things they depict, and the complex set of relations that can exist between images and their viewers. Any given image contains a number of such representational and interactive relations. In figure 6.1, an image from Bergman's *Through a Glass Darkly* (1961), we see Karin (Harriet Anderson), who suffers from an incurable mental disease, and her younger brother Minus (Lars Passgard). From the point of view of representation, the shot contains what we have called a 'non-transactive reaction' (Karin looks out of the frame, at something the viewer cannot see) and a 'transactive reaction' (Minus looks up at his sister). These choices relate to the themes of the dramatic action: Karin has visions, sees things other people cannot see; Minus is caught in the here and now of his problematic relations with the other characters in the film. From the point of view of interactive meaning, the viewer is positioned closer to Karin ('medium shot') than to Minus ('long shot'); and while Minus is seen from behind, Karin faces the viewer frontally. Clearly, the viewer is meant to be most centrally involved with Karin, and with her mental turmoil.

These patterns do not exhaust the relations set up by the image. There is a third element: the composition of the whole, the way in which the representational and interactive elements are made to relate to each other, the way they are integrated into a meaningful whole. Minus, for instance, is placed on the left, and Karin on the right. If this were turned around, the representational and interactive meanings would not be affected. Karin's reaction would still be 'non-transactive' and Minus' reaction 'transactive', and Karin would still be in medium shot, Minus still in long shot. But the meaning of the whole would no longer be the same. The placement of the elements (of the participants and of the syntagmas that connect them to each other and to the viewer) endows them with specific information values relative to each other. We will discuss the value of 'left' and 'right' in the next section.

In addition, Karin is the most *salient*, the most eye-catching element in the composition, not just because she is placed in the foreground and because she forms the largest, simplest element in the picture, but also because she is in sharper focus and receives the greatest amount of light. Throughout much of the film Karin is dressed in light colours and made to bathe in light, in an almost supernatural fashion, this in contrast to the other characters. For these reasons she is also the most salient element in the shots where one of the other characters, for example her husband, is placed in the foreground. Her white clothes and the light on her pale face draw attention to her, even when she is placed in the background. To generalize, pictorial elements can receive stronger or weaker 'stress' than other elements in their immediate vicinity, and so become

Fig 6.1 Harriet Anderson and Lars Passgard in *Through a Glass Darkly* (Bergman, 1960)

more or less important 'items of information' in the whole.

A vertical line formed by the left edge of the door of the shed, and continued by the dividing line between a particularly light and a darker board on the roof of the shed, runs through the middle of the picture, dividing it into two sections, literally and figuratively 'drawing a line' between the space of Karin, who can 'look into the beyond', and the space of Minus, who cannot. The world of Karin is thus separated from the world of Minus, in this pictorial composition as in the dramatic action of the film as a whole, where Minus' desire for contact and communion with his sister remains unfulfilled. There is yet another demarcation line in the picture, the horizon, which divides the picture into the zone of 'heaven' and the zone of 'the earth'. In his discussion of Titian's *Noli Me Tangere* Arnheim (1982: 112–13) describes how the staff of Christ forms a 'visual boundary' between Christ, who is already 'removed from earthly existence', and Magdalen, and how 'the lower region is separated by the horizon from the upper region of free spirituality, in which the tree and the buildings on the hill reach heavenward'. In figure 6.1 Karin straddles the two zones, half still of the earth, half already in the realm of 'free spirituality', while Minus is 'held down by the horizon into the region of the earth'. More generally, composition also involves *framing* (or its absence), through devices which connect or disconnect parts of the picture, so proposing that we see them as joined or as separate in some way, where without framing, we would see them as continuous and complementary: there would be no visual 'directive' of this kind.

Composition, then, relates the representational and interactive meanings of the picture to each other through three interrelated systems:

(1) *Information value*. The placement of elements (participants and syntagms that relate them to each other and to the viewer) endows them with the specific informational values attached to the various 'zones' of the image: left and right, top and bottom, centre and margin.

(2) *Salience*. The elements (participants and representational and interactive syntagms) are made to attract the viewer's attention to different degrees, as realized by such factors as placement in the foreground or background, relative size, contrasts in tonal value (or colour), differences in sharpness, etc.

(3) *Framing*. The presence or absence of framing devices (realized by elements which create dividing lines, or by actual frame lines) disconnects or connects elements of the image, signifying that they belong or do not belong together in some sense.

These three principles of composition apply not just to single pictures, as in the example we have just discussed, they apply also to composite visuals, visuals which combine text and image, and, perhaps, other graphic elements, be it on a page or on a television or computer screen. In the analysis of composite or *multimodal* texts (and any text whose meanings are realized through more than one semiotic code is multimodal) the question arises whether the products of the various codes should be analysed separately or in an integrated way; whether the meanings of the whole should be treated as the sum of the meanings of the parts, or whether the parts should be looked upon as interacting with and affecting one another. It is the latter path we will pursue in this chapter. In considering, for example, the picture of the train (figure 3.41) we do not seek to see the picture as an 'illustration' of the verbal text, thereby treating the verbal text as prior and more important, nor treat the visual and verbal text as entirely discrete elements. We seek to be able to look at the whole page as an *integrated* text. Our insistence on drawing comparisons between language and visual communication stems from this objective. We seek to break down the disciplinary boundaries between the study of language and the study of images, and we seek, as much as possible, to use compatible language, and compatible terminology in speaking about both, for in actual communication the two and indeed many others come together to form integrated texts.

In our view the integration of different semiotic codes is the work of an overarching code whose rules and meanings provide the multimodal text with the logic of its integration. There are two such integration codes: the code of spatial composition, with which we will be concerned in this chapter, and rhythm, the code of temporal composition. The former operates in texts in which all elements are spatially co-present, for example, paintings, streetscapes, magazine pages. The latter operates in texts which unfold over time, for example speech, music, dance (see Van Leeuwen, 1985, 1988). Some types of multimodal text utilize both, for example film and television, although rhythm will usually be the dominant integrative principle in these cases.

It follows that the principles of information value, salience and framing, apply, not only to pictures, but also, for example, to layouts. Figure 6.2, an advertisement for Fenjal bath cosmetics, contains two photographs and two main verbal elements (the headline and the copy in the bottom part of the advertisement). The larger photo is a pictorial representation of the 'promise' of the advertisement, and it is placed in the top section. The photo of the product (or rather, range of products) is smaller, and placed in the bottom section. Reversing this would produce an entirely different effect, and probably result in a rather anomalous layout. Just what information values this arrangement accords to the two sections of the page will be discussed below. As far as salience is concerned, we can note that this page is not divided into two equal halves. The top section is the most salient, not only because of its size, but also because of the salience of its central element, the woman, whose fleshtones stand out against the blue background, and

⬙ **Fig 6.2 Fenjal advertisement (*Women's Weekly*, November 1987)**

because the female figure has cultural salience in any case. Thus the advertisement gives greater stress to the promise of the product than to the factual information it also offers. Finally, a sharp line provides a boundary between the photo and the verbal text, dividing the page into two separate sections, two spaces, reserved for two different kinds of meaning, one for the promise of the product, the sensation of luxury in pampering one's body, the other for more down-to-earth information about the product, its uses, its range, and so on. Just as there is a dividing line between heaven and earth in Titian's *Noli Me Tangere*, and in the still from Bergman's *Through a Glass Darkly*, so there is, in this advertisement, a dividing line between the world of 'what might be', the projected happiness the product might bring, and the world of 'what is', the product itself.

Early printed pages still treated text as 'visual material'. Walter Ong (1982: 119ff.) describes how sixteenth-century title pages broke up words without regard for syllable boundaries, and used different type sizes in a way that was not related to the relative importance of words, but served to create pleasing visual patterns. However, the printed page soon developed into the 'densely printed page' in which reading is linear and textual integration is achieved by linguistic means (conjunctions, cohesive ties, etc.). In books of this kind it seems that the page has ceased to be a significant textual unit. The page shown in figure 6.2, on the other hand, is a semiotic unit, structured, not linguistically, but by principles of visual composition. In such pages verbal text becomes just one of the elements integrated by the codes of information value, salience and framing, and reading is not necessarily linear, wholly or in part, but may go from centre to margin, or in circular fashion, or vertically, etc. And this is the case, not only in contemporary magazines, but also, as our later examples will show (e.g. figure 6.8), in many modern school textbooks, where each double page may become a 'chapter', a self-contained section, a semiotic unit.

It should be noted of course, that the layout of the densely printed page is still visual, still carries an overall cultural significance, as an image of progress. The densely written pages of other cultural traditions are laid out differently, as, for example, in the Talmud, which has the oldest text, the Mishna, in the centre, the Gemara written around it, and later, medieval commentaries again, around the Gemara, in concentric layers. In such cases, however, every page is still read the same way. In the case of magazine pages and the pages of modern computer screens each successive page may have a different reading path.

This development beyond the densely printed page began in the late nineteenth-century mass press, in a context in which the ruling class, itself strongly committed to the densely printed page, attempted to maintain its hegemony by taking control of popular culture, commercializing it, and so turning the media *of* the people into the media *for* the people (see Williams 1977: 295). Their own comparable media – 'high' literature and the humanities generally – became even more firmly founded on the single semiotic of writing. Layout was not encouraged here, because it undermined the power of the densely printed page as, literally, the realization of the most literary and literate semiotic. The genres of the densely printed page, then, manifest the cultural capital ('high' cultural forms) controlled by the intellectual and artistic wing of the middle class, to use Bourdieu's terms (1986). Yet it is this same class which has been instrumental in spreading the new visual literacy to those who were not, or not yet, to be initiated into the forms of literacy which constituted its own mark of distinction (the 'masses', or children), *and* to embrace it, for example in 'high' culture avant-garde manifestations, as an expression of their opposi-tional role within the middle class as a whole. As so often in this century, they turned out, in the end, to have been sawing off the branch on which they were sitting. The distinction between 'high' and 'low' forms is now everywhere in crisis, and new ways of maintaining cultural hegemony are required, for instance the development of different and differently valued ways of *talking* about forms which, themselves, are no longer differentiated in the old way (the 'discourses' of different 'audiences'). But the most highly valued ways of talking (and semiotics is one of them) remain themselves bound to methods that cannot adequately describe the new forms. If we are to understand the way in which vital text-producing institutions like the media, education and children's literature make sense of the world and participate in the development of new forms of social stratification, a theory of language is no longer sufficient and must be complemented by theories which can make the principles of the new visual literacy explicit, and describe, for instance, the role of layout in the process of social semiosis that takes place on the pages of the texts produced by these institutions as we will try to do in this chapter.

GIVEN AND NEW: THE INFORMATION VALUE OF LEFT AND RIGHT

Many of the double-page spreads in women's magazines use the layout shown in figure 6.3, a feature article from the *Australian Women's Weekly*. Their right pages are dominated by large and salient photographs from which the gaze of one or more women engages the gaze of the viewer (what, in chapter 4, we called 'demand' pictures). These pages show women in specific and sometimes contradictory roles, with which the readers of the magazine are invited to form a positive identification: a mother; a former 'soapie star' turned housewife and happy in that role; working women capable of coping with 'tough', 'masculine' jobs. Their left pages contain mostly verbal text, with graphically salient photographs on the right. The spread shown in figure 6.3 has a photograph on the left also, but this photo is smaller and, in contrast to the photo on the right page, it is a 'fly on the wall' photograph, which does not acknowledge the presence of the photographer, nor therefore, that of the viewer. It is what, in chapter 4, we called an 'offer' picture. On such pages there often is a sense of complementarity or continuous movement from left to right, as in figure 6.3, where the photograph on the left is tilted to form a vector that leads the eyes to the photograph on the right, and where the colour gold, with its less obvious connections to the theme of the story, is used as another integrating device: it occurs in the photograph as the colour of the helmets and of the liquid being poured, and is used also as the background against which the verbal text is printed.

On such pages the right seems to be the side of the key information, of what the reader must pay particular attention to, of the 'message' – whether it is the invitation to identify with a role model highly valued in the culture of the magazine or something else, for example an instance of what is to be learned in a textbook. It follows that the left is the side of the 'already given', something the reader is assumed to know already, as part of

● Fig 6.3 Gold-diggers (*Women's Weekly*, November 1987)

the culture, or at least as part of the culture of the magazine. In figure 6.3, gold mining is Given, and the fact that *women* can engage in it, and that you, the reader, should identify with such 'tough' women, is New, the message, the 'issue'.

Looking at what is placed on the left and what is placed on the right in other kinds of visuals confirms this generalization: when pictures or layouts make significant use of the horizontal axis, positioning some of their elements left, and other, different ones right of the centre (which does not, of course, happen in every composition) the elements placed on the left are presented as Given, the elements placed on the right as New. For something to be Given means that it is presented as something the viewer already knows, as a familiar and agreed-upon point of departure for the message. For something to be New means that it is presented as something which is not yet known, or perhaps not yet agreed upon by the viewer, hence as something to which the viewer must pay special attention. Broadly speaking, the meaning of the New is therefore 'problematic', 'contestable', 'the information "at issue"'; while the Given is presented as commonsensical, self-evident. This structure is ideological in the sense that it may not correspond to what is the case either for the producer or for the consumer of the image or layout: the important point is that the information is presented *as though* it had that status or value for the reader, and that readers have to read it within that structure, even if that valuation may then be rejected by a particular reader.

A similar structure exists in the English language, in the information structure of the clause (see Halliday, 1985: 274ff.). In language, as in visual communication, this is not a constituent structure, with strong framing between elements, but a gradual, wave-like movement from left to right (or rather, from 'before' to 'after', since in language we are dealing with temporally integrated texts), and it is realized by intonation. Intonation creates two peaks of salience within each 'tone group', one at the beginning of the group and another, the major one (the 'tonic', in Halliday's terminology) as the culmination of the New, at the end. Just as in figure 6.3 we have one peak of salience on the left, in the bold headline and the red bar which separates it from the article itself, and another on the right, in the photo of the two women, so we would have one peak of salience on the syllable *gold* and another on the syllable *wo-* of *women* in:

> GOLD-digging can now be done by *wo*men

And just as the image of the two women is the New in figure 6.3, so the word *women* would be the New, the key point of the message, in the clause above. In other words, there is a close similarity between *sequential* information structure in language and *horizontal* structure in visual composition, and this attests to the existence of deeper, more abstract coding orientations which find their expression differently in different semiotic codes.

So far we have taken a composite text as our example, but the Given–New relation applies also within an image. Figure 6.4 shows a fourteenth-century relief depicting the creation of Eve. God is the Given, agreed origin and departure point of all that exists.

⬤ Fig 6.4 *The Creation of Eve* (Lorenzo Maitani, fourteenth century) (from Hughes, 1969)

'Woman', on the other hand, is New and, in the context of the Genesis story, problematic, the temptress who leads Adam into sin. Michelangelo, on the other hand, in his famous painting *The Creation of Adam* on the ceiling of the Sistine Chapel, placed God on the right, in keeping with the new, humanistic spirit of the Renaissance. In this period God suddenly became New, and problematic. Generations of philosophers were to attempt to redefine Him in ways commensurate with the new science, and to try to prove His existence by the use of logic. In this picture the movement is no longer from God to 'Man', but from 'Man' to God. 'Man' reaches out, aspiring to divine status, and almost achieving it – but not quite. Figure 6.5 is just one of many modern advertisements which play with this image. The computer is treated as Given, as something to be taken for granted in today's world, and the 'problem', the 'issue', now lies, not in the machine, but in values commonly opposed to the machine – art, religion, humanity.

In many magazine layouts, the space of the Given is filled by verbal text, the space of the New, or at least a large part of it, by one or more images. But this is not always the case. A double-page advertisement for Mercedes-Benz showed, on the left, a Mercedes, photographed objectively (rather than, for example, from the driver's point of view), and with the well-known Mercedes emblem in the centre of the composition. The right page contained only verbal text, with a headline saying 'Mercedes-Benz agrees with its competitors. You

⬤ **Fig 6.5 Sharp advertisement (*Sydney Morning Herald*, July 1991)**

should drive their cars before you drive a Mercedes-Benz.' In other words, the advertisement treated the Mercedes as an already-known, 'Given' symbol of status, and the message that 'you, too might own a Mercedes' as the New. More generally, if the left contains a picture and the right verbal text, the picture is presented as Given, as a well-established point of departure for the text, and the text contains the New. If the left page has text and the right page a picture, the text contains the Given, and the picture the New.

The Mercedes advertisement points to the social effects and uses of this structure. What is taken for granted by one social group is not taken for granted by another. We might expect to find, therefore, systematic differences in the dispositions of material in layout across different magazines, for instance according to their readership. The Fenjal advertisement (figure 6.2) appeared on the left of a two-page layout, with a story about a family reunion on the right. In a magazine aimed at a readership from a more affluent social group, advertisements might appear on the right – as they tend to in Australian *Vogue*. In one case, what is advertised are necessities; in the other case, what is advertised are means of constructing a 'lifestyle'.

The concepts of Given and New can be applied also to the design of diagrams. In

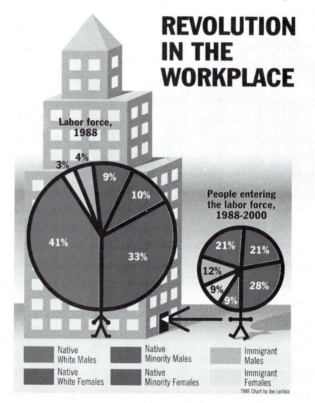

◗ Fig 6.6 Revolution in the workplace (*Time*, special issue *Time Australia*, Summer 1990)

Shannon and Weaver's communication model (figure 2.2) it might seem that the horizontal order of the elements is motivated representationally: the process of 'sending information', for instance, must take place before the information can be received. On the one hand, this means that left signifies 'before', on the other hand, arrows do not always point to the right.

Figure 6.6, a diagram from *Time Magazine*, uses a pie chart to display the composition of the workforce today and in the year 2000. The pie chart which represents the future composition of the workforce is moving towards the present, gradually 'coming closer' – but it is not moving towards the right, because the current composition of the workforce must be treated as Given, and represented as a massive, solid edifice, while future additions to the workforce (of women and minorities!) must be treated as New, and problematic. This shows how the Given–New structure can be ideological even in diagrams. If the horizontal order of the communication model were re-arranged in a similar way, it would no longer depict communication from the point of view of the 'sender', with the 'receiver' as New, and problematic (Will the message 'hit the target'?

Fig 6.7 Reversed communication model

Will it have the intended effect?). Instead, the *reader* would become the origin and departure of the communication process, and the 'sender' ('author') problematic, as has indeed happened, for instance, in literary reception theory.

Given–New structures can also be found in film and television. Media interviews, for example, usually place the interviewer on the left of the interviewee (from the viewer's point of view). Thus interviewers are presented as people with whose views and assumptions viewers will identify and are already familiar, indeed, as the people who ask questions on behalf of the viewers. The interviewees, on the other hand, present 'New' information – and are situated on the right (see Bell and Van Leeuwen, 1994: 160–4). The relation between Given and New may be emphasized by horizontal camera movements ('pans'). In a current affairs item from an ABC *7.30 Report* (March 1987), the children from a Muslim Community School were initially shown as 'ethnic', 'different' from 'us', viewers – there was much emphasis on their non-Western dress, and there was Arabic music in the background. But it was the point of the programme to establish that they were, despite this, 'just like ordinary Australian children', playful, spontaneous, creative, etc. This was realized, among other things, by various horizontal camera movements: a shot which panned from children in non-Western clothes to the teacher, a young woman in a Western dress, tying a bow in the hair of a little girl; a shot which panned along a classroom wall from an Arabic sign to a picture of a clown, etc. In other words, 'difference', ethnic prejudice, was treated as Given; the fact that at least these children

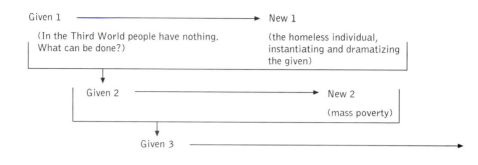

Given 1 ────────────────────────► New 1

(In the Third World people have nothing.   (the homeless individual,
What can be done?)   instantiating and dramatizing
                                             the given)

Given 2 ────────────────────────► New 2

                                             (mass poverty)

Given 3 ───►

▲ **Fig 6.8 Cumulative Given–New structure**

should be accepted as 'like us' was treated as New, and formed the message the programme was trying to get across.

The Given–New structure does not only apply to what we would conventionally regard as a single text. As we have suggested, magazines may have an advertisement on the left page and a feature article on the adjoining right page, so treating advertisements as the commercial Given of the magazine, and suggesting that the magazine is principally read for the editorial material, for the information about the 'real world' which it offers. This is the case in the example above of the *Australian Women's Weekly*. In *Vogue*, on the other hand, the advertisements are treated as New. The magazine presents itself as one which is principally read for clues about the commodities that can express the readers' 'lifestyle' and status. The feature articles then form the 'Given' without which magazines would no longer be magazines.

In ongoing texts, each New can, in turn, become Given for the next New. The opening pages of the chapter 'In search of a straw' from the Dutch junior highschool geography textbook *Werk aan de Wereld* (Bols *et al.*, 1986) have, on the far left, a single column of text, occupying about a fifth of the page, which has a 'landscape' format, favouring a horizontally oriented layout. The text contains assertions such as 'Many people in the Third World have nothing' and questions such as 'What prospects do all these people have?' Given is, in the first place, the Third World as a problem. The remainder of the left page has a large colour photo of a man sleeping on the street, covered by a blanket (there is no indication where this photo is taken). This more emotive way of presenting the 'problem' therefore functions as New in relation to the text. The right page features a single photograph, showing a large crowd of people searching a rubbish dump, armed with cane bags and baskets. In relation to this photo, the image of the homeless man (an image now also familiar in Europe) becomes Given, while the photo itself, with its, in Northern Europe, less familiar image of shocking mass poverty, is presented as New. Together with the introductory text, the two images constitute the Given of the chapter as a whole . Thus each new item of information, once received, becomes, in turn, Given for the information which follows, as shown in figure 6.8. This pattern of the New becoming Given is characteristic of language also, both in speech and in writing.

IDEAL AND REAL: THE INFORMATION VALUE OF TOP AND BOTTOM

Like many other Western advertisements (see Myers, 1994: 139), the Fenjal bath cosmetics advertisement (figure 6.2) is structured along the vertical axis. In such advertisements the upper section visualizes the 'promise of the product', the status of glamour it can bestow on its users, or the sensory fulfilment it will bring. The lower section visualizes the product itself, providing more or less factual information about the product, and telling the readers where it can be obtained, or how they can request more information about it, or order it. There is usually less connection, less ongoing movement, between the two parts of the composition than in horizontally oriented composition. Instead, there is a sense of contrast, of opposition between the two. The upper section tends to make 'emotive' appeal and show us 'what might be'; the lower section tends to be more informative and practical, showing us 'what is'. A sharp dividing line may separate the two, although, at a less conspicuous level, there may also be connective elements. In figure 6.2, for instance, an axis runs down the centre of the page, indicated by the head/neck/cleavage line of the figure, and continued in the graphic composition of the lower element; the woman's glance provides a vector to the text below, particularly to the emphasized 'Fenjal Bath Cosmetics. Indulge yourself'; and some of the visual motifs from the upper section (the references to fragrance and moisture, the gestural reference to indulgence, the flowers, the colour blue) are repeated in the lower section, either verbally or visually. Overall, however, the opposition between unreal (image) and real (language) is strongly emphasized, with the product itself placed firmly in the realm of the real, as the solid foundation of the edifice of promise, and with the top section as the realm of the consumer's supposed aspirations and desires.

In other contexts, the opposition between top and bottom takes on somewhat different values. In a fairly conservative but still widely used Dutch geography textbook (Dragt *et al.*, 1986 [1972]) the upper half of the first page of a chapter on, again, 'The Third World', is fully verbal, presenting generalized assertions and definitions such as 'A large part of the world has a low development' and 'These underdeveloped countries we call poor countries or developing countries.' This provides a more neutral and less emotive (but not less ideological) kind of idealization, a representation of the world which is divested of contradictions, exceptions and nuances. The lower half of the page is given over to a map of the world which uses colour coding to divide the world into regions according to the average income of the inhabitants, thus providing specific and detailed evidence to support the assertions in the top half. Directions for action, for instance coupons for ordering a product in advertisements, or assignments or questions in textbooks, also tend to be found on the lower half of the page, usually at the bottom right (hence also New).

The information value of top and bottom, then, can perhaps be summarized along the following lines. If, in a visual composition, some of the constituent elements are placed in the upper part, and other different elements in the lower part of the picture space or the page, then what has been placed on the top is presented as the Ideal, what has been placed at the bottom as the Real. For something to be ideal means that it is presented as the idealized or generalized essence of the information, hence also as its, ostensibly, most salient part. The Real is then opposed to this in that it presents more specific information (e.g. details), more 'down-to-earth' information (e.g. photographs as documentary evidence, or maps or charts), or more practical information (e.g. practical consequences, directions for action). This of course is no less ideological.

As is already evident from the examples given so far, the opposition between Ideal and Real can also structure text–image relations. If the upper part of a page is occupied by the text and the lower part by one or more pictures (or maps or charts or diagrams), the text plays, ideologically, the lead role, the pictures a subservient role (which, however, is important in its own way, as specification, evidence, practical consequence, and so on). If the roles are reversed, so that one or more pictures occupy the top section, then the Ideal, the ideologically foregrounded part of the message is communicated visually, and the text serves to elaborate on it.

As with the Given and New, the Ideal–Real structure can be used in the composition both of single images and of composite texts such as layouts. Figure 6.9, reproduced from one of the Dutch geography textbooks we have discussed (Bols *et al.*, 1986) includes a photo which may have been taken in India – its origin is not mentioned, but to the left of the picture, as its Given, we see a map of India. A young mother, carrying a baby, occupies, by herself, the top section of the vertically composed photo, as a 'Third World' Madonna with child. The bottom section shows a group of women and children, sitting on the ground, tightly packed together. The young mother looks at this group, an expression of worry crossing her face. In this way the picture as a whole expresses a contradiction between the deep-rooted Ideal of motherhood and the Real of overpopulation. Immediately below the photo we find a collage of newspaper headlines ('India struggles against overpopulation'; 'Unemployment nightmare in India') as Real (the newspaper as source of 'hard facts', of evidence) with respect to the more symbolic, idealized and emotive representation of the problem in the picture.

Ideal and Real can also play a role in diagrams. It is striking, for instance, that diagrams based on a vertical time line sometimes idealize the present, sometimes the past. The already mentioned Dutch geography textbook *Werk aan de Wereld* (Bols *et al.*, 1986) features a diagram which represents the decrease of living space per head of the population, by means of a vertical arrangement of what looks like chessboards of different sizes. On these 'chessboards' stand cartoon figures. On top we see a gentleman from 1900, complete with top hat, on a large ('6285 m²') 'chessboard'. At the bottom, on the smallest 'chessboard', we see a 'punk' character from 1980. Here, as in many advertisements, the past, the 'good old days', is presented as Ideal. The other Dutch geography textbook we mentioned (Dragt *et al.*, 1986 [1972]) features a 'geological calendar' in which the present ('development of vertebrates', complete with a small drawing of a naked woman) becomes the Ideal, the culmination of progress and evolution.

Many visuals combine horizontal and vertical structuring. In figure 6.10 (as in figure 6.4) God is Given, and Adam and Eve are New. But their fall from grace has introduced a (New) opposition, between the Ideal of Paradise, of the Garden of Eden, and the Real of death and decay – and the two are visually separated by the river which surrounds the Garden of Eden.

⬤ **Fig 6.9 Overpopulation (Bols *et al.*, 1986)**

The communication model in figure 6.11 also combines horizontal and vertical structuring, in an intricate piece of visual thinking about the impossibility of knowing reality 'as it is', objectively. Given is the 'event', as it exists 'out there', separate from our perception of it. New, and therefore problematic, is our perception of the event, and at the lower level, the way we communicate our perceptions through language. Ideal is the 'empirical', the world 'as it is', and our perception of it, unmediated by communication, culture, language (which are positioned in the lower section). Real are our interpretations of these perceptions, as mediated by communication. Clearly, this diagram could have been vertical, or horizontal. But it is not. Communication is positioned *below* the 'event' and its perception. The 'empirical' world and 'pure' observation are Ideal. But this Ideal is also depicted as isolation from our 'statements' about it, and our perceptions of these statements. This is what the lower section of the diagram, the Real, tells us. Perception is second-hand, filtered through culture and language, which, as the double-headed arrows indicate, feed back into our perception of nature, and hence into nature itself. The diagram tells us that reality *does* exist, but that our perception of it can only be 'subjective, selective, variable and unpredictable' (McQuail and Windahl, 1993: 25).

Figure 6.12 shows a page which is fairly typical of many magazines; in this case it is a page from the *Australian Women's Weekly*. Ideal is the moment, one might say, that 'marriage was made in Heaven'. Modality is 'distant', representing the 'not now', the 'out of time'. The bottom section, by contrast, represents the world of 'is', 'now', 'in our time'.

⬯ Fig 6.10 *God Shows Death to Adam and Eve* (French, fifteenth-century miniature from ms. of *De civitate Dei*)
(from Hughes, 1969)

Given, is the royal couple, presented as the quintessential couple, the well-established symbol of family values. New are Sydney's Gwen and Ray Kincade, an instance, an example of these values. Hence what is Given is the pre-eminence (historically, socially, semiotically) of the royal couple as the paradigm example of the married couple. What is New is one instance of the paradigm – where many others of a set of acceptable instances would have served equally well. This distinction is perhaps sharpest in the bottom part. The two pictures in the top part become, at the safe distance of forty years, almost identical, an equation between equal terms.

   In one, and a very real, sense the place of the New seems merely perfunctory: it is the place of the replication of the paradigm, of the reproduction of the existing classifications of the culture, the place where the underlying values of the culture are reaffirmed. The New instantiates and 'naturalizes' these values. But that very fact also makes the position problematic, for it is at the same time the place of the affirmation of what is, the place of the reproduction of social meanings, and the place where the contestation of paradigmatic values can take place, the place therefore of the constant production of social meanings (e.g. of new definitions of 'women's work' in figure 6.3), even when that

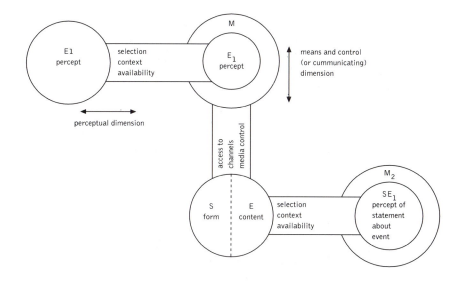

Fig 6.11 Gerbner's communication model (Watson and Hill, 1980: 77)

production seems to be mere reproduction and hence conservative in its effects. Could there, for instance, have been a Vietnamese or Lebanese or Aboriginal couple in this position (in 1987), not to mention a gay couple? This contestation over 'established', 'Given' values may happen in one or two ways: a reader who is not Anglo-Australian will identify either with the syntagm of Anglo-Australianness, 'assimilate', in other words; or refuse the syntagm as having no relevance or value to him or her. In the latter case there will be pressure on this place in the syntagm, and this in turn will result in pressure on the paradigm as a whole.

There is another aspect to this: while the syntagm declares itself as unquestionably established, its appearance points at the same time to a problem with the paradigm, to the need precisely for a testing and (re-)affirmation of its legitimacy. Read from the right to the left, the syntagm declares that it is the willingness of readers to read it as a relation of identity (within a hyponymic structure) which gives legitimacy to the royal couple. Royalty is the established, the Given. What has to be reaffirmed anew is that subjects are still prepared to enter into this paradigmatic relation. A monarchy trying to establish itself, on the other hand, might need to utilize a structure where the power of the people is represented as Given, and the identity of the monarch is to be established – that is, the royal couple would appear on the right.

Thus this syntagm reveals a number of social facts: what is regarded as established and Given; what the cultural classification system is with respect to a certain feature; and whether the system is progressive or reactionary. It is above all a syntagm which does not permit deviance; or rather, once an item is in the syntagm, it has to be read as being in the paradigm. Where it does permit deviance is on the part of the reader, who can refuse

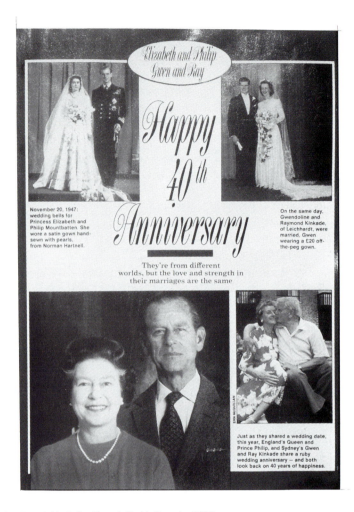

Fig 6.12 **Royal couple (*Australian Women's Weekly*, November 1987)**

to be part of the community defined by this paradigm.

In the Western visual semiotic, then, the syntagmatic is the realm of the process of semiosis, and the top–bottom structure the result and record of semiosis, the realm of order, the paradigm, the mimetic representation of culture (Hodge and Kress, 1988). To maintain and unsettle top–bottom structures, one has to work on the left–right structures. That this system goes back a long way in Western art can be seen in genres such as fifteenth-century Flemish diptychs, which, for instance, may have the Virgin and the Child as Given, and a donor or Saint as New, as in the diptych by the master of Bruges in the Courtauld Gallery, and polyptychs from the same period, which may parallel a Real (earthly) and Ideal (heavenly) version of the same theme in the lower and upper part of the panels, as in Bosch's *Last Judgement*, where the lower part of one of the left panels shows Adam and Eve being driven from the Garden of Eden and the upper part the expulsion of the Rebel Angels from Heaven.

As we have said in the Introduction, we are largely concerned with the description of the visual semiotic of Western cultures. Cultures which have long-established reading directions of a different kind (right to left or top to bottom) are likely to attach different values to these positions. In other words, reading directions may be the material instantiations of deeply embedded cultural value systems. Directionality as such, however, is a semiotic resource in all cultures. All cultures work with margin and centre, left and right, top and bottom, even if they do not all accord the same meanings and values to these spatial dimensions. And the way they use them in their signifying systems will have relations of homology with other cultural systems, whether religious, philosophical or practical.

We will end this section with two further examples of the uses of Given and New, one in paintings by Rembrandt and the other in paintings by three European impressionists, Sisley, Pissarro and Monet. In discussing Rembrandt we will draw attention to the way he uses Given and New for the expression of affective aspects of meaning, and this especially in relation to the source and direction of light and the effect produced by that. In many, perhaps the majority, of Rembrandt's paintings, whether in landscapes such as *Landscape with a Stone Bridge* or in portraits such as *A Young Woman in Bed* or *Double Portrait of the Mennonite Preacher Cornelius Claesz Anslo and his Wife Aeltje Gerritsdr Schouten* (figure 6.13), the light source is outside the left frame of the picture and illuminates mainly the left part, leaving the right of the painting in greater or lesser darkness. Iconographically speaking the metaphoric range of light is wide – light can signify 'the divine', 'illumination', 'hope', etc. In these paintings light, whatever its meaning, is in the area of the Given, the taken for granted, the now/present. 'Light' is Given, 'darkness' New.

The height of the unseen light source also varies: in *Young Woman* it is on or just below the centre; in *Double Portrait* it comes from a position above the halfway mark, perhaps two-thirds of the way up; and in *Landscape* it comes from somewhere high up, near the top corner and in the near middle distance. That is, light may be in the area of the Real coming from a 'mundane' source, or it may be 'divine'. In other paintings the light comes from within the painting, for instance in *The Holy Family on the Flight to Egypt*, where it forms the (divine) light 'in the world' (there is also a second, faint light coming from outside, in the sky above). In *Belshazar's Feast*, by a most unusual contrast, the light source (the glowing script announcing the doom of the king) is situated in the top-right quadrant – the space of the New and the 'Ideal'/'divine'. The variation in the source and directionality of light thus has a complex set of meanings. It can contrast the secular/mundane and the divine/ideal; light as Given and taken for granted and light as New and astonishing: and all these in variable combinations. In *Double Portrait*, for example, the light comes from outside the depicted world, is situated in the area of the Given (the area where the scriptures are depicted); and comes from just above the midway point between Ideal and Real, so that it could be interpreted as 'divine', yet close to the Real. One overwhelming effect is the brightness of the area of the Given, and the total

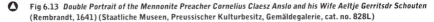

Fig 6.13 *Double Portrait of the Mennonite Preacher Cornelius Claesz Anslo and his Wife Aeltje Gerritsdr Schouten* (Rembrandt, 1641) (Staatliche Museen, Preussischer Kulturbesitz, Gemäldegalerie, cat. no. 828L)

darkness of the area of the New (the future?) to which the two figures have, in any case, turned their backs. Are we entitled to read from this autobiographical, affective meanings – perhaps a deep, pervasive pessimism about both the future, the New, and the present, the Real, which then contrasts with a feeling of security about what was, a faith in a divine light from the past certainty, which entails that we must turn our back on the New, on the future? If so, these affective, personal meanings are surely as significant as social and cultural meanings, and of course, related to them.

Turning to our second example, Sisley, Pissarro and Monet belonged to the same 'school' and the paintings we show were made within a four-year period during which they were in constant and close interaction with each other. Yet their use of the left–right structuring shows characteristic differences. In most of Pissarro's paintings the centre dominates, and is the space of the 'topical' element (figure 6.14). In Sisley's paintings the left carries the major weight, and features, for instance, buildings or towns, while the right is relatively open, and empty, or more diffuse (figure 6.15). In Monet's paintings, by contrast, the right is generally full and 'closed' and the space of the 'topical' elements

Fig 6.14 *Chestnut Trees in Louvecienne* (Camille Pissarro, 1872) (Musée d'Orsay, Paris)

(figure 6.16). Our attention was drawn to this during a visit to the Musée Quai d'Orsay in February 1994, where three paintings by these artists were exhibited as a triptych – in one frame, with Sisley on the left, Pissarro in the centre, and Monet on the right, a perfectly symmetrical composition, due to the left–right and central disposition of material in the three paintings.

Such dispositions are probably largely unconscious, just as the dispositions of elements in handwriting are largely unconscious. Yet there is clear regularity, and there are deep, affective meanings behind this regularity. Profound, and profoundly metaphysical orientations to the world are or can be encoded in this particular feature, revealing aspects of affective states, ways of being in the world, at least as strongly as other, perhaps more readily apparent, elements: a sense of security or insecurity about the past or about the future, for instance, or a sense of permanence and solidity or impermanence and fragility. Clearly, systems such as the Given–New system are both stable and long-lasting *and* always productive, both inert and conservative and, always at the same time, dynamic and innovative, allowing the production of new, complex and infinitely nuanced meanings. And although we have tried to render some of them in words, meanings of this kind are rarely, if ever, articulated other than in the visual, which is why they are so difficult to express, transpose, transform into language.

⬤ Fig 6.15 *Boat during the Flood* (Alfred Sisley, 1876) (Musée d'Orsay, Paris)

⬤ Fig 6.16 *Yachts in Argenteuil* (Claude Monet, 1872) (Musée d'Orsay, Paris)

THE INFORMATION VALUE OF CENTRE AND MARGIN

Visual composition may also be structured along the dimensions of centre and margin. The most typical manifestations of this can be found in children's drawings, or, for example, in Byzantine art. As Arnheim (1982: 73) notes:

> In the Byzantine churches the dominant image of the divine ruler holds the centre of the apse. In portrait paintings, a pope or emperor is often presented in central position. More generally, when the portrait of a man shows him in the middle of a framed area, we see him detached from the vicissitudes of his life's history, alone with his own being and his own thoughts. A sense of permanence goes with the central position.

Figure 6.17 is an example – a Buddhist painting in which the central figure is surrounded by a circle of subordinates. Arnheim in fact makes the centre the crucial element of his theory of composition, conceiving of the visual objects in a composition as 'so many cosmic bodies attracting and repelling one another in space' (1982: 207).

In contemporary Western visualization central composition is relatively uncommon, though here too there may be changes in train. Most compositions polarize elements as Given and New and/or Ideal and Real. But when teaching on a media design course in Singapore, we found that central composition plays an important role in the imagination

Fig 6.17 Buddhist painting (Arnheim, 1982)

Fighting for Their Lives

The world's airlines, battered by war and recession, slug it out in a brawl that will reshape the industry for years to come

By THOMAS MC CARROLL

Planning a trip? You'll be happy to know that Pan Am, American and Northwest airlines have drastically cut U.S. fares for travelers buying tickets before March 1. British Airways would like to cut transatlantic fares one-third, and TWA, USAir and Pan Am want to cut them that much or more, if the government lets them. Air carriers are offering dramatic bargains —and not out of benevolence. They're desperate.

In 1990, their all-time worst year, the world's airlines lost a record $3.5 billion and nearly half their passenger traffic to the threat of war and the pain of recession, and they figured things couldn't get any worse. They were wrong. With bombs falling in the Middle East and the world economy almost motionless, this year is shaping up as an even bigger disaster. From passenger airlines to aircraft makers, the aviation business is in a tailspin. Losses and failures are mounting, planes are flying half empty, and the transatlantic fare war is certain to create more ruin. Says Lee Howard, chief executive of Airline Economics: "This is the most serious crisis in the history of the airline business."

The crisis signals an end to a decade of unprecedented expansion. Passenger travel, which soared to record levels in the aftermath of U.S. deregulation, is paralyzed by corporate belt-tightening and fear of terrorism. So far this year, international traffic is down 40%. In the U.S. 2 of every 5 seats is flying empty. As the war and the recession roll on, carriers are lightening their loads by suspending unprofitable routes, flying remaining ones less often and cutting costs. Airlines have reduced new orders for aircraft as much as 50%; 44,000 airline workers worldwide, from machinists in Kansas City to flight atten-

dants in Amsterdam, have lost their jobs since January. USAir, which reported $221 million in losses for the fourth quarter, last week laid off 3,600 workers. Belgium's national airline, Sabena, and Spain's flagship carrier, Iberia, each announced plans to eliminate more than 2,000 jobs. British Airways, which suffered a 72% profit decline last quarter, cut 4,600 jobs while taking out of service five Boeing planes worth $1.5 billion.

Even before Iraq invaded Kuwait, America's stalling economy was forcing

the U.S. industry to consolidate. With passenger revenues slowing, the airlines separated into two groups: healthy carriers with strong balance sheets, like American, United and Delta, and those weighed down by excessive debt from buyouts and overexpansion, such as Pan Am, Eastern, TWA and Continental. To remain aloft, the weaker carriers sold routes, planes and other assets piecemeal to their stronger competitors, widening the chasm. Desperate for cash, Pan Am offered its London routes to United for $290 million, while financially troubled TWA agreed to unload its Heathrow landing rights to American for $445 million.

The Middle East crisis and the resulting rise in jet-fuel prices hastened the consolidation. Fuel ranks second only to labor in

airline expenses, accounting for about 20% of operating budgets. Overleveraged carriers couldn't take the hike. After its annual fuel costs rose 33%, to $1 billion, Continental failed. Faced with a similar bill, Pan Am filed for bankruptcy a month later. Last week Northwest raised the possibility of merging with a stronger airline or selling its lucrative Pacific routes. Analyst Julius Maldutis of Salomon Brothers says, "The industry is being separated into the big eagles and the sitting ducks."

The still regulated airlines across the Atlantic are asking the European Commission to reduce red tape, approve joint operating ventures and allow the carriers to raise fares. European airline traffic has dropped 25% since January. Italy's Alitalia, with its transatlantic business down 30%, wants government assistance for workers scheduled to be laid off.

The surest way to bring back passengers is also the most painful: a fare war. British Airways fired the first shot Feb. 9 with its plan to cut transatlantic fares for summer travel one-third. U.S. carriers responded with fare cuts of up to 50%, but U.S. Transportation Secretary Samuel Skinner rejected all cuts, including the British Airways request. The decision is widely viewed as retaliation for London's foot dragging in approving the sale of Pan Am's and TWA's London routes. TWA said it will be forced into bankruptcy if the sale isn't approved soon. Skinner permitted Pan Am fare cuts for domestic and international flights before March 1, an offer that American and Northwest immediately matched. While consumer response has been positive, the impact on the industry will probably be negative. Says David Swierenga, airline economist at the Air Transport Association: "The fare war will only increase the bloodshed."

The U.S. industry received a boost last week when First Lady Barbara Bush took a commercial flight to Indianapolis to show terror-stricken Americans that air travel was safe. Said she: "I'm not afraid to fly." Her gesture may diminish fears, but it will take a stronger economy and probably an end to the gulf war to get the industry—big eagles and sitting ducks alike—airborne again. ∎

TIME, FEBRUARY 25, 1991

Fig 6.18 Fighting for their lives (*Time*, 25 February 1991)

How Can You Expect To Have Staying Power If The Vitamins You're Taking Don't?

Whilst no vitamin pill can promise instant vitality, Blackmores can promise Naturetime.* A range of high potency Sustained Release vitamins and minerals designed to be more effectively absorbed by your body over a longer period of time. Just as they would be from the food you eat. Just the way nature intended.

Our modern, unbalanced lifestyles can put additional demands on our bodies. Blackmores can help restore the balance. You'll find them wherever quality nutritional products are sold.

The Celloid* minerals in Naturetime Multi help your body absorb nutrients more effectively, so you can get more of the vitamin you take.

Naturetime Multi's staying power comes from a unique combination of vegetable gums that allow nutrients to be released over 8 hours.

Nothing is added that isn't needed. Naturetime Multi has no artificial colours, preservatives, yeast, wheat or milk derivatives.

NATURETIME

BLACKMORES
DEDICATED TO THE BODY HEART & SOUL *

Fig 6.19 Blackmores advertisement (*Women's Weekly*, November 1992) of young Asian designers. Perhaps it is the greater emphasis on hierarchy, harmony and continuity in Confucian thinking that makes centring a fundamental organizational principle in the visual semiotic of their culture. Much of the work produced by these students had strong dominant centres, surrounded or flanked by relatively unpolarized marginal elements.

While many Anglo-Western tabloid newspapers tend to adhere to a basic left–right structure in the layout of their front pages, others place the main stories and photographs in the top section. The front pages of the business sections of the *Sydney Morning Herald*, however, for a time invariably used central composition, featuring a large photo (or, frequently, drawing) in the centre of the page, for instance Asian students entering the neo-Gothic Quadrangle of the University of Sydney when the page featured articles on education as 'business'; a cartoon-like drawing of two men playing Monopoly (based on Van Doesburg's *Card-players* – see figure 5.9), when corporate take-overs dominated the news, and so on. Such pictures provided a symbolic kernel for the issues of the day, and a centre for the elements arranged around them – news stories at the top and to the left, as, still, the Ideal and the Given of the newspaper, even if now somewhat marginalized; advertisements as the Real; and a column of expert commentary as New, hence as the element to which readers should pay particular attention. In other contemporary layouts the centre is often a symbolic drawing, a kind of logo almost, unifying the information surrounding it around a central meaning (e.g. figure 6.18). Advertisements may also use centred compositions, as in figure 6.19, where the unencumbered female body is depicted as the essential and dominant expression of 'naturalness', from which the surrounding elements draw their value and meaning.

To generalize, then, if a visual composition makes significant use of the centre, placing one element in the middle, and the other elements around it, we will refer to the central element as Centre and to the elements around it as Margins. For something to be presented as Centre means that it is presented as the nucleus of the information on which all the other elements are in some sense subservient. The Margins are these ancillary, dependent elements. In many cases the Margins are identical or at least very similar to each other, so that there is no sense of a division between Given and New and/or Ideal and Real elements among them. In other cases, for instance the newspaper pages we discussed above, Centre and Margin combine with Given and New and/or Ideal and Real.

Not all Margins are equally marginal. Circular structures can create a gradual and graded distinction between Centre and margin, as for instance in the communication model in figure 6.20, where the process of 'structuring' is more marginal than the process of 'evaluating'. In this model, nature (the 'environment') is Centre, origin and prime mover of communication. Compared to the dominant position of nature, communication is a marginal phenomenon, just as, in the medieval maps of cities we discussed in chapter 3, the cities themselves were placed in the centre and depicted with topographical accuracy, while the surrounding countryside was represented on a smaller scale, and with less accuracy. Verbal commentaries do not necessarily 'transcode' such meanings. Watson and Hill (1980: 76), for example, say that Andersch *et al.* (1969) show the 'message' as 'interacting with factors in the environment'. Yet, the model itself represents the relation

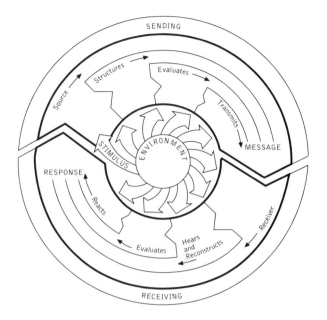

○ **Fig 6.20 Communication model (from Watson and Hill, 1980: 14)**

between communication and the 'environment', not as interaction, but as a one-way process, a 'non-transactive reaction', according to our terminology in chapter 2 (there is an arrow only from the 'environment' to the communicative processes that surround it). And 'interacting' suggests greater equality between the 'message' and the 'factors in the environment' than does the centred composition of the model.

As we have seen, Given–New and Ideal–Real can combine with Centre and Margin. Dividing visual space according to these dimensions results in the figure of the Cross, a fundamental spatial symbol in Western culture (see figure 6.21). Just how marginal the Margins are will depend on the size and, more generally, on the salience of the Centre. But even when the Centre is empty, it continues to exist *in absentia,* as the invisible (denied) pivot around which everything else turns, the place of the 'divine ruler'. The relative infrequency of centred compositions in contemporary Western representation perhaps signifies that in the words of the poet, 'the centre does not hold' any longer in many sectors of contemporary society.

One common mode of combining Given and New with Centre and Margin is the triptych. In many medieval triptychs there is no sense of Given and New. The Centre shows a key religious theme, such as the Crucifixion or the Virgin and Child, and the side panels show Saints or donors, kneeling down in admiration. The composition is symmetrical rather than polarized, although the left was regarded as a slightly less honorific position. In the sixteenth century altar pieces become more narrative, showing, for instance, the birth of Christ or the road to Golgotha in the left panel, the Crucifixion on the centre panel, and

⬤   **Fig 6.21 The dimensions of visual space**

the Resurrection on the right panel. This could involve some polarization, albeit subordinated to the temporal order, with the left as the 'bad side' (e.g. the transgression of Adam), the right as the 'good side' (e.g. the Resurrection) and the middle panel representing Christ's role as Mediator and Saviour (e.g. the Crucifixion). Bosch's *Last Judgement* (and also his *Earthly Delights*) inverts this, showing on the left the Garden of Eden and on the right a cataclysmic vision of Hell in which there is no place for the 'ascent of the blessed'.

The triptychs in modern magazines and newspaper layouts are generally polarized, with a 'Given' left, a 'New' right, and a centre which bridges the two, and acts as 'Mediator'. The top section, hence the Ideal, of a feature article on Downs Syndrome children in the *Australian Women's Weekly*, for instance, featured three photos side by side, the middle one larger than the others. The left-hand photo showed a perhaps fifteen-year-old Downs Syndrome boy who might well look a little repulsive to most readers. The right-hand photo showed a young Downs Syndrome child with an angelic smile. The centre photo showed a mother with another young, but somewhat less angelic-looking, Downs Syndrome child. Motherly love was thus presented as the Mediator, the factor that could overcome one's 'Given' repulsion and make the New (the proposition that the Downs Syndrome child can be as lovable as any other child) acceptable. We have encountered similar triptychs in other magazines, and in newspapers. Figure 6.22, for instance, is a triptych from the *Sydney Morning Herald*. On the left, as the Given, we see Australia's Labour Prime Minister and Labour ex-Prime Minister, together with Papua New Guinea's then Opposition Leader Somare. On the right, as the New, we see the Liberal Opposition Leader, who, at the time, was campaigning for a forthcoming Federal election. The woman on his left (Given within the right-hand picture) is the widow of the former long-reigning Liberal Prime Minister, Menzies. Labour, in power at the time, is Given, the Liberal contender for the next election is New. The Mediator is the former Governor-General whose funeral the various leaders were attending, hence a man who stands above the political parties. But the Mediator is less salient than the Given and the New. The polarization of Given and New dominates the triptych.

Triptychs can also be used to structure diagrams. Iedema (1994: 217) shows how the left column of the organizational chart of a Local Council lists that Council's 'Corporate Services', so making the 'administrative and financial backbone of the organization' Given, while the Council's 'Development and Environmental Services', the department which 'connects all other departments', is described in the central column, as the Mediator. In a lecture on social cognition attended by the authors, the lecturer used the blackboard (conventional blackboards also have a triptych structure!) to list, on the left panel, a number of key issues in linguistics (this was Given because most of those present were linguists and students of applied linguistics), on the right panel a number of issues in sociology (this was New as the linguists were meeting to discuss the social relevance of discourse analysis), and on the central 'panel' an outline of his own theory of social cognition, which he presented as the necessary link between the two fields, and as an issue that should be the central concern of those present at the meeting.

Triptychs continue to be used in art. Figure 6.23 shows a triptych by Brett Whiteley. The monkey in the left panel (and placed low in the space of the Real) refers to the artist's heroin addiction, and is a 'bad' Given. The 'good' New (placed high in the space of the Ideal) is a humanized portrait of the artist. Mediating between the two, bridging the extremes, is a portrait of Whiteley as an artist: his eye and hand are shown in detail, his body, his physical self, is only lightly sketched and represented as evanescent and insubstantial.

Vertical triptychs are less common than horizontal triptychs. Colour plate 6 taken from a German junior highschool politics textbook (Nitzschke, 1990) is an example. As the Ideal we see, in colour, immigrants (*Ausländer* 'foreigners') in high-status professions. As the Real we see 'foreigners' in low-status professions. This Real is divided into a Given and

Fig 6.22 Australian political triptych (*Sydney Morning Herald*, 21 January 1990)

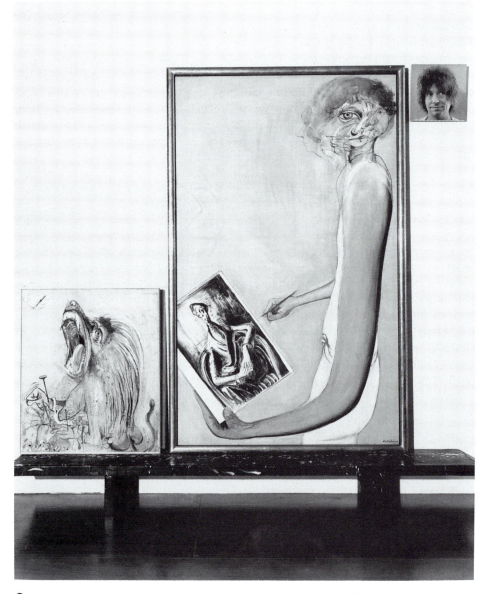

⬥ Fig 6.23 *Art, Life and the Other Thing* (Brett Whiteley (1978), Australia (1939–92)), oil, glass eye, hair, pen and ink on cardboard, plaster, photography, dried PVA, cigarette butts and hypodermic syringe on board. 90.4 × 77.2cm, 230 × 122 cm, 31.1 × 31.1cm. Collection: The Whiteley Studio Museum, NSW Government a New, with a colour photo as Given and a black-and-white photo as New, as though, in the 1990s, the low status of immigrants should be looked at in a more sober light, and no longer as 'Given' as it once was. In the Centre we see, again in black and white, a single immigrant worker, cleaning a train. The accompanying text encourages students to explore what would happen if 'one day all foreign workers had to leave the *Bundes-republik*'. What, it asks, would be the consequences for the building industry, the children of the workers, the owners of hostels, the workers themselves, the managers of hospitals and cleaning firms? In other words, this triptych (itself the New on the double page in which it appears) tells us that foreign workers should, perhaps, ideally be able to move into high-status positions, but in reality are needed to do 'our' menial jobs. The central image is an attempt to overcome, or at least mitigate, this contradiction. It shows a worker who, like the high-status immigrants in the Ideal, is depicted as an individual, and as involved in 'clean' work, but who, also like the workers shown in the Real, has a low-status job – and is shown in the sober, documentary modality of black-and-white realism.

The structure of the triptych, then, can be either a simple and symmetrical Margin–Centre–Margin structure or a polarized structure in which the Centre acts as a Mediator between Given and New or between Ideal and Real (see figure 6.24).

In this and the preceding section of this chapter we have not drawn any parallels with language. While language, like visual communication, has a specific 'grammatical' form for realizing the Given–New structure, this is not the case with the Ideal–Real and the Centre–Margin structures. This is not to say that the meanings these structures express cannot, in some form, be expressed in language, but rather, that they are more readily and frequently expressed visually, and that language, unlike visual communication, has not developed 'grammatical' forms to express them. Throughout the book we have emphasized that language and visual communication can in many cases express the same kind of relations, albeit in very different ways. But we must also keep in mind that there are relations which are more often and more easily expressed visually – just as there are others which are more often and more easily expressed linguistically.

Given	Mediator	New

Ideal
Mediator
Real

Fig 6.24 Horizontal and vertical triptychs

SALIENCE

The fundamental function of integration codes such as composition is textual. Integration codes serve to produce text, to place the meaningful elements into the whole, and to provide coherence and ordering among them. So far we have discussed how composition determines 'where things can go' and how the positioning of the elements in a composition endows these elements with different information values in relation to other elements. But the composition of a picture or a page also involves different degrees of salience to its elements. Regardless of where they are placed, salience can create a hierarchy of importance among the elements, selecting some as more important, more worthy of attention than others. The Given may be more salient than the New, for instance, or the New more salient than the Given, or both may be equally salient. And the same applies to Ideal and Real and to Centre and Margin. The Mediator in figure 6.22, for instance, is considerably less salient than the Mediators in figures 6.27 and 6.28 below.

The same phenomenon occurs in temporally integrated texts. Rhythm always involves cycles which consist of an alternation between successive sensations of salience (stressed syllables, accented notes, etc.) and non-salience (unstressed syllables, unaccented notes) and these cycles repeat themselves with the time intervals that are perceived as equal even when, measured objectively, they are not. The perception of salience, in speech as in music, results from a complex interplay between a number of auditory factors: the duration of the strong and weak elements of the cycle ('long'–'short'), the pitch of the strong and the weak elements ('high'–'low') their loudness ('loud'–'soft'), and in speech also the vowel colour (vowels may be fully pronounced, for instance the first *e* in *element*, or pronounced as a 'schwa', like the second *e* in *element*, or the second *a* in *alabaster*). Indeed anything that can create an auditory contrast between successive sounds can serve to realize salience. And even when objective clues for salience are absent, the first element of each cycle can be perceived as 'stronger': perception imposes rhythm, waves of salience and non-salience on sound (and on movement) even when, strictly speaking, there is none.

When composition is the integration code, salience is judged on the basis of visual clues. The viewers of spatial compositions are intuitively able to judge the 'weight' of the various elements of a composition, and the greater the weight of an element, the greater its salience. This salience, again, is not objectively measurable, but results from complex interaction, a complex trading-off relationship between a number of factors: size, sharpness of focus, tonal contrast (areas of high tonal contrast, for instance borders between black and white, have high salience), colour contrasts (for instance the contrast between strongly saturated and 'soft' colours, or the contrast between red and blue), placement in the visual field (elements not only become 'heavier' as they are moved towards the top, but also appear 'heavier' the further they are moved towards the left, due to an asymmetry in the visual field), perspective (foreground objects are more salient than background objects, and elements that overlap other elements are more salient than the elements they overlap, as in figure 6.28 below, where the Mediator overlaps the Margins), and also quite specific cultural factors, such as the appearance of a human figure or a potent cultural symbol. And just as rhythm creates a hierarchy of importance among the elements of temporally integrated texts, so visual weight creates a hierarchy of importance among the elements of spatially integrated texts, causing some to draw more attention to themselves than others.

Being able to judge the visual weight of the elements of a composition is being able to judge how they 'balance'. The weight they put into the scales derives from one or more of the factors just mentioned. Taken together, the elements create a balancing centre, the point, one might say, from which, if one conceived of the elements as part of a mobile, this mobile would have to be suspended. Regardless of whether this point is in the actual centre of the composition or off-centre, it often becomes the space of the central message, and this attests to the 'power of the centre' (Arnheim, 1982) to which we have alluded already, a power which exerts itself even if the Centre is an empty space around which the text is organized (cf. Barthes' remarks about the 'empty heart of Tokyo' (1970: 44)).

Perspective produces centres of its own, and by doing so contributes to the hierarchization of the elements in compositions. As a result viewers may relate to compositions in two ways: perspectivally, in which case the composition is ostensibly based on the viewer's perspective/position; or non-perspectivally, in which case the composition is not based on the viewer's position/perspective. In the former case the viewers, face to face with the infinite recess of perspective, become themselves the centre of the composition, thus taking the place of, for example, the deities in Byzantine or Buddhist paintings. In the latter case the representation is coded from an internal point of view, as is borne out by the fact that what is left and what is right is judged from the point of view of the represented participants rather than from the point of view of the viewer. Uspensky (1975: 33–9) has documented this with respect to icon-painting. He cites traditional guides for icon-painters which state, for instance, 'On the right, or good side, is Mount Sinai, on the left, or bad side, Mount Lebanon', and then shows how from the viewer's point of view, Mount Sinai is on the right and Mount Lebanon on the left. He adds that this is a general feature of pre-Renaissance art, and also of primitive cartographic drawing.

In the theory of art, composition is often talked about in aesthetic and formal terms ('balance', 'harmony', etc.). In the practice of newspaper and magazine layout it is more often discussed in pragmatic terms (does it 'grab the readers' attention'?). In our view these two aspects are inextricably intertwined with the semiotic function of composition. In the Fenjal advertisement (figure 6.2) the top section, the 'promise of the product', is the most salient element due to its size, to the central position of the figure, its place in the top section of the page, its contrasting and more salient colour (towards the red end of the spectrum against a blue background), and the culturally given salience of the human female figure. This suggests, not only that this advertisement, like so many others, attempts to make the viewers notice the attractive picture first, so as to 'hook' them, but also that Ideal and Real are ranked in importance and opposed to each other in this way. Composition is not just a matter of formal aesthetics and of feeling, or of pulling the readers (although it is that as well), it also marshals meaningful elements into coherent text and does this in ways which themselves follow the requirements of code-specific structures and themselves produce meaning.

Rhythm and balance also form the most bodily aspects of texts, the interface between our physical and semiotic selves. Without rhythm and balance, physical co-ordination in time and space is impossible. They form an indispensable matrix for the production and reception of messages and are vital in human interaction. Moreover, it is to quite some degree from the sense of rhythm and the sense of compositional balance that our aesthetic pleasure in texts and our affective relations *to* texts are derived.

FRAMING

The third key element in composition is framing. In temporally integrated texts framing is, again, effected by rhythm. From time to time the ongoing equal-timed cycles of rhythm are momentarily interrupted by a pause, a *rallentando*, a change of gait, and these junctures mark off distinct units, disconnect stretches of speech or music or movement from each other to a greater or lesser degree. Where such junctures are absent, the elements are connected in a continuous flow. In spatially integrated compositions it is no different. The elements or groups of elements are either disconnected, marked off from each other, or connected, joined together. And visual framing, too, is a matter of degree: elements of the composition may be strongly or weakly framed.

The stronger the framing of an element, the more it is presented as a separate unit of

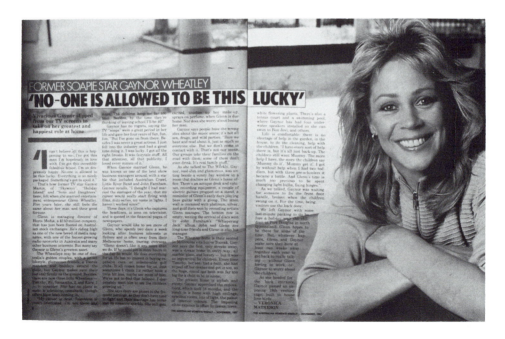

Fig 6.25 Gaynor Wheatley (*Women's Weekly*, November 1987)

⬥ **Fig 6.26 Greta Scacchi (*Women's Weekly*, November 1987)**

information. Context then colours in the more precise nature of this 'separation'. The members of a group, for instance, may be shown in a group portrait (as in group photos of school classes or employees of a company) or in a collage of individual photos, marked off by frame lines and/or empty space between them (as with photos of the managers of a company in a company brochure). The absence of framing stresses group identity, its presence signifies individuality and differentiation. In figure 6.1 framing acquires dramatic significance. The left post of the door and the dividing line between the light and dark boards on the roof create a frame line which, literally and figuratively, separates Minus from his sister, expressing the communicative gap between them. In film and video a similar effect can be created by the choice between showing two or more actors together in one shot, or editing between individual shots of the actors in which each is isolated from the others by frame lines.

The more the elements of the spatial composition are connected, the more they are presented as one unit of information, as belonging together. In figures 6.25 and 6.26, for instance, the text is Given and the picture of a woman looking at the viewer New. In figure 6.25 the text tells of a woman who used to be a television star but is now happy and fulfilled as a wife and mother. Between text and picture there is a strong sense of connection: the Given leads to the New, to the friendly smile which so reassuringly addresses 'us' readers. In figure 6.26 the text is printed in white letters on a black background. It is a *negative* Given. It describes, not the world of the reader, but a world

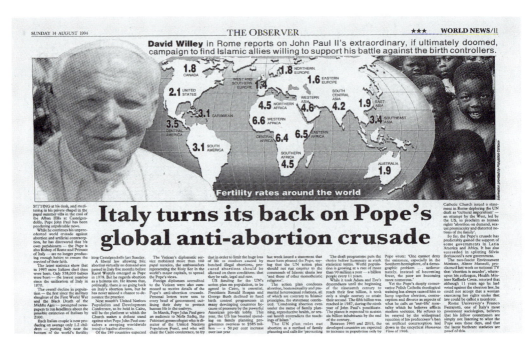

SUNDAY 14 AUGUST 1994

THE OBSERVER ★★★ WORLD NEWS/11

David Willey in Rome reports on John Paul II's extraordinary, if ultimately doomed, campaign to find Islamic allies willing to support his battle against the birth controllers.

Fertility rates around the world

Italy turns its back on Pope's global anti-abortion crusade

◆ Fig 6.27 Triptych (*The Observer*, 14 August 1991)

unreachable for the reader, the world of the stars and screen, the glittering path to Hollywood. A sharp demarcation line separates this story from the picture of Greta Scacchi, who looks at the reader in a pensive and self-absorbed way. Here the reader's world and the world of the woman in the picture are quite separate, quite irreconcilable: you, the reader, are not 'the most beautiful woman in the world' (you can, however, be a happy and fulfilled housewife).

Framing can be realized in many different ways. We have already seen how objects such as a doorpost or, in Titian's *Noli Me Tangere*, the staff of Christ can realize framing in pictures. Framing can also be realized by frame lines (the thickness of which then indicates the strength of the framing), by discontinuities of colour or shape (as with the transition between black and white in figure 6.26) or simply by empty space between the elements.

Connectedness can be emphasized by vectors. We have already commented on the vectorial function of the tilted photograph in figure 6.3. Vectors can be realized by depicted elements (structural elements of buildings, perspectively drawn roads leading the eye to elements in the background, etc.) or by abstract graphic elements, leading the eye from one element to another, beginning with the most salient element, the element that first draws the viewer's attention. Figure 6.3 has a number of framing devices (a red frame around the smaller photo, discontinuity between the gold colour of the pages and the off-white background of the right-hand photo), but it also has connective elements: the tilting of the left-hand photo, for instance, and the repetition of the colour gold in all the

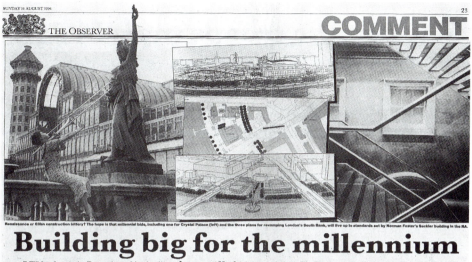

SUNDAY 14 AUGUST 1994   23

THE OBSERVER   **COMMENT**

Renaissance or £8bn construction lottery? The hope is that millennial bids, including one for Crystal Palace (left) and the three plans for revamping London's South Bank, will live up to standards set by Norman Foster's Sackler building in the RA.

Building big for the millennium

Laurence Marks assesses the chances that public projects for the year 2000 will change the face of Britain for the better.

●   Fig 6.28 Triptych: public building for the year 2000 (*The Observer*, 14 August 1994)

elements of the two pages – visual 'rhyme' of this kind, repetition of colours and shapes in different elements of the composition, forms another key connection device, often used in advertisements to stress the connection between the 'promise of the product' and the product itself. In figure 6.25 all framing between text and photo is removed: the double page simply consists of a single photo. One part of it, the female figure, is made salient, the rest becomes a background on which the verbal text is superimposed. The headline, made salient by bold type, red colour and strong framing, not only balances the visually heavy figure of the woman on the right, but also forms a strong vector towards her, and from her another vector, the airbrushed edge of the table on which she leans, leads back to the text.

We noted that horizontal and circular compositions often have weak framing, while vertical compositions tend to have strong framing. But this is only a tendency. Figure 6.26, for instance, has a horizontal composition with strong framing. Framing and information values are separate systems. Every element, Given or New, Ideal or Real, Centre or Margin, can either be framed strongly or weakly (or not at all). Figures 6.27 and 6.28 show two triptychs from the *Observer*. In the former the Pope's crusade against all forms of birth control is Given, its effect, overpopulation, is New. The Mediator between the two is a map showing fertility rates in the world (Centres are often conceptual pictures with abstract or scientific modality): scientific information links the 'Given' cause and the 'New' effect.

The triptych in figure 6.28 forms the Ideal of an article about major public building projects for the year 2000. Given is a photo of Crystal Palace, a familiar example of past styles of public building. New is a detail from the Sackler Building in the Royal Academy, presented as an example of good contemporary building. The Mediator is formed by the architects' drawings which will transform the Given into the New. But here framing is stronger, the flow from Given to New less uninterrupted and continuous, and this introduces a note of doubt about the connection between the elements. As the article says: 'The greatest anxiety for the Millennium Commission is that all this celebratory vision may be lost in the entrails of bureaucracy.'

It should finally be noted that, at a deeper level, there is also an element of framing in styles of drawing and painting. In line drawings, for instance, the outlines of objects strictly demarcate them from their environment. In certain styles of painting (e.g. Impressionism) they are set apart from their environment only by subtle transitions of colour.

LINEAR AND NON-LINEAR COMPOSITIONS

In densely printed pages of text, reading is linear and strictly coded. Such texts must be read the way they are designed to be read – from left to right and from top to bottom, line by line. Any other form of reading (skipping, looking at the last page to see how the plot will be resolved or what the conclusion will be) is a form of cheating and produces a slight sense of guilt in the reader. Other kinds of pages (e.g. traditional comic strips) and images (e.g. time line diagrams) are also designed to be read in this linear way.

The pages we have described in this chapter are read differently – and can be read in more than one way. Their reading path is less strictly coded. Readers of magazines, for instance, may flick though the magazine, stopping every now and again to look at a picture or read a headline, and perhaps later returning to some of the articles which drew their attention. But they may also move straight to their favourite columnist and read him or her from the beginning to end. Newspapers, similarly, are not read in linear order, but selectively and partially. Many such pages nevertheless have their reading paths. Their composition sets up particular hierarchies of the movement of the hypothetical reader within and across their different elements. Such reading paths begin with the most salient element, from there move to the next most salient element, and so on. Their trajectories are not necessarily similar to that of the densely printed page, left–right and top–bottom, but may move in a circle, as in figure 6.25, where the photo of Gaynor Wheatley is the most salient element, the headlines the next most salient element, and where, as we have noted already, one vector (the arrow-like profile of the frame of the headline) leads the eye from headline to photo, and another (the airbrushed edge of the table on which Gaynor Wheatley leans) from the photo back to the text. In other words, the reading path moves from the most salient element, the woman, to the text, and from the text back to the woman again, in circular fashion. Whether the reader only 'reads' the figure and the headline, or also part or all of the verbal text, a complementarity, a to-and-fro between text and image, is guaranteed. For any one reader the photograph or the headline may form the starting point of the reading. Our assumption is that the most plausible reading path is the one in which readers begin by glancing at the photo, and then make a new start from left to right, from headline to photo, after which, optionally, they move to the body of the verbal text. Such pages can be 'scanned' or read, just as pictures can be taken in at a glance or scrutinized for their every detail. We deliberately make a modest claim here and speak of the 'most plausible' reading path, for this type of reading path is not strictly coded, not as mandatory, as that of the densely printed page or the conventional comic strip. Different readers may follow different paths. Given that what is made salient is culturally determined, members of different cultural groupings are likely to have different hierarchies of salience, and perhaps texts of this kind are the way they are precisely to allow for the possibility of more than one reading path, and hence for the heterogeneity and diversity of their large readership.

As non-linear texts become more common, even densely printed pages of text begin to be read differently. The scientist, reading a journal of organic chemistry, will glance at the diagrammatic representations of organic compounds before deciding whether or not to read the paper, or, when reading that only one rat has been used in the experiment, skip to find out first why this was done (Gledhill, 1994). Students preparing for their exams will use the index of the textbook to find out and highlight the passages they need, rather than read the textbook from cover to cover. The more a text makes use of subheadings, emphatic devices (italics, bold type, underlining), numbered lines of typical elements or characteristics of some phenomenon, tables, diagrams and so on, the more likely it is to be scanned, skipread, 'used' rather than read: linear reading is gradually losing ground.

We noted that reading paths may be circular, diagonal, spiralling and so on. As soon as this possibility is opened up, as soon as there is a choice between differently shaped reading paths, these shapes can themselves become sources of meaning. If the reading path is circular, one reads outwards, in concentric circles, from a central message which forms the heart, so to speak, of the cultural universe. If the reading path is linear and horizontal, it constitutes a progression, moving inexorably forwards towards the future (or backwards, towards the 'origin' of all things). If it is vertical, a sense of hierarchy is signified, a movement from the general to the specific, from the 'headline' to the 'footnote'. The shape of the reading path itself conveys a significant cultural message.

Sixteenth-century books of emblems explicitly described the meanings of different kinds of reading path. The reading path of figure 6.29, an illustration from a Flemish book of emblems, is a spiral, which was an emblem for the inexorable progress of time. It is also a serpent, so that the reading proceeds from the tail, a low, base element, to the head, a superior element. Alain-Marie Bassy (1975: 303–5) explains the sequence of the emblematically expressed meanings one encounters as one follows the spiral from the centre outwards: the hand ('work'), the head ('intelligence'), the tail of the serpent (a 'base' element), the hand which holds down and imposes its will on the tail. Joining these meanings together results in the visual proposition also expressed in the title of the picture: 'Ex literatum studiis inmortalitem acquiri' ('Through intellectual endeavours I gained immortality').

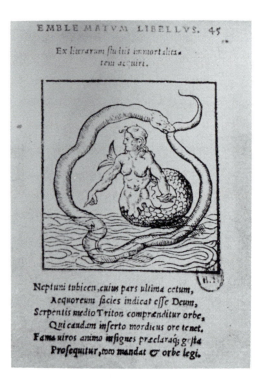

Fig 6.29 A page from Alciates' *Book of Emblems* **(from Bassy, 1975)**

Analysing reading paths with students, we found that some are easy to agree on, others harder, again others impossible. This was not, we think, because of a lack of analytical ability on our part or on the part of our students, but because of the structure of the texts themselves. Texts encode reading paths to different degrees. Some, though no longer densely printed pages, still take the readers by the hand, guiding them firmly through the text. Others (we might call them 'semi-linear' texts) at best provide readers with a few hints and suggestions, and for the rest leave the readers to their own devices. In again others we can, with the best will in the world, not detect any reading path that is more plausible than any number of others. In figure 6.30, a comic strip from the magazine *Cracked*, the headline stands out and this, together with the strong vector formed by the waterslide on the left page predisposes us to start our reading top left. But where the eye will move from here is difficult to predict. There is neither chronology (despite the resemblance to a flowchart), nor a clear hierarchy of salience.

Though nowhere near as anarchic, the spread shown in figure 6.31, taken from an Australian junior highschool science textbook, is not all that different. It features a salient photo in the top half of the left page, and the most salient element is perhaps formed by the three boxes at bottom right. But which of these will be read first is, again, difficult to say. Many newspapers (billboards, comic strips, advertisements) are of this kind. They

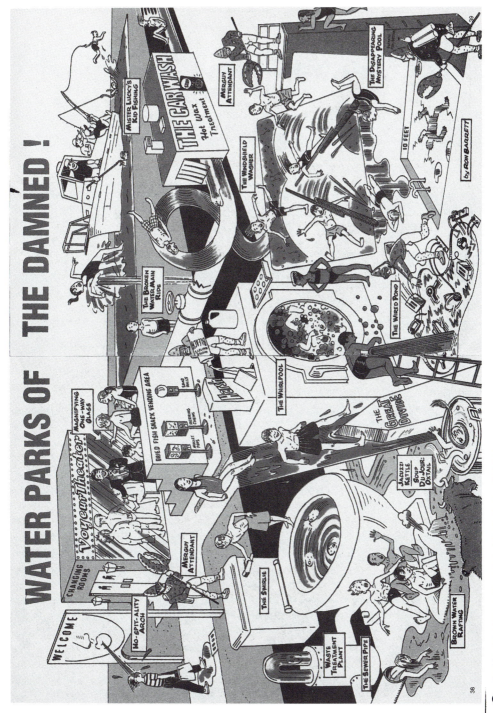

Fig 6.30 Water parks of the damned (*Cracked*, no. 293, October 1994)

Fig 6.31 Highschool science textbook (Jenkins, 1990)

offer the reader a choice of reading path, and, even more so than in the case of texts where a plausible reading *can* be discerned, leave it up to the reader how to traverse the textual space. To use the currently fashionable term, they are 'interactive' – and it is perhaps no accident that they have their clearest antecedent in the genre of the 'activities' books which offer children a choice of puzzles, riddles, colouring-in pictures, etc. for a rainy day during the holidays.

This is not to say that the order of the elements on such pages is random. The comic strip, for instance, still has its 'welcome' sign at top left, and its most gruesome images in the Real, a division between depictions of holiday fun and of sadistic torture that recalls the division between the Garden of Eden and Death in figure 6.10. The photograph of the countryside in figure 6.31 is still Given and Ideal – an image of an ideal, 'well-managed' environment with which the student readers are assumed to be familiar. And the 'activities' are still placed in the New.

Linear texts, then, are like movies, where the viewers have no choice but to see the images in an order that has been decided for them, or like an exhibition in which the paintings are hung in long corridors through which the visitors must move, following signs, perhaps, to eventually end up at the exit. Non-linear texts without any clear reading paths are like the new technologies now being introduced, in which viewers can select their own images and view them in an order of their own choosing, or like an exhibition in a large room which visitors can traverse in any way they like. But, again, the way these exhibits are arranged will not be random. It will not be random that a particular major sculpture is placed in the centre of the room, or that a particular major painting has been hung on the wall opposite the entrance, to be noticed first by all visitors entering the room.

Linear texts thus impose a syntagmatics on the reader, describe the sequence of and the connection between the elements. As a result the meanings of individual elements can be less strictly coded, as for instance in documentary films, where the meaning of the individual shots can be largely determined by the editing, rather than by the intrinsic meanings of the shots. Non-linear texts impose a paradigmatics. They select the elements that can be viewed and present them according to a certain paradigmatic logic, the logic of Centre and Margin or of Given and New, for instance, but leave it to the reader to sequence and connect them. In the design of such texts there will be pressure to put more of the meaning in the individual elements of the composition, to use more highly coded images – symbolic and conceptual images, stereotyped characters, drawings or highly structured images rather than realistic photographs and so on. Linear and non-linear texts thus constitute two modes of reading and two regimes of control over meaning, exactly in the same way as we discussed in chapter 1, in connection with *Baby's First Book* and the page from Dick Bruna's *On My Walk*.

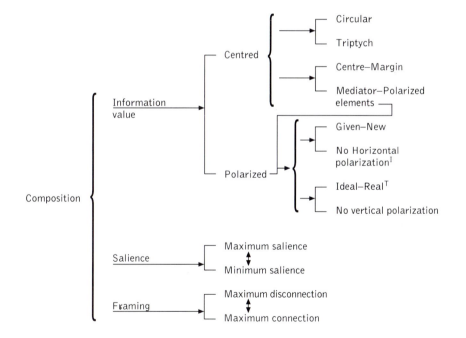

Fig 6.32 The meaning of composition

A SUMMARY

Figure 6.32 provides a summary of the distinctions we have introduced in this chapter. The double-headed arrows ($\updownarrow$) stand for graded contrasts ('more or less', rather than 'either–or'). The superscript 'I' means 'if' and the superscript 'T' means 'then'. In other words, 'if there is no horizontal polarization, then there must be vertical polarization' – the opposite follows from this. In the next section we will discuss a number of examples in greater detail.

REALIZATIONS

Centred	An element (the Centre) is placed in the centre of the composition.
Polarized	There is no element in the centre of the composition.
Triptych	The non-central elements in a centred composition are placed either on the right and left or above and below the Centre.
Circular	The non-central elements in a centred composition are placed both above and below and to the sides of the Centre, and further elements may be placed in between these polarized positions.
Margin	The non-central elements in a centred composition are identical or near-identical, so creating symmetry in the composition.
Mediator	The Centre of a polarized centred composition forms a bridge between Given and New and/or Ideal and Real, so reconciling polarized elements to each other in some way.
Given	The left element in a polarized composition or the left polarized element in a centred composition. This element is not identical or near-identical to the corresponding right element.
New	The right element in a polarized composition or the right polarized element in a centred composition. This element is not identical or near-identical to the corresponding left element.
Ideal	The top element in a polarized composition or the top polarized element in a centred composition. This element is not identical or near-identical to the corresponding bottom element.
Real	The bottom element in a polarized composition or

	the bottom polarized element in a centred composition. This element is not identical or near-identical to the corresponding top element.
Salience	The degree to which an element draws attention to itself, due to its size, its place in the foreground or its overlapping of other elements, its colour, its tonal values, its sharpness or definition, and other features.
Disconnection	The degree to which an element is visually separated from other elements through framelines, pictorial framing devices, empty space between elements, discontinuities of colour and shape, and other features.
Connection	The degree to which an element is visually joined to another element, through the absence of framing devices, through vectors and through continuities or similarities of colour, visual shape, etc.

GIVEN AND NEW IN CHILDREN'S TEXTS AND NEWSPAPER FRONT PAGES

In any sequential structure, that which is about to be said or shown is by definition always New, not yet known. By contrast, what has (just) been seen, heard, discovered, is, by comparison, now known, Given. In visual media, sequence can of course be represented in a number of dimensions, right to left, bottom to top, in a spiral from outside, etc. (and in medieval painting perspective can indicate sequence, with the foreground as the present and the background as the future). Such dimensions have been used throughout history, and are still used by different cultures, as primary visual sequencing orientations. The medium of the book, bringing the possibility of turning the page, adds a further means of representing sequence visually, the left page/right page structure and the possibility of the two-page structures (right page and following left page).

Figure 6.33 shows a double page from a book produced by a six-year-old boy, while staying in Paris for half a year with his parents. It records events and experiences he was involved in and sights and objects he encountered during his stay in Paris. Clearly, in this situation everything was New for the child, literally. He was faced with the question of how to represent new information, new ideas, new objects, without the possibility of relating them to already established, known domains.

The book opens with the name and address of the author, on the first left-hand page. This is the Given for the book as a whole, an element of security and familiarity in the new environment. On the first right-hand page that new environment is represented visually: a picture of the Eiffel Tower. It is only when this page is turned that the picture is named, commuted into language. Once named, the Eiffel Tower becomes Given, and on the adjoining right-hand page the child faces the next aspect of his new environment. Thus the

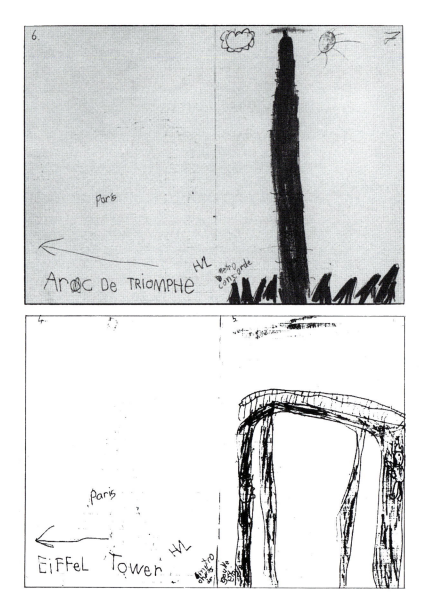

⬡　　**Fig 6.33 Paris diary of a six-year-old boy**

book continues: the new picture, too, is only identified on the next left-hand page – the Arc de Triomphe. The child obviously realized that this structure could be misunderstood, and used left-facing arrows to refer the reader to the picture on the previous page. But his impulse was to first visually represent Paris as the New, and then to master it, make it known and Given by means of language, by means of naming it. His attitude was empirical and he used language as an 'anchorage' in his effort to come to terms with his new experiences.

We have, throughout the book, insisted on the cultural specificity of visual semiotics. With the global expansion of information, communication and the mass media, this factor

Fig 6.34 Front page of *The Sun*

becomes increasingly important. We cannot hope to know or understand all the visual semiotics of all the cultures of the world; we can, however, hope to make viewers and readers conscious of such cultural specificities as still exist in visual communication. Three examples may help to make the point. They are from the front pages of two newspapers, *The Sun* from Britain (figure 6.34) and the *Bildzeitung* from Germany (figure 6.35).

Despite our stress on cultural specificity, we assume that all front pages have common communicational functions and elements. They are the first point of 'address' for the readers, and they present what are the most significant events and issues of the day for the paper and its readers. But this leaves room for differences. Some front pages, such as that of *Le Monde* and the *Frankfurter Allgemeine*, for instance, remain stubbornly un-visual, even today, although they do of course employ such non-verbal semiotic modes as layout, typeface, line length, etc.

The front page of *The Sun* has a fundamentally left–right, Given–New organization. There is usually one 'story', carried visually and verbally, with the image on the right, as the New, and the written text on the left, as the Given. The written text, in turn, has screamer headlines as the Ideal and tightly printed text as the Real, as if the readers of *The Sun* are, in part, still caught in the tradition of the former, Given modes of communication, while at the same time already embracing the New of the visual, in colour.

The *Bildzeitung* presents to an Anglo-Saxon eye an image of anarchy. There is no suggestion of left and right, Given–New ordering. If it was thought that the layout of *The Sun* could be explained in terms of the social class of its readers, it would have to be said that the readership of the *Bildzeitung* is quite similar in those terms. The explanation of the differences must lie in (national) cultural characteristics rather than in class. In the apparent confusion of elements it is the salience of the elements which provides the means of reading. The daily news forms a jumble of disconnected events, distinct only in the degree to which they catch the attention. Top–bottom and right–left structures do have a small role, of course, but, in contrast to *The Sun*, it is very much a subsidiary one. The left–right, Given–New structure has a strongly conservative effect. It habituates the readers to a daily dose of 'paradigm' and 'instance of paradigm', an insistently classificatory act of great regularity. While the items which appear in the place of the Given and the place of the New do vary (an investigation of the range of variance would be revealing), this structure of classification of 'what is Given' and 'what is an example of this Given' recurs day after day, to reproduce and reaffirm an unchanging set of norms and values. If the British paper thus tends towards the synthesis of stasis, the German paper, by contrast, tends towards the analysis of anarchy. And each produces quite different habits of reading and quite different orientations to the world, questions which must be at the forefront of semiotic/ideological analysis.

7 The materiality of meaning: surface and inscription

INSCRIPTION AS A SEMIOTIC RESOURCE

When, some time in 1988, we first presented our initial ideas on the visual, one of our friends said 'But what about brushstrokes? How can you describe brushstrokes as semiotic units?' Our fumbled response was to say 'You have to start somewhere. We'll get to brushstrokes later, when we are further on with our work.' But the question stayed with us, and regularly kept coming up in our discussions. It was and is an important question.

Six years on, our answer would be different. We now think the question was misconceived, or rather, framed within an older, now superseded, mode of thinking. It arose, we think, out of a totalizing view, in which, on the one hand, all the aspects which go into the making of a painting (or of any image) are treated as part of a single representational system, a single semiotic mode (in this case the system of 'painting'), but which, on the other hand, is seen also as a homogeneous system, in which, while there are differences in size of units, all the units are of the same kind. So all texts are, in the end, built up from a single kind of 'minimal unit', be it the brushstroke, the 'iconic figure' (Eco, 1976a) or the 'coloureme' (Saint-Martin, 1987). By contrast, we would maintain that 'painting' involves a multiplicity of signifying systems, and that the means and processes of inscription (e.g. applying paint to canvas with a brush) constitute one such system among the many which make a 'painting'. Inscription is a *semiotic* resource, one among the many available to the makers of images.

This is borne out by the fact that the means and processes of inscription can be changed while other aspects of the production of an image are held constant. Any given configuration of choices from all the signifying systems which we have so far discussed, any of the examples we have so far given, can, at least in principle, be realized as a painting, or as a photograph, or as a drawing, to mention just some types of inscription. And any given type of inscription can, at least in principle, realize all the choices from all the ideational, interpersonal and textual networks we have presented in this book. In practice there are of course historically and culturally specific restrictions on the combination of choices from these signifying systems. For example, there are more or less severe restrictions on what is painted and how, but this does not diminish the point. Any one of the combinations is, in principle available, and can, at any time, be taken up as part of the ongoing change of the semiotic landscape.

In the realm of art this is a relatively acceptable point of view. It means something quite specific whether a painting is executed in watercolours or in oil, whether a knife is used to apply the paint or a spraygun. But the idea that inscription is a semiotic resource also applies to language. We can ask the seemingly simple question 'What is a text?' Is a written text the same object or a different one when written with pen and ink or with a word-processor? The answer of most linguists would be 'No question. It is the same text.'

The material, graphic expression of the text would not be seen as a relevant matter in linguistics. If we asked a non-linguist the same question the answer might be different. The teacher who responds negatively to an essay presented on scrappy bits of paper, badly handwritten (perhaps badly spelled), but responds very favourably to a 'well-presented', typed version of the same text, uses a quite different criterion. So does the marketing executive, when presenting a proposal to a client. Their notion of what a text is differs from that of the linguist. They see 'presentation' as a significant part of the making of the text, perhaps equal to other aspects. For them, as for the painter or the viewer of a painting, the mode of inscription changes the text. It is our impression that this aspect of text is rapidly gaining in importance, perhaps aided by new technologies of writing.

The boundaries between the criteria prevailing in art and those prevailing in writing are no longer as sharply drawn as they once were. We do not want to engage in an argument with linguistics here. But we do want to say that the linguistic notion of text is an artefact of linguistic theory; as indeed our notion of text, whether written and linguistic or painted and visual, is an artefact of our social semiotic theory. The question about the significance of brushstrokes comes, we think, out of a deeply logocentric view in which everything representational is seen as belonging to the same unified, homogeneous representational system (language, or painting) and in which, at the same time, by a deep-seated paradox, not everything within that representational system is given the same, or even any, attention.

In our view the material expression of the text is always significant; it is a separately variable semiotic feature. Texts are material objects which result from a variety of representational practices that make use of a variety of signifying systems, each of which contributes to the meaning of the text in its own particular way. In this chapter we will explore this idea, focusing on the material aspects of representation, and enquiring into 'material' as meaningful and as signifier. We are interested therefore in the surfaces on which inscriptions are made (paper, rock, plastic, textile, wood, etc.), in the substances with which inscriptions are made (ink, gold, paint, light, etc.) and in the tools used for making the inscriptions (chisel, pen, brush, pencils, stylus, etc.). In exploring these issues a real distinction appears between the linguist's concern and the semiotician's. For the linguist, we think, surfaces and substances tend to be non-material until the very last, when an utterance is spoken or written, so that this last link in a chain of inscription ('realization' in Hallidayan linguistic theory) may seem less or even least significant. For the sculptor, on the other hand, the surface is utterly material from the start and remains so right to the end of the sculpting process. For the marketing executive the material surface may be at least as important as the more abstract surfaces which interest the linguist. In other words, representational practices differ in the degree to which the materiality of the text plays a role in semiosis – although materiality always does play some role, even if only by virtue of its negation.

In this chapter we will discuss the complex set of issues around inscription from a social semiotic point of view, focusing on inscription as a culturally and socially produced resource for meaning-making. We regard inscription as significant particularly because it is in the process of inscription that unsemioticized materiality is drawn into semiosis.

It is therefore somewhat less subject to the various forms of semiotic policing than are other regions of the semiotic landscape, and it leaves more room for the individual's possibilities of expression than those regions which have better-known cultural histories and better-understood conventions. To explore inscription is to explore the boundaries between the semiotic and the non-semiotic, and between individual expression and social semiosis.

It may help at this point to try to locate our enterprise. Our attempts have been in the area of visual grammar, of visual syntax – the taxis of the visual. We have paid next to no attention to visual lexis, to iconography. Generally speaking, that has been dominant in debates around the visual – it is as important an area in the visual as it is in the linguistic, so our decision not to make it focal in this study does not reflect our view of the importance of visual lexis. There is a further area which we will not consider here in detail, even though it needs detailed description in a fuller treatment of visual representation: it is the question of the materials which are (made) available in a culture for the purposes of representation. This applies to *surfaces of inscription*, to the *materials which are applied to surfaces* and to the *tools which are used in the processes of representation*.

Every culture has systems of meanings coded in these materials, and in the means of processes of inscription. It is an area which is fully semioticized in every culture, even though it is the point where the natural comes closest to the semiotic. Here, as in all areas of semiosis, signs as materials are fully motivated, though as always the motivations are those of a particular culture and are not global. Precious metals are precious because of their scarcity, and perhaps because of their malleability. But scarcity is not a globally uniform characteristic, and the preciousness of one metal need not be equally marked in another culture. It was one of the particular calamities of Central and South American cultures that they had attached different semiotic values to the material signifier *gold* from those of the invading Spaniards.

The systems of signs expressed in the materiality of substance can be documented for any one culture, and the relations of signifieds and signifiers elucidated. The hastily torn out scrap of paper has different sets of potentials as a signifier than does the beautifully made, weighty sheet. Glossy paper has the possibility of signals of a different kind to matt – and here the complexities of materials as signifiers already appear: 'glossy' paper can serve as a signifier of value, and yet, in different contexts, it can also serve as the signifier of the pretence of value. It is not our intention here to provide an inventory, but to point to the existence of semiotic systems, and to the motivated relation of material signifier and signified at this level. Stone has a potential range as a signifier; as polished stone that range is already narrowed due to actual physical work done on the stone, which is also semiotic work. Oil-paint has potentials of meaning which differ from those of water-based paint, due to cost, ease of working, durability, effects.

In a book on the syntax of the visual this is not the appropriate place for this exploration. It seems crucial to point to its effects nevertheless.

INSCRIPTION SYSTEMS AND TECHNOLOGY

Forms of inscription are closely related to technology. Indeed, dependence on technology may be one of the defining features of the visual semiotic, and distinguish it from semiotic modes in which signs are articulated by the body, without any technological aids – for instance speech, singing, 'non-verbal communication', dance. Modes like music would straddle the two categories, and the boundaries between them would, in any case, always be fuzzy: one can draw or write with one's finger in sand, using only the body and a natural surface. But generally the surfaces, substances and tools of the visual semiotic are made available by technologies, and this as much in the case of pencil and paper as in the case of the modern word-processor. Thus technology enters fundamentally into the semiotic process: through the kinds of meaning which it facilitates or favours, and through the differential access to the means of production and reception which it provides.

We will distinguish three major classes of inscription technologies: (1) inscription in the narrower sense, that is, technologies of the hand, technologies in which representations are, in all their aspects, articulated by the human hand, aided by handtools such as chisels, brushes, pencils, etc.; (2) recording technologies, that is, technologies of the eye (and ear), technologies which allow the more or less automated analogical representation of what they represent, for instance audio tape, photography and film; and (3) synthesizing technologies which allow the production of digitally synthesized representations, and, while remaining tied to the eye (and ear), reintroduce the human hand, but now via a technological 'interface', at present still in the shape of a tool (keyboard, mouse), but in future perhaps increasingly through direct articulation by the body (e.g. through issuing spoken commands to the computer, or through other gestures).

The boundaries between these categories are not clearcut. A photograph can be hand-coloured, for instance, or digitally altered, and many artists experiment with precisely these mixed inscription systems. It should also be noted that the possibility of 'mechanical reproduction', to use Benjamin's term, is not uniquely tied to any of the three categories. Printing can be done from a hand-carved master, photographically, or with a modern laser printer. But our categories remain useful, particularly as they can be tied to major periods in the history of inscription, and to the epistemologies that went with them.

While inscription technologies, technologies of the hand, have continued to play a role, the development of recording technologies has dominated the visual semiotic from the moment Renaissance artists began to use the camera obscura as an aid in painting, and particularly during the last two centuries or so, when a variety of recording technologies were developed, beginning with photography. They are now beginning to be superseded by synthesizing technologies. Quite different ontological orientations go with these different technologies. Walter Benjamin (1973) commented on the transition between inscription and recording, stressing reproduceability rather than the modes of representation themselves, and linking it to the dissolution of traditional forms of social organization in 'mass society' and to the disappearance of the 'aura' of the work of art.

Today the transition from recording to synthesizing inscription technologies is the more pressing issue. The 'crisis of representation' which has characterized theoretical debate over the last two decades or so may be an indication of this. 'Recording' leads, we believe, to ontologies of referentiality, of representation being founded on direct, referential relations between the representations and the world. In another publication we developed this idea in more detail (van Leeuwen and Kress, 1992). Synthesizing inscription technologies undermine or even abolish such notions of referentiality. Whereas, as recently as in the 1970s, 'Electronic News Gathering' was ubiquitous enough to have developed an acronym, ENG (with its increasingly and deceptively naive metaphor reminiscent of other unproblematic gatherings – apples, the children), that metaphor is now untenable: news does not need to be gathered simply because the technology exists literally to *produce* it – a development anticipated by the critical media theory of the 1970s. 'Reference' has given way to 'signification', the production, out of existing semiotic resources, of new semiotic means, new signs, new texts, new images, new visions, new worlds. This does not mean that representation has ceased. Rather, the formerly naturalized relation, the identity of representation and reference, has broken down, irreparably for the time being; instead a new relation is becoming established between representation and signification. If present social and technological developments continue, this relation will, in its turn, become naturalized.

These technological and semiotic developments perhaps help understand contemporary theoretical developments. With 'recording' goes an older semiotics of 'representation' and of naturalistic modality – which itself gave rise to particular ontologies of truth, fact (hence the interminable debates around 'bias'). To deconstruct this form of inscription, representations ('texts') had to be deconstructed, which happened by emphasizing 'production' and therefore the 'constructedness' of the representations in texts, images, etc., and in doing so already theorizing the next stage of semiotic practice – synthesis, construction, production. From this history, which both heralds and legitimizes the present stage of synthesis, we could project a further development, which will be to deconstruct production by showing that 'underneath' production there is an already existing, already produced 'programme', a system which defines the limits of production. This system, of course, is still a system of representation – a representation of the social/cultural system. We could also point to the present tendencies in semiotic theories (in cultural studies, in education, in literacy theory) to collapse reading into writing, or vice versa. The dissolution of that distinction ('reading is writing') was initiated in theory but is now enacted in electronic technologies which combine the acts of reading and (re)writing someone else's text. In other words, when the analogically based mode of 'recording' is dominant, the tendency of critical theory is to deconstruct representation-as-reference, and to emphasize the 'constructedness' of the sign, or the text. As the synthetically based mode of production is becoming the dominant technology, critical theory will have to turn to deconstructing representation-as-programme, representation-as-design, that is, deconstructing the combinatorial possibilities. It is for this reason that we concentrate on representational *systems* in this book, rather than (only) on texts.

Before we leave this subject, we should note two other aspects of the relation between inscription and technology. Our classification of inscription modes was based on the way representations are produced: by hand, by more or less automated recording, by electronic synthesis. But different inscription technologies also favour different *modes of reception*, and here the surface plays a particularly important role. Some surfaces (walls, cinema screens) favour public reception, for instance, and others (pages, and paper generally, the computer screen) favour private reception. Also, more difficult to describe, there is the effect of the physicality, the tangibility of the surface – the difference between the forms carved in the hard rock and the fleeting flickers of light on the glass screen (we return to this in the next section). What matters here is, of course, the surface on which the text is *received*, and this surface is no longer always the same as the one on which the text is produced. Transcodings may take place. An image may be produced in an inscription mode, as a painting, for instance, and received in a recording mode, for instance as a photograph. Or it may be produced in a recording mode, as a photograph, for instance, and received in a synthesis mode, retrieved from the image bank of a computer, for instance.

Finally, technology has also developed different *modes of distribution*, and it is here that the issue of (mass) reproduceability belongs, together with the issue of long-distance communication. The latter, although of crucial social importance, bears less directly on our subject. Whether images are distributed via electrical wires, optical fibres or the airwaves is semiotically irrelevant. What matters is the inscription mode in which they are produced, and the inscription mode in which they are received, where the latter is different from the mode in which they were produced, be it because of transcoding (e.g. the photographic reproduction of paintings) or because of re-inscription on the other end of the telecommunication channel. Or, to be more precise, we would say that the mode of transmission is relevant only in relation to the limitations which it imposes on reception, (re-)production and technology.

BRUSHSTROKES

If one looks at Rothko's *Seagram Murals* from a distance of 4–5 metres, the boundaries between the large blocks of colour seem sharp and clearcut. The closer one moves to the paintings, however, the more uncertain and fuzzy the boundaries become, the more they begin to overlap and run into each other. A postcard of one of the paintings, taken from much more than 5 metres' distance, shows nothing of this. An aspect of meaning is lost, because of the distance from which the photograph was taken, and because of the transcoding, from painting to photograph, from one inscriptional mode into another. And this brings us back to the starting point of this chapter, the argument about brushstrokes and about the status of 'text'.

Painting, the 'inscription' mode, allows the viewer a choice between different ways of relating to the text, even though this choice may in practice be restricted, as when a line in front of a painting prohibits the gallery visitor from coming too close to the painting. I may wish to view the painting as a representation, to concentrate on what the painting is about ('the effective use of colour', or 'depression'), and in that case I will stand at a distance. Or I may wish to engage with its materiality and with the very way in which the hand of the artist 'inscribed' the canvas, and in that case I will move close up. Photography does not allow this choice. The 'recording' mode is representational and can only be representational. It abstracts away from the imprint of the hand that made it, even when it reproduces art.

A certain discourse about art puts much emphasis on inscription, particularly in relation to a handful of great painters: the fine brushstrokes of Rembrandt, the violent brushstrokes of Van Gogh, the treatment of volume by the Pointillists. It encourages us to focus on the 'graphology' of the painting, as a symptom, a trace of the individual temperament of the artist. Most of the descriptions of paintings in art galleries and in catalogues, however, focus on representation rather than on inscription. And the preference of art historians for black-and-white reproductions or even drawings of paintings also points to an overriding concern with representation. Like linguistic discourses, commonsense art discourses focus on overtly present content and treat painting as articulated through a unified representational system, in which inscription is part of a homogeneous practice of painting.

The question of transcoding is closely related to this. What does it signify when I purchase a print of Monet's *Poppies* to hang on my living-room wall? That I want to show my appreciation and admiration of Monet? That I have been to a gallery where the painting was exhibited? That I like the theme of the painting? That I am familiar with the intellectual histories of which Impressionism is a part? The print will allow me to signify all of these, but it will not allow me to signify my interest in inscription, simply because it does not enable me to focus on that: it does not even make it available as a question.

To take another example, in an original painting by Mondriaan the lines are, in close-up, not straight, and overpainted, and there is modulated rather than plain, flat colour in the various rectangles. Postcards and other reproductions of the same painting make the lines appear straight, remove the overpainting and present flat, unmodulated colour. It is these reproductions which produce the Mondriaan of innumerable highschool art lessons, and so reinforce and reproduce a particular (incorrect) version of Mondriaan and a particular (ideological) version of abstract painting. And it is through these ideologized readings that such paintings have their effect on and in other practices.

As a final example, consider Kandinsky's *Cossacks* (colour plate 7). Representation is strongly reduced in this painting: one can 'see' Cossacks on horseback and drawn and flashing sabres, but figuration is not foregrounded. Colour differentiation, on the other hand, is amplified. And colour is used, not in a representational/referential function (shades of white to represent the 'real' shades of the white of uniforms, for instance), but to allow the substance of the inscription and the traces of the act of inscription to signify themselves. Colour is, in this painting, *the* inscriptional medium: jagged blocks of white, flashes of red, curves of yellow and blue. Action, energy, movement and violence are represented through the inscriptional resources of the painter. And this takes us back to the issue of individuality with which we ended the first section of this chapter, and perhaps also to the distinction between 'art' and 'design'. The handling of inscriptional resources is close to the individuality of handwriting, and it was precisely this mark of individuality which came to be lauded as the distinguishing characteristic of art and as its mark of difference from 'recording'. On the other hand, this celebration of individuality was also somewhat of a last ditch stand for art, in its losing battle with photography, and the very same art which came to stand for individual expression had its principal social effects in the form of photographic reproductions, that is, without the marks of individuality, while the originals became the priceless relics of a past ethos. In most other domains such marks of individuality became proscribed. Handwriting, for instance, has become unacceptable in all but the most private forms of writing, despite the increased emphasis on 'presentation' which we noted earlier: this new valuation of 'presentation' is in no way a return to the kind of individual expressiveness that hovers on the border between the individual and the social, the unsemioticized and the semioticized – it is thoroughly semiotic and social.

The individuality of the brushstroke not only became a symbol of individual expression, of 'the essence of things seen through an individual temperament', it also came to be drawn into the domain of the semiotic, the domain of culture. It 'made school'. It was reproduced, faked, developed, imitated, and so entered into the world of semiosis as a transformative element, in a process which then transformed the brushstroke itself, as witnessed by Roy Lichtenstein's pop art parody (figure 7.1). Thus the brushstroke becomes a paradigm case of how inscription (the 'how' of painting) is allowed to play a key role in some domains, for instance the domain of the great Modernist art of the

○ Fig 7.1 *Big Painting 1965* (Roy Lichtenstein)

immediate past, but required to play a humbler role in others, where representation (the 'what' of painting) dominates, and where product matters more than process and practice. The division exists within painting also. A painter such as Robert Ryman, whose work we discussed in chapter 5, focuses on the 'how', on the inscriptional practices of painting. A painter such as Gainsborough focused on the 'what', on the analysis of social arrangements, the recording of social states of affairs, in short, on the referential.

Such shifts of emphasis are themselves 'signs'. Interest in the materiality of representation and representational practices reflects wider social and cultural concerns with questions of substance and materiality in a world in which the concrete becomes abstract, the material immaterial, the substantial insubstantial and reality 'virtual'. Today we have, side by side, a hankering for the individual, the subjective, the affective, the non-semiotic and non-social 'punctum' of the photograph or 'grain' of the voice (Barthes, 1977, 1984), and the increasing semioticization of all these phenomena and more. As we have noted already, it is as representations rather than as inscriptions that modern art has informed and shaped practices in other domains, that paintings such as those of Mondriaan came to be transformed into blueprints for designed objects, buildings, cities, and that paintings such as those of Kandinsky had their effect on the layout of European newspapers such as the *Bildzeitung* and *The Sun*, which are further translations/reductions of other translations/reductions, but none the less potent for that.

Any systematizing semiotics of inscription (of the brushstroke, or of handwriting) would follow the trend of semioticizing the not yet semioticized. Reluctance to do so would follow the trend set by Barthes to 'protect' the non-semiotic, to protect the 'unspoilt nature' after which the tourist hankers. In this chapter we clearly are at least a little reluctant. We do not present 'networks', for instance. Nevertheless as inscription is drawn into semioticization, it becomes more important to be able to talk about it, and not stop at asserting the value of the non-semiotic at the very moment when it is everywhere around us, semioticized, or marginalized, or repressed.

THE MEANING OF MATERIALITY

From the 1920s onwards, there has been a 'functionalist' current in Modernism which is only now beginning to change, a trend to 'let materials speak for themselves'. This had various roots, but it culminated in now happily clichéd styles of plain steel or timber furniture, and of 'brutalist' architecture, with its love of unadorned concrete. Behind this trend are notions of 'authenticity', themselves explicit or implicit critiques of the 'distortions' of representation, the 'falsities' introduced by 'decorative' art and its ideologies. Again, this trend had its origins in art, where it could even become the subject-matter of artworks, as in Ryman's paintings. In some periods or genres of art, artists have no choice of materials: all paintings are painted on canvas, with oil-paints, all photographs are printed on paper. In other periods or genres, the material becomes a fully exploited resource. Modern sculpture is perhaps the best example. The smoothly turned wood of Brancusi's *Head* 1919–23 or the veined redness of the alabaster of

Epstein's *Jacob and the Angel* (1940) (see figure 8.1 below) become part of the meaning.

In some cases it is precisely the opposition between the materiality of the material and the mimetic quality of the product which becomes the issue. In Rodin's *The Kiss* (1880) (see figure 8.3 below) the figures are perfectly worked when seen from the front. The material resistances of marble have been entirely and successfully overcome. The material has become 'invisible', just as the materiality of the canvas is invisible in most paintings. If we change our viewing position by walking around the sculpture, however, we are permitted to see that this first impression is 'produced', and therefore ideological. The contrast then poses the question of the sculptor's work, his semiotic action. It forces us to reflect on the borderlines between the unsemioticized materiality of the representation and the semioticized, fully cultural work of the sculptor, and on the dialectic between the expression of individuality and the social–semiotic framework in which it takes place. The two are connected: the 'handwriting' effect, so clearly visible in the less 'polished' parts of Rodin's sculpture, becomes increasingly possible as we move from the highly policed, the highly conventionalized, the fully semiotic, towards the less semioticized, therefore less policed and less conventionalized. The uncertain lines of a Mondriaan painting signal individuality, affect and art as clearly as the certain lines of a blueprint signal conventionality, reference and design. Figure 7.2, a painting by Nicholson (1945), makes the same point in a different way. It consists, quite simply, of two circles, a perfect, compass-aided circle on the left, as the Given, and a hand-drawn circle on the right, as the New. Drawing by hand, with all its subtle marks of individuality, may have once been unproblematic, as there was no other way of drawing, but has now become problematic, an issue for concern.

Architects who develop blueprints for buildings are of course also working with 'unsemioticized' materials. Their intentions, too, are usually less semiotic, or, to put it another way, it is harder for them to put the semiotic in the foreground. Other considerations may weigh more heavily: functional considerations (the fact that they are designing an office building, for instance), financial considerations, the wishes of a client. Art, on the other hand, has, since the 1960s, attempted critiques of mass society and in particular of mass production methods, which led it towards the very practices it sought to critique. When the American artist Jeff Koons commissions sculptures from factories, from artisans or from other artists and signs them with his name, he works with attenuated, abstract surfaces: the whole global domain of cultural production becomes the material of the work. Choice serves as the inscriptional tool, and industrialized cultural production as the surface of inscription. Our focus on physical materiality should therefore be taken as a metaphor. In the highly semioticized world we live in, Jeff Koons' work may be both more relevant and more usual than that of Giacometti or Moore, or Rothko or Ryman. The notion of artists producing objects 'with their own hands' dates back to the pre-industrial period, and had already come into crisis in the period of industrialization. It may be that in the post-industrial world it has lost much of its relevance.

The relative freedom of the artist, perhaps greater in the visual than in the verbal, remains, for the time being, in force, albeit on the margins. It lies in the possibility of *foregrounding* – either of the materiality of the means of inscription or of the object

◭   Fig 7.2 *Two Circles* (Ben Nicholson, 1945) (Tate Gallery)

produced, or of the semioticization of this material in (referential or significatory) acts of representation. Wallpaper draws attention away from the materiality of a plastered brick wall. A room without a hint of decoration on concrete or pine walls draws attention away from the facts of the wall itself and onto the materiality of the material.

What, then, is the meaning of material? Our assumption remains that signs are motivated. It is no accident that the statues erected to commemorate heroic figures are made of durable materials, or that we still carve in tombstones: the durability of these materials makes them signifiers for the meanings we intend to produce. Nor is it an accident that certain flowers or stones become signifiers for love: their rarity may make them precious, or else their colour, shape or perfume may make them suitable signifiers. Bone china teacups do not produce the same meanings as tin mugs. Important documents are written on paper with a certain weight, texture and colour. The marketing executive's report is likely to be produced on heavy glossy paper. Australian money is now printed on plastic – a shock to the returning expatriate, as if it is too boldly a signifier of what it should not signify.

To summarize, inscription comprises the interrelated semiotic resources of surface, substance and tools of inscription. Each has its own semiotic effects, and in their interaction they produce complex effects of meaning. The inscription system exists on many planes, that is, there are serial relations between surfaces. As with Hjelmslev's and Barthes' notion of the sign, signs at one level become available as signifiers at a higher level. And there are serial relations of translation *between* inscription systems also, as in the case of the relation between paintings and their photographic reproductions.

The brushstroke is not the smallest unit of meaning. That image is, as we suggested in the beginning of this chapter, misconceived – as misconceived as the idea of the *phone* as the smallest unit of a text. Texts, whether linguistic or visual or both, deploy a multiplicity of signifying systems, and semiotic theory should allow us to focus on the way each is used in the text, and on the configurations in which the text brings them together. Among these signifying systems, inscription is just one, but significant enough to be considered as productive of meaning in its own right.

8 The third dimension

THE THIRD DIMENSION: FROM 'READER' TO 'USER'

So far we have restricted ourselves to still rather than moving images, and to two-dimensional forms of visual communication rather than three-dimensional ones such as sculpture, designed objects, architecture or stage sets. In this chapter we will explore to which degree the descriptive framework we have developed in this book can be applied also to the three-dimensional visual. Our examples will mainly be drawn from the fields of sculpture and children's toys — objects which occupy a space somewhere in between sculptures, which are primarily symbolic objects, objects for contemplation and veneration, and 'designed objects', which are primarily objects for use, even though they may also convey symbolic messages. In addition we will consider everyday objects such as cups and motorcars, and architecture. The chapter is intended as a first exploration. We are not yet ready to present a systematic account of the three-dimensional visual similar to that we have presented in the preceding chapters for the two-dimensional visual. But we will at least be able to indicate in which ways three-dimensional visual communication is similar to and different from two-dimensional visuals, and to outline the theoretical issues which follow from this.

As far as the moving image is concerned, we have already given some film and television examples and drawn attention to some of the similarities and differences between still and moving images. However, the added factor of time involves so many new and complex issues that a more comprehensive account will have to wait for another occasion. The composition of moving images, for instance, is predominantly temporal and structured by rhythm. The role played by vectors in still images is, to a large extent, taken over by movement — movement of the represented participants as well as of the camera, which involves additional 'interactive' dimensions: social distances, involvement and power relations become dynamically variable. Although non-linear forms of compositional coherence can and do play a role in the moving image, temporal coherence is by nature linear, and this makes possible forms of semantic conjunction which have no equivalent in still images (van Leeuwen, 1991). Transactional relations can be realized at different levels, within or between shots, for instance. And text–image relations depend, not on spatial positions such as Given and New or Ideal and Real, but on complex uses of the dimensions 'before', 'at the same time' and 'after'. We intend to address these and other issues in a separate book.

Returning to the three-dimensional, we found that the key categories of our account of visual representation (see chapters 2 and 3) can be applied also to three-dimensional visuals, and do indeed seem sufficient to describe a wide range of such objects. Many sculptures, for example, have what we called in chapter 2 a 'narrative' structure. Take Epstein's *Jacob and the Angel* (1940), shown in figure 8.1: the arms of Jacob and the

Fig 8.1 *Jacob and the Angel* (Jacob Epstein, 1940) (Granada Television Ltd)

Angel form powerful vectors, relating the two participants in a complex and interesting way. The Angel's action is transactive. It has a Goal, as he holds Jacob in a firm grip. But Jacob's action, though foregrounded, is non-transactive – his arm hangs limply, and he does not hold or grab anything.

Kenneth Armitage's *People in the Wind* (1952), shown in figure 8.2, also has strong vectors, formed by the way the figures are bent forwards as they struggle against the wind. But here (as in sculptures of discus throwers, ballerinas and other active subjects) the action is 'non-transactional'. The vectors do not point at or lead to another participant, a Goal. The figures, it seems, 'strain forwards', but they do not 'strain towards something'.

'Reactions' are also common, although in sculpture the eyes do not usually form as strong a focus of attraction as they do in two-dimensional images, because they lack the strong tonal contrast between the whites of the eyes and the pupils, which, in pictures as in nature, makes eyes so salient. It is as if the added naturalism of the third dimension must be counteracted by greater abstraction in other means of expression, such as colour, to prevent sculpture from crossing the line between art and the uncannily real make-believe of the waxworks show (or of certain contemporary forms of art). Nevertheless, the man and the woman in Rodin's *The Kiss* (1880), shown in figure 8.3, not only hold each other within their arms, they also hold each other with their gaze, in

Fig 8.2 *People in the Wind* (Kenneth Armitage, 1952) (Tate Gallery)

a 'transactional reaction'. It is not difficult to find examples of 'non-transactional reactions' also. Jacob (figure 8.1) looks up, in a non-transactional reaction, while the Angel looks at Jacob, in a transactional reaction. Again, the Angel acts on Jacob, but Jacob does not act on the Angel. Arnheim's description of Michelangelo's *Moses* provides another example. 'The deflection of the lawgiver's head and the fierce concentration of his glance introduce an oblique vector that moves outwards like the beam of a lighthouse. But no goal object is included' (Arnheim, 1982: 46).

Even the design of objects and buildings can be vectorial and hence 'narrative', as shown in figure 8.4. The vector formed by the tailfins of 1950s cars, for instance, represented, in an abstract way, the idea of dynamic motion, as if it was not enough that cars *are* in fact dynamic moving objects, regardless of whether they have tailfins or not. The fact that cars do not have tailfins now points to the ideological dimension of sculptural representation: the meanings represented were those of the 'jet age'. But here an important complication occurs. In the case of objects, the ideational relations we have discussed in chapters 2 and 3 can be realized in two ways: they can be realized by the designer, as forms to be 'read' by a viewer, as when a cup has a 'dynamic', vectorial handle (and also, of course, in the case of the pictorial or decorative designs printed or painted on, or moulded or carved in, the cup); or they can be realized by the *user* of the object,

△ Fig 8.3 *The Kiss* (Auguste Rodin, 1880) (Tate Gallery)

as when the cup is held or drunk from, in a 'transactional action' with its user – the vectorial handle is then a 'non-transactional action' from the point of view of the design of the cup, and a potential for transactional action, a means, from the point of view of its use.

Even reactions can occur in objects. The toy telephone shown in figure 8.5 not only includes the dog's tongue, as an oblique vector signifying a non-transactional speaking, it also has eyes. The inclusion of eyes is in fact quite common in toys for young children, particularly in toys with the themes of time (clocks), communication (toy telephones) and transport (toy locomotives and cars), as if to encourage the child to form an emotive, personalized bond with these three key technologies as early as possible.

In contrast to two-dimensional visuals, sculptures rarely include a Setting. Their setting is the environment in which they are displayed, a gallery, a niche in a church, or a public square. It is not a *represented* Setting. Of course, sculptures *can* include a Setting, as in the works of Edward Kienholz and George Segal, for instance, or Asian sculpture gardens, such as the Tiger Balm Gardens in Singapore. But in contemporary Western sculpture the inclusion of a Setting is relatively rare. Decontextualization, it seems, has

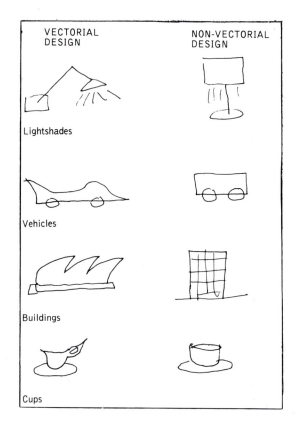

Fig 8.4 Vectorial and non-vectorial lightshades, cups, cars and buildings

Fig 8.5 Toy telephone

to counteract the added naturalism of the third dimension. Sculptures do, however, often have another participant, the pedestal on which they stand. Such pedestals can be (mere) framing devices, creating a degree of separation between the sculpture and its environment, and so enhancing its status as a representation, an object for contemplation, set apart from its environment. But they can also and at the same time form part of the representation, as in Canova's *Paolina Borghese* (1805), which has Paolina resting on a couch which forms also a sarcophagus-like support for her reclining body. The absence of such framing can have a strong effect, as in the life-size bronze of a middle-aged, corpulent man in a raincoat and hat placed as if mingling with the shoppers in the middle of the footpath of a busy shopping street in Amsterdam.

Turning now to 'conceptual' rather than 'narrative' structures of representation these,

Fig 8.6 *Woman* (Joan Miró, 1970) (Parellada, Barcelona)

too, can be found in sculpture. Miró's *Woman* (1970), reproduced in figure 8.6, is what, in chapter 3, we called an 'analytical' representation. The sculpture does not just play with the forms of found objects, making eyes of the headlights and a mouth of the windscreen of a car, it is also an 'analysis' of 'Woman'. 'Woman', in all its generality, is the 'Carrier', and the parts, the 'Possessive Attributes', are, in Miró's conception: a head which is also the empty shell of a car; an upper body which is also a tray on which two aggressively pointed breasts are presented to the viewer; and a lower body which is a barrel-shaped container with a vagina-like slit and two handles to hold her by. When we visited an exhibition of Miró's sculptures we noted that the misogynistic quality of Miró's analysis was not lost on many viewers. There was a guest book in which the visitors of the gallery could write down their impressions and many had used the opportunity to draw a quick caricature of Miró women with contemptuous comments like 'WOMAN????' These readings contrasted sharply with the artspeak in the catalogue, which described the formal qualities of the sculptures only, and did not dwell on Miró's way of representing the female gender.

Giacometti's *Hour of the Traces* (1930), shown in figure 8.7, is an analysis of the genderless human being, of the human condition in general. The parts: a kind of antenna, with an abstract eye, forms an active sensory tentacle and protrudes from the sculpture at an angle, constituting an oblique vector; a rigid rusty frame, the body; and, within the open frame, a plaster heart, suspended on a thin string, and moving slightly to and fro. Thus two actions are embedded in the analysis, both non-transactional: the action of the sensory apparatus, and the movement of the heart – the human being as a skeletal frame that is alive and surveys its environment.

We might add that analytical sculpture is used not only in art but also in science, for instance to show the construction of a molecule, or as a teaching aid, for instance in anatomy, in which case the parts can often be detached from the whole.

The third dimension creates an additional option in representation, a relation between the representational structure and the position of the viewer. Seen from the side (figure 8.1) Epstein's *Jacob and the Angel* has a narrative structure ('transactional action'). It is in the first place, about what Jacob and the Angel *do*. But if we look at the Angel from behind (figure 8.8) we are faced with the 'analysis' of the Angel, and a very striking one: the three principal 'Possessive Attributes' Epstein emphasizes are the Angel's long hair, his wings – and his balls.

Not all sculptures use this possibility. One can imagine a continuum running from reliefs which perhaps differ from two-dimensional images only in terms of modality, to fully 'multifaceted' sculptures such as *Jacob and the Angel*. In between there are sculptures which, though freestanding, are clearly not designed to be seen from behind and leave the back 'unworked', perhaps because they were meant to be placed against a wall or in a niche. And even when a sculpture is a fully multifaceted representation, like *Jacob and the Angel*, its placement in a particular environment can block access to alternative viewing positions, and hence to alternative readings. This may be because the work is placed with its back against the wall, or because a barrier prevents the viewer from access to other than more or less frontal viewing positions. But it may also be done in subtler ways. When

⬤   Fig 8.7 *Hour of the Traces* (Alberto Giacometti, 1930) (Tate Gallery)

we first discussed *Jacob and the Angel*, it was placed in the centre of the octagonal entrance hall of the Tate Gallery, in such a way that the viewer first saw it from the side, with the Angel on the left. In other words, its position favoured the narrative reading, the drama of the sculpture, rather than Epstein's striking 'analysis' of the Angel. But the viewer did have access to the other sides, as the sculpture was placed in the centre of the hall.

Playmobil figures such as those placed in figure 8.9 are also analytical structures. They show the significant attributes, the significant characteristics of, for example, an 'ethnic family'. The family has five members, a father, a mother and three children. Each member of the family has black hair and dark skin. Note the difference from the neutrally labelled 'family set': the composition of the family is the same, and all the members of the family have pink skin, but they differ in the colour of their hair and therefore have individual characteristics as well as social characteristics whereas (lesson number one) the members of the 'ethnic family' are 'others' who 'all look the same'. The children of the two families are dressed identically, but the parents are not. Lesson number two: second-generation immigrants are already 'more like us'. The Playmobil company brochure says that these toys 'form an aid to the training of your minds' and will 'acquaint children with what they will meet in the big real world' – but not in an entirely neutral fashion. As we have said in chapter 3, any analytical structure is only one of the many ways in which a given 'Carrier' can be analysed.

We have to remember, of course, that Playmobil figures enter into representation in

⬤ Fig 8.8 *Jacob and the Angel* from behind (Jacob Epstein, 1940) (Granada Television Ltd)

⬤ Fig 8.9 Playmobil 'family set' and 'ethnic family'

two ways, like our earlier example of cups with vectorial handles. On the one hand, they are like sculptures, predesigned representations, to be 'read' by the child; on the other hand, they have movable limbs and detachable parts and they can hold objects in their hands. Children can therefore use them to create a variety of representational structures, narrative 'scenes', and they can even subvert the predesigned representations, for instance by giving an 'ethnic' child red hair. They can also create their own classificatory or analytical arrangements, for instance by making a display of different kinds of Playmobil children on their toy shelf or by creating a new analysis of the 'family', with only a mother, perhaps, or with six children of different 'ethnic' origins (the arrangement of *Our Society and Others*, figure 3.40, could be reconstructed with Playmobil figures!). In the same way a cup can be used, not only in the 'transactions' of holding or drinking, but also to create an analytical structure, as when the cup is arranged on a sideboard together with the other parts of the set to which it belongs, or on the kitchen shelf, to become a 'Possessive Attribute' of the 'Carrier' 'dishes'; or to create a classificational structure, as when a number of different cups are arranged symmetrically in a shop window, or a design exhibition.

The *Vitrinen* (display cases) of the German avant-garde artist Joseph Beuys are an intriguing example of the classificational sculpture. They are the kind of sculpture which is usually referred to as an 'installation' – glass display cases containing a variety of objects, some of them altered by Beuys. *Vitrine 2* (1960–70), for instance, contains a film can (itself containing a film which features a performance by Beuys), a pair of boxing gloves, a sausage, a cassette player (with a tape of music performed by Beuys), a Beethoven score with a small blackboard eraser on it, two wineglasses (one coated with a white substance, the other looking as though something has been burnt in it), and a zinc box. Clearly a work like this raises the question of what these objects have in common (what their 'superordinate' is, in our terms), and this is exactly the question Beuys' interpreters have asked. According to Theewen (1993), 'Verwandschaft' (relatedness) is the key to understanding Beuys' *Vitrinen*: 'By bringing related objects together an association between them is created' (p. 139), and in the case of the *Vitrine* we have just described this association is that all the objects 'have played a role in performances of Beuys, and [that they] all contain something' (p. 29).

The third kind of conceptual structure discussed in chapter 3 was the symbolic relation. We saw how in pictures an overall colour – a blue haze, or a golden glow – could realize what we called a 'suggestive symbolic' process, endowing the depicted scene with an overall significance, 'saying', as it were, 'this scene is cold and desolate' (in the case of the blue haze) or 'these objects are very valuable' (in the case of the golden glow). Colour can play this role also in the case of three-dimensional objects – think of the colours of cars, for instance, the difference between a black, a bright red and a white Mercedes, say. But in addition to colour there are other factors, such as the material from which an object is made, the way the surface of a sculpture or other object is 'worked', or the overall shape of the objects, in so far as these are not determined by considerations of naturalistic representation, or by the functions served by an object. Giacometti's *Man Pointing* (1947), shown in figure 8.10, is much less 'analytical' than the sculptures we have so far discussed. It places no emphasis on the distinctness of the parts of the human body. Even the facial features are hardly stated – small indentations to indicate a mouth and eyes. The sculpture does of course have a clear vector in the oratorical gesture. Its most striking characteristic however is its rough, black craggy, surface. It is difficult to put into words exactly what is suggested by this surface, but whatever transcoding we attempt, it will have

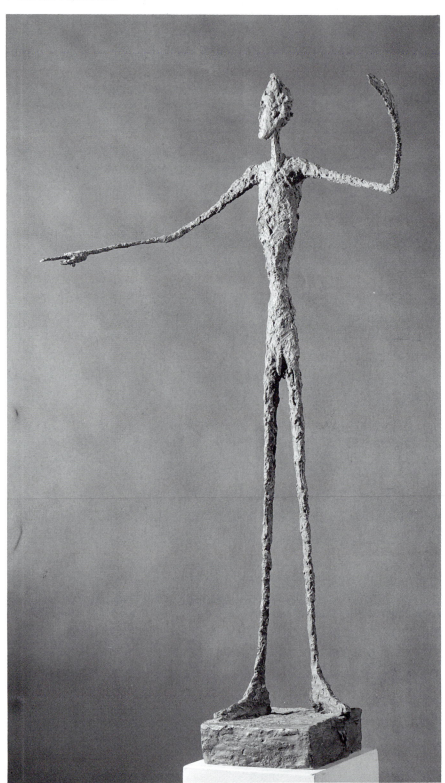

to express somehow that this figure is 'weather-beaten', affected by exposure to – but here we can fill in a number of things: the elements suffering, ageing and so on. The sculpture is abstract enough to allow all these readings and more.

The same applies, again, to other kinds of three-dimensional objects. Cups can be smooth, made of delicate china, suggesting, perhaps, an overall quality of elegance and refinement; or they can be sturdy and solid and made of brick-red terracotta suggesting, perhaps, an overall quality of down-to-earth simplicity. Cars can be elongated and streamlined, suggesting power and speed, or, as in the case of the currently fashionable 'retro' look, rounded and egg-like, suggesting a safe cocoon, a kind of womb.

The second kind of symbolic relation we discussed was the 'symbolic attributive' process, where one represented participant has no other function than to endow another with symbolic significance. This occurs, for instance, in some of Miró's sculptures, where birds and eggs attribute symbolic qualities to the figures depicted (usually 'women'). But it occurs also in toys for young children, where telephones can have wheels (an early lesson about the concept of communication as 'transport of information' and 'bridging the distance' rather than 'sharing of information'), and 'interactive learning centres' for children aged $2\frac{1}{2}$ to 5 ('6 built-in functions which teach the alphabet, numbers, shapes, colours, sound effects and nursery rhymes' and all this for £29.50) have a steering wheel and dashboard, as a symbol of the power and control afforded by knowledge. Or in adult toys: emblems and other decorations on cars, for instance. Or in architecture, where sculptures and murals can become symbolic attributes for buildings.

On the whole, then, we feel that the account of visual representation we have presented in chapters 2 and 3 can be applied to three-dimensional visual communication. At the same time, however, there are some significant differences. First, three-dimensional objects can be placed on a continuum which runs from objects that allow only one reading (by offering the reader only one aspect, usually the front) to objects which allow more than one reading, depending on the position of the viewer relative to the object.

Second, three-dimensional objects can be placed on a continuum which runs from objects which have been designed only to be looked at, only to be 'read', to objects which enter into representational relations in three ways: (1) the relations encoded in the design of the object itself, to be 'read' only by the viewer; (2) *interactive* relations between the object and its *user* (e.g. holding the cup, or drinking from it); and (3) *conceptual* relations created by the user (e.g. creating a classificational syntagm with a number of different cups).

Third, even when an object does have a potential for multifaceted representation and/or for being 'used' as well as 'read', external conditions can inhibit this potential, block the viewer's access to alternative reading positions, or to interactive engagement with the representational potential of the object.

Fig 8.10 *Man Pointing* (Alberto Giacometti, 1947) (Tate Gallery)

INTERACTIVE VIEWING

We will now turn to the interactive relations we discussed in chapter 4, trying to explore, again, how applicable they are to three-dimensional visual communication. In that chapter we distinguished between 'demand' pictures from which represented participants address the viewer directly with their gaze and 'want something from the viewer', and 'offer' pictures which position the viewer as an observer only, and offer the represented participants as 'information' to be taken in by the viewer.

Clearly, this distinction can be applied also to sculpture, but, again, with a difference. Henry Moore's *Recumbent Figure* (1938), shown in figure 8.11, addresses the viewer powerfully. Although the eyes are little more than indentations in the surface of the stone, the whole attitude of the figure suggests a concentrated look. But, as viewers, we can take up a position from which that look *will* directly address us (as did the photographer, in the case of figure 8.11), so that the picture forms a 'demand'; or a position from which the figure looks past us, at something else, or at nothing in particular, in any case, at something not included in our view, and in that case the look will become a 'non-transactional reaction'. In the two-dimensional medium we cannot, as viewers, decide whether or not we will allow ourselves to be directly addressed by a represented participant; the decision has been made for us. In the three-dimensional medium we can – that is, if the placement of the sculpture allows us to do so. In the Tate Gallery Moore's sculpture could have been placed in such a way that the figure's gaze would fix the viewer immediately upon entering the room. But this was not done when we viewed the sculpture there, and as a result the figure became just one of a number of Moore's works, presented as part of a classificational syntagm, and favouring the 'offer' rather than the 'demand'.

The same would be true of the toy telephone (figure 8.5). The gaze of this telephone can only become a 'demand' by virtue of an active decision on the part of its user. Some toys, of course, lend themselves more to this than others. Playmobil characters have small black dots for eyes. They are biased more towards the 'offer for information' than towards the interactive 'demand'. And the eyes of many boys' dolls (Batmen, Crash-dummies, Megazords, etc.) are often obscured by helmets, masks, or dark glasses. The eyes of girls' dolls (and of many cuddly animal toys), on the other hand, tend to be large and highly detailed. While boys are steered towards a more manipulative relation to their dolls, for girls the look, the interactive dimension, is made to matter more. And the same is true for very young children: even their bedclothes, pillow-cases, cups, plates may have eyes, and are thus personalized, animated, capable of entering into a direct address of relation with the child. As with many other things, some of this may well live on, unconsciously, in the adult relation with objects.

The same reasoning can be applied to the other interactive dimensions we discussed in chapter 4. In principle the viewer can decide whether to see the object from close up or from a distance, frontally (hence with 'involvement') or from an oblique angle (hence with 'detachment'), from above (hence from a position of power over the object) or from below (hence from a position in which the object has power over the viewer). We say 'in principle', because here too the viewer's choice may be restricted by external factors, by

Fig 8.11 *Recumbent Figure* (Henry Moore, 1938) (Tate Gallery)

barriers that prevent viewers from coming up close or seeing the object from a different angle. And large objects can make the high-angle viewpoint and the close distance impossible. What towers over us has, by design, power over us, and is, by design, socially distant: the vertical dimension is the dimension of power and reverential distance, the dimension of 'highly placed' people, places and things. In this connection it is also significant that sculptures, as works of 'high' art, cannot usually be approached from the most intimate distance, the distance that makes touching possible: as soon as the gallery visitor comes too close, a guard will become alert.

When sculptures are taken out of their original context and moved into another, their interactive meanings may change significantly. They may be, literally, taken down from the pedestal, in a church perhaps, where they were to be looked at from below, with reverence, to be moved into a gallery, where they are positioned at a level of equality, and viewed from a more 'familiar' distance: Michelangelo's *David*, removed to the rotunda of a museum, no longer calls to the citizens of Florence and is unaware of their calling on him and now 'can be explored by the viewer, but makes no advances to him' (Arnheim, 1982: 50; also Hodge and Kress, 1988: 201–3).

MODALITY IN THREE DIMENSIONS

In chapter 5 we described visual modality as resulting from the degree to which certain means of pictorial expression (colour, representational detail, depth, tonal shades, etc.) are used. Each of these dimensions can be seen as a scale, running from the absence of any rendition of detail to maximal representation of detail, or from the absence of any rendition of depth to maximally deep perspective. And on each of these scales there is a point that represents the way the given pictorial dimension is used in what could be called standard naturalism. To the degree that the use of a dimension is reduced, it becomes, at least in one respect, more abstract, 'less than real'. To the degree that it is amplified, it becomes 'more than real', and we associated this with a 'sensory coding orientation', an emphasis on sensory pleasure (or displeasure, as in the case of 'more than real' horror images), and an attempt to come as close as possible to a representation that involves all the senses.

Some of these play much the same role in three-dimensional visuals. Clearly, sculptures and toys can represent what they represent in naturalistic detail or more abstractly. And when the shape of everyday design objects no longer betrays their function, when, for instance, refrigerators, washing machines and kitchen storage cabinets all become sleek featureless white boxes, there is also a strong sense of abstraction. The same can be argued for buildings. Also, like pictures, three-dimensional representations can include several levels of modality. The heads of Henry Moore's *King and Queen* (1952–3), for instance, shown in figure 8.12, are abstract symbols, while their hands are rendered in naturalistic detail. This expresses the contradictory nature of the powerful. Their minds may have lost touch with the detail of everyday concrete reality, but look at their hands – they are after all still human, and their work, their doing, is still the work of humans.

The representation of detail in toys is particularly interesting. Barthes' still highly readable essay about the semantics of toys (1973: 53ff.) is now perhaps overtaken by semiotic events. He describes French toys as highly detailed, highly naturalistic miniature versions of adult objects – and notes how unsatisfactory they are, therefore, both from the point of view of pleasure, of the sensory dimension, and from the point of view of their interactive potential, as objects to play with: 'the child can only identify himself as owner, as user, never as creator; he does not invent the world, he uses it: there are, prepared for him, actions without adventure, without wonder, without joy' (*ibid.*: 54). Toys of this kind can be seen in museums such as London's Museum of Early Childhood. One's first impression on seeing Victorian toys is that children are addressed as miniature adults, their subjectivity 'scaled down', but not 'reduced', from that of the adult world. This is represented through a large number of semiotic modes: the materials (glass, clothes of various kinds, metals, etc. – all of them rarely, if at all, used in contemporary toys) as much as the miniature naturalism of the represented objects. Today's toys vary in their detail. Toys for young children are abstract. Shapes and textures are brought down to their essentials. Locomotives have featureless wheels, one featureless chimney, two yellow circles for windows. They are, from the point of view of detail of representation, like the simplest line drawings. As the child gets older, detail increases. The wheels of the

Fig 8.12 *King and Queen* (Henry Moore, 1952–3) (Tate Gallery)

locomotives get spokes and drive-shafts. The texture of the machine's body acquires detail. Headlights with miniature fresnel lenses are added. But on the whole the contemporary toy remains simple, essentialized, as for instance, again, in the popular Playmobil figures, where the eyes are two dots, the mouth a curved line, the hair an almost featureless helmet, with a few indentations suggesting texture and the length signifying gender. Girls' dolls, on the other hand (and other girls' toys: realistic washing machines, 'beauty shops', vacuum cleaners, dolls' cots), imitate the adult world, or at least that of the glamour girl, the housewife and the mother, much more so than boys' toys, which depict a make-believe world of science-fiction vehicles and weapons, or a world of dinosaurs and other monsters. The latter are often 'more than real', with highly textured, glistening scales, and irregular teeth, and menacing eyes, set behind wrinkled lids. They are designed to create the kind of sensory, visceral reaction also sought, for instance, in horror films. Cuddly animal toys also tend to be 'more than real', with exaggeratedly soft furs and large moist eyes, this time to enhance the sensory pleasures of holding and touching. Researching this chapter, we spent many hours in toy shops as well as in toy museums, and the contrast is striking. The former world of toys is the one Barthes describes, the world of the 'bourgeois' naturalistic toy. The latter, with the exception of some girls' toys (especially dolls), is a make-believe world of brightly coloured plastic and creatures and objects from fantasy stories.

The role of colour in the modality of three-dimensional visual representation also resembles that of the two-dimensional visuals. Some of Miró's sculptures of 'women', for instance, are painted in bright, primary colours – yellow, blue and red. As a result they are schematic and analytical from the point of view of representational detail, a simplified, abstract view of 'woman', but 'more than real', 'sensory' from the point of view of colour. Miró's women are not just machine-like assemblages of parts, they are also pleasurably colourful ('woman' as a machine for pleasure). Many toys, especially toys for young children have exactly the same kind of modality configuration: abstract and schematized, 'conceptual', from the point of view of colour; 'un-naturalistic' primary colours, colours for the sake of pleasure rather than naturalistic representation. This 'sensory' aspect is then further enhanced by the way these toys appeal to all the senses, and include touch and sound, as stressed in this description of the 'Chicco animal train': 'a locomotive featuring 8 different animal sounds and four different train sounds. Sounds are activated by pressing appropriately shaped buttons.' Again, for older children colour can become more naturalistic, as in Thomas the Tank Engine, which replaces bright reds, yellows, blues and greens with more mute steel blue, grey and black, and just a touch of red. And while the colour in all these examples is unmodulated, the colour of girls' dolls becomes more varied, with blushes on the cheeks, shadows under the eyes, a shine on the lips. And the same applies to the slimy greens and greys and pinks on dinosaurs and monsters.

The materials used in three-dimensional representation, similarly, can be motivated naturalistically, as when toy cars are made of metal, or cuddly animals of soft, furry materials (though, on the other hand, even toy pigs can be furry!). But they can also be 'less than real', abstracting from the variety and specificity of the range of materials available, as in the case of plastic. To quote Barthes again:

> Many toys are now moulded from complicated mixtures; the plastic material of which they are made has an appearance at once gross and hygienic, it destroys all the pleasure, the sweetness, the humanity of touch.... Henceforth, toys are chemical in substance and colour; their very material introduces one to coenasthetics of use, not pleasure.
>
> (1973: 55)

Again, materials can have 'more than real' modality, when their choice is motivated, not by an attempt to make the object look like what it represents, but by an attempt to create

Fig 8.13 *Family Romance* (Charles Ray, 1993) (ICA)

pleasure or displeasure. And this can apply also to everyday objects, and to buildings, if we replace naturalism by an attempt to reveal the material from which the object is actually made and divergence from naturalism by attempts to conceal these in one direction (say, plain sheets of a synthetic material over bricks) or another (say, timber cladding over bricks or concrete).

In other respects, however, three-dimensional modality differs from two-dimensional modality. There is no need to *represent* depth: the object already has depth, by virtue of its three-dimensionality. And there is no need to *represent* the play of light and shade: it already occurs, naturally. It is to compensate for these intrinsic naturalistic qualities that most Western sculpture (1) is decontextualized, lacking a Setting; (2) refrains from using colour as a means of representation, except in the sense of overall, symbolic colour; and (3) increasingly tends towards highly reduced forms of representation. In this way 'high art', which seeks to go beyond the mere replication of reality by representing an ideal of beauty or an abstract truth, distinguishes itself from everyday sculpture – from the dummies in shop windows, from girls' dolls, from miniature dinosaurs and so on. These need not themselves be naturalistic in every dimension in any case, and may use reduced naturalism either for didactic purposes, as in toys for young children, or to create class distinctions in taste, as with the more stylized dummies in expensive shops. When sculpture becomes naturalistic in too many dimensions, it becomes uncanny, 'freaky', as in Charles Ray's *Family Romance* (1993), shown in figure 8.13 – which still is not naturalistic in every dimension, as all the members of the family have been given the same size, and as it was displayed, at least when we saw it at the ICA in London, in a decontextualized way, as the only exhibit in a stark white, bare gallery room.

COMPOSITION IN THREE DIMENSIONS

Many sculptures and other three-dimensional objects do not clearly polarize between left and right; top and bottom, centre and margin, but when they do, the values of Given and New, Ideal and Real and Centre and Margin apply, we think, in the same way as they do in two-dimensional visual communication. Yet the third dimension does introduce additional factors.

In figure 8.1 we saw Epstein's *Jacob and the Angel* as it would have been seen by visitors entering the Tate Gallery when the work was positioned in the centre of the Gallery's octagonal entrance hall. The Angel, against whose force Jacob is so helpless, is Given, as was God in figures 6.4 and 6.10. Jacob's helplessness is New, the focus of the drama. But moving to the other side, the viewer can reverse this, and make Jacob Given and the Angel New, provided access to the other side is not blocked. The same is true for other multifaceted sculptures with two (or more) 'polarized' participants, such as Rodin's *The Kiss* (figure 8.3), where either the man can be the Given and the woman the New, or the woman the Given and the man the New. This is why photographs cannot do justice to multifaceted sculptures – a photo can always give only one angle, and hence one reading. The same is not true, however, for Ideal and Real and Centre and Margin. These relations cannot be inverted by changing the angle from which the work is viewed. In other words, the horizontal dimension allows interactivity; the vertical dimension and centrality do not.

Ideal and Real and Centre and Margin are often the most significant compositional dimensions in three-dimensional visual composition. Architecture provides perhaps the clearest example. Left and right are not usually polarized. Horizontally there is symmetry. But vertically there is not. The vertical dimension is used to polarize, to produce difference, with the Ideal, the element(s) that give(s) the building its more general and 'ideal' significance on top – the tower, for instance, with its significant emblems, the cross, or the clock, the gable stone on Amsterdam canal houses, the frieze high up on the Greek temple. Below, on the other hand, is the space of the Real – the forecourts where we meet, the doors through which we enter. More generally, the façade of a building, its vertical dimension, is the building we 'read'; the horizontal dimension, the floor plan, is the building we 'use':

the compositional spectacle in the upright dimension is essentially visual. It restricts the user to observation from a distance. . . . In the horizontal plane, the corresponding dynamics involves the user directly and is therefore largely social. The level plan is the arena of human action.

(Arnheim, 1982: 213)

Figure 8.14, shows an example of centrality in an architectural façade: the canopy with the Madonna, in the centre of the façade of the Church of Santa Maria della Spina in Pisa.

The design of objects can also make use of these dimensions. Differences between what is on top and what below, or what is on the left and what is on the right cannot always be explained ergonomically. As can be seen in any shop or catalogue, some contemporary telephones may have the receiver on top and the dial or buttons below, while others have

○ **Fig 8.14 Church of Santa Maria della Spina (Arnheim, 1982)**

⬛ **Fig 8.15 Telephone with dialogue balloon (Argos catalogue)**

a flatter, more horizontal design, with the receiver invariably on the left, and the buttons that operate the electronic gadgetry on the right. Although, in our observation, most right-handed people transfer the receiver to the right hand after dialling, it must be picked up and returned to the left, because of the design which treats the traditional use of the telephone as Given and the electronically generated 'messages', the communication with the machine, as New, as shown by the dialogue balloons in figure 8.15.

In toy telephones, similarly, dot matrix displays, talking Teddies, 'picture pop-ups' and so on are also placed on the right, and on top, above the buttons, with the receiver on the left. Multifaceted objects add further dimensions to three-dimensional composition, and allow, at least in principle, front and back, and the left and right side (and, in the case of open structures, an interior centre and the exterior) to be used for the production of difference. Of the latter we have already seen an example in figure 8.7 – the plaster heart in the centre of the rigid frame of Giacometti's *Hour of the Traces*. But not all multifaceted objects use these dimensions. As in nature, where trees or mountains do not have a front or back (other than one which stems from our positions towards them, e.g. which side of the mountain we live on), objects can be the same, and have the same meaning, whichever side we view them from. Sculptures of the 'Three Graces', for instance, are usually composed in the round, offering essentially the same view from whichever side one approaches them. And the same pattern can be observed in some children's toys, for instance a kind of ball with symmetrically distributed pictures illustrating nursery rhymes (although 'the one that ends up on top determines which song is heard'). Or in buildings, such as the Queen Victoria Building in Sydney, which, in its latest reincarnation as a shopping centre, has, on every side, a central entrance and shop windows; or perfectly round buildings such as the Temple of Vesta in Rome, or the Pantheon. In other cases, however, front and back especially differ in meaning. We have not studied enough examples to generalize confidently about the informational values of these dimensions of space. But it is tempting to take the human body as a metaphor with the front as the public side, the side where we articulate how we want to be read, and the back as the non-social side, the private side which is not meant to be viewed and often has no meaning except perhaps for those with whom we are most intimate – this is why, paradoxically, it can also be the most revealing, as in the case of Epstein's Angel (figure 8.8).

In chapter 3 we argued that the structures of diagrams (the top–down path of the taxonomy, the left–right path of the flowchart, the digital network) are modelled on forms of social organization. Perhaps it can be argued along the same lines that composition, both two- and three-dimensional, is ultimately modelled either on the 'non-social' roundness of the natural forms such as trees and mountains, or on the polarized human body, with the head as the Ideal, the feet as the Real, the heart as the Centre, movement and action as the more interactive and dynamic horizontal dimension, and the front and the back as, respectively, the social and public and the non-social and private side. As Lakoff and Johnson said (1980: 14):

> Spatial orientations arise from the fact that we have bodies of the sort we have and that they function as they do in our physical environment. Orientational metaphors have a basis in our physical *and* cultural experience. Though the polar opposites, up–down, in–out, etc., are physical in nature, the orientational metaphors based on them can vary from culture to culture.
>
> (our italics)

9 Colourful thoughts (a postscript)

We have, in this book, attempted to present a 'grammar of visual design', to make explicit how the available resources of visual grammar form a potential for the production and communication of meaning through spatial configurations of visual elements. We have travelled a certain distance along the road, but, as we conclude the book, we realize that we have only just begun, and find ourselves thinking more about the limitations of what we have done and the amount of work that still remains than about what we have achieved so far. Social semiotics is an attempt to describe and understand how people produce and communicate meaning in specific social settings, be they 'micro' settings such as the family or settings in which sign-making is well institutionalized and hemmed in by habits, conventions and rules. But social semiotics, sign-making in society, is so varied an activity that any attempt to capture it in a general theory must look crude by comparison with the richness of the actual semiotic world.

  We were aware of this and we have tried to write our grammar not as one which seeks to capture the detail of everything people can and do do in visual communication, but as a flexible set of resources that people use in ever new and ever different acts of visual sign-making, and we have included as many examples as we have to try and bring out just how many uses these resources allow. But even given this qualification, we feel we have only made a beginning. We wish, for instance, that we could have more fully documented and interpreted the social history of scientific–technical image-making, or the question of modality configurations in different schools of modern art, to mention just some of the questions on which we have touched all too lightly. And in beginning to explore the 'third dimension', we saw a whole new field of problems and questions opening up – one which no doubt will itself open up further questions when we begin to delve into it more deeply. However, it was our aim to provide a broad overview, to map one – large – region of the semiotic landscape, and this we have done, with all the faults that will inevitably cling to such a broad enterprise. The broadness of our approach will, we hope, at least have the advantage that it begins to show up some of the connections which have often been obscured by the limited and highly specialized objects of, for instance, so many art-historical studies. One of these connections is that between the history of art (and visual communication generally) and the theory of language, in which the social and historical dimensions have, too often, been absent. Another is the connection between the 'micro' and 'macro' accounts of the social world which characterize different schools of sociology. For us, the child's relatively 'free' act of sign-making, which for its understanding requires very specific, 'biographical' contextualizations, is of as much interest as is representation within highly institutionalized genres in which sign-makers must follow well-established rules and conventions, and which, for their understanding, require broader social and historical contextualizations.

  To emphasize, once more, the nature of the 'grammar of visual design' as a resource for making and communicating meaning through the convergence of many different signifying systems, we will discuss one final example. This example will also help reiterate another point. In writing a book such as this, one sometimes feels that one is applying a cold, clinical approach to semiotic practices which are, in reality, strongly coloured by affective factors. How to write about affect? How to steer a path between the mere assertion, or celebration, of the role of affect, which will leave no room for analysis and interpretation, and the cold dissection which threatens to destroy its object as one is writing about it? We have, from time to time, reminded the reader of the omnipresence of affect which we asserted in the Introduction: for instance, in chapter 4, where we discussed the relations between the image and the viewer, relations which are always affective relations, relations of identification or its opposite; in chapter 5, where we discussed the affective quality of 'more than real' values of modality markers; in chapter 6, where we discussed 'balance' as an interface between the biological and the semiotic; and in our discussion of 'handwriting' in chapter 7. Yet we feel that affect has perhaps been too thin a thread in the tapestry. The production and communication of meaning is always affective and constitutive of subjectivities, in the domains we tend to regard as self-expressive (e.g. children's drawing and art) as much as in the domains we see as objectivating and impersonal (e.g. scientific and technical drawings). Even the maximally abstract modality of diagrams is an affective choice, by the very fact that it attempts to negate affect. The productive subject is as central here as anywhere else. In much contemporary theory, the old body–mind dichotomy again manifests itself in the strict boundaries drawn between rational and cognitive approaches and more affective approaches, be they grounded in the discourses that eulogize the 'pleasure of the text', in psychoanalytical discourses, or otherwise. We have tried to avoid this. We feel strongly that the cognitive and the affective are not antithetical, and it is for this reason that we have given such a central place to children's representation. Our final example will therefore be another example of children's visual sign-making, and its title, *Colourful Thoughts*, indicates that the child who made it sought to fuse the cognitive ('thoughts') and the affective ('colourful'). A painting, on plywood, measuring, in reality, 120 by 90 centimetres, it was made by a ten-year-old girl. It is reproduced in colour plate 8. The mother of the girl who made this painting is a professional artist, and in the size of the work, the medium and the way she has signed the painting, the girl has, perhaps, imitated her mother. But the work itself very much represents her own style of visual thinking. It was painted as a present for her father (separated from her mother), an academic whose study, the girl felt, was too bare and functional, and lacked not only sufficient pictures on the wall, but also and above all colour.

Looking at the painting from the point of view of ideational meaning, we note first of all that there are no vectors between the main participants, the shapes in the foreground. It is a conceptual picture. Like many of the conceptual pictures discussed in chapter 3, it lacks a concrete setting, shows the participants front-on and at eye level, includes a linguistic element in the picture space and uses abstract representation. The participants are distributed across the picture space in a symmetrical way, and this suggests that the relation between them is classificational. The symmetry is in fact quite striking and the objects are delicately balanced: even though, by itself, the yellow shape top left is heavier than the yellow shape middle right, the balance is restored by the higher position of the small blue 'thought balloon' top right. The title, in black, is balanced by a horizontal, slightly curved black line on top. And the participants are placed in a kind of circle around the central participant, which differs from the others in that it is not completely enclosed by a thick black line, but open at the bottom, so that the red colour, literally, drips out of it.

The title indicates what these participants represent. Their shapes and colours may be different, but they all represent 'thoughts'. What is a thought, according to this painting? Here we can make four observations: thoughts are (1) differently coloured (red, blue and yellow); (2) differently shaped; (3) mostly enclosed by a thick, black crust (black, the colour of words!); and (4) sometimes not quite enclosed, in which case their content 'bleeds out of them', so to speak. These strongly saturated colours (the same palette as the Miró sculptures and the children's toys we discussed in the previous chapter) are 'more than real' and hence motivated by affect, rather than on naturalistic grounds (resemblance to reality) or conventionally (colour 'codes'). It is difficult to go into detail about the meanings of the different colours. The literature on the emotive meanings of colour is quite inconsistent. Some psychologists have reported that 'people' prefer saturated colour over unsaturated colour, others that they prefer unsaturated colour over saturated colour. Blue has been described as 'depressing and sad' and as representing 'calm pleasure'. Goethe called yellow 'gay and softly charming', Kandinsky said it 'never contains a profound meaning and is akin to utter waste'. One thing is certain, however: colour (and colour contrast) is used to realize affect in the sensory coding orientations that inform, for instance, certain types of art and art appreciation, certain forms of dress and interior decoration and their appreciation, and so on. In *Colourful Thoughts*, thoughts are thus represented as affects of different kinds: red, blue and yellow (among other things, for they also have a shape, a frame, etc.). As far as the enclosing black lines are concerned, we might perhaps say that the child represents thoughts as mostly 'dammed up', repressed, kept inside, except in the one, central case. On the shapes we will comment below.

The background may not be a concrete setting, but it is not a neutral background either: a green field, with yellow diagonal stripes and pink dots. It is difficult not to think of these stripes as downward vectors, going from top left to bottom right, particularly since there is, in the right bottom corner, a darkening of the green field in the form of an arrowhead: the painting as a whole thus converges towards the name of the artist, and might be seen as a kind of mental self-portrait. In conceptual visuals (maps, diagrams, heraldry) colours often have conventional meanings, and we would suggest reading these somewhat less saturated colours in this way: green as the colour of nature, pink as the colour of femininity. In other words, the strongly emotive, but bottled-up, thoughts of the child exist against a background of nature 'dotted with femininity'.

As far as the interpersonal meanings of the painting are concerned, the viewer is not positioned by any form of perspective, although there is a separation between foreground and background, through overlapping and through differences in colour saturation. Nor does the picture form a 'demand'. And as no human subject is represented, the issue of social distance does not arise. However 'colourful', the painting is, in many ways, 'objective'. It exists as an object in its own right, regardless of the viewer. Something can be said, however, about its modality. The painting abstracts from naturalistic depiction in almost every respect except one: the vibrant and strongly saturated colours. These colours, as we have noted already, are 'more than real', and thus suggest a coding orientation in which the affective forms the cornerstone of reality. Like Roderic O'Conor's *Yellow Landscape* (plate 5), the painting mixes the 'intellectual' and 'analytical' with the 'emotive' and 'expressive', albeit through a different modality configuration, namely within a conceptual rather than a naturalistic framework.

We turn finally to compositional, textual meanings. Three things can be noted. The painting is, first of all, a balanced composition with a strong sense of Centre and Margin. The child has, literally, balanced and centred her emotions in this picture. Second, the title is at the bottom, and so coded as, on the one hand, more concrete and real but, on the other hand, less valued and less 'ideal' than the visual element. At the top we find merely the shadow of this title: the colour, but not the substance of the verbal; its emotive quality, but not its content. Third, there is a difference between left and right – a difference in the shapes of the thoughts and a difference in colour (red is most strongly represented on the right).

On the meaning of this we can only speculate. It is tempting to read the shape of the participants on the left as phallic, and those on the right as, by contrast, representing the female. The centrality, and hence the mediating function (since left and right are polarized), of the central participant derives from this: the child herself is the central 'thought' in the middle, caught between the father and the mother. Remember also that the colour of the central participant (red) is most strongly represented on the right, the female side, and lies most clearly on the path of the vectors which lead to the artist's name.

We mentioned that the picture was painted as a gift to the father. In the picture the father is Given, the mother New. In other words, what the father, as the addressed viewer, is asked to pay attention to is the mother, the female, while the link between the two is formed by the 'thought' of the child which here, unlike all the other thoughts, escapes from its encapsulation, and expresses itself in the act of producing the painting and giving it to the father.

Thus the child not only brings together choices from all the available resources of visual sign-making in a piece of intricate and complex visual thinking, but also fuses her thinking, her cognitive work, with her affects in an active process of working through some of the problems connected with her identity and subjectivity.

References

Allen, J. (1977) 'Self-reflexivity in documentary', *Cinetracts* 2: 37–44.

Arnheim, R. (1969) *Visual Thinking*, Berkeley and Los Angeles, University of California Press.

—— (1974) *Art and Visual Perception*, Berkeley and Los Angeles, University of California Press.

—— (1982) *The Power of the Center*, Berkeley and Los Angeles, University of California Press.

Bakhtin, M. (1981) *The Dialogic Imagination*, Austin, University of Texas Press.

—— (1984) *Problems of Dostoyevski's Poetics*, Manchester, Manchester University Press.

Bal, M. (1985) *Narratology: Introduction to the Theory of Narrative*, Toronto, Toronto University Press.

—— (1990) *Verf en Verderf: Lezen in Rembrandt*, Amsterdam, Prometheus.

Barthes, R. (1967a) *Elements of Semiology*, London, Cape.

—— (1967b) *Système de la mode*, Paris, Seuil.

—— (1970) *L'Empire des signes*, Geneva, Skira.

—— (1973) *Mythologies*, St Albans, Paladin.

—— (1977) *Image–Music–Text*, London, Fontana.

—— (1984) *Camera Lucida*, London, Fontana.

Bassy, A.-M. (1975) 'Du texte à l'illustration', *Semiotica* 11(4): 297–335.

Bell, P. and Van Leeuwen, T. (1994) *The Media Interview: Confession, Contest, Conversation,* Sydney, University of New South Wales Press.

Belting, H. (1990) *The Image and its Public in the Middle Ages,* New Rochelle, N.Y., Aristide D. Caratzay.

Bender, L. (1988) *France,* London, Macmillan.

Benjamin, W. (1973) *Illuminations,* London, Fontana.

Berger, J. (1972) *Ways of Seeing,* Harmondsworth, Penguin.

Bernstein, B. (1981) 'Codes, modalities and the process of cultural reproduction: a model', *Language and Society* 10: 327–63.

Bindon, H. and Williams, H. (1988) *Geography Research Projects: a Senior Student's Handbook,* Melbourne, Edward Arnold.

Bogatyrev, P. (1971) *The Function of Folk Costume in Moravian Slovakia,* The Hague, Mouton.

Bols, P., Houppermans, M., Krijger, C., Lentjes, W., Savelkouls, T., Terlingen, M. and Teune, P. (1986) *Werk aan de Wereld,* Den Bosch, Malmberg.

Booth, W.C. (1961) *The Rhetoric of Fiction,* Chicago, Chicago University Press.

Bourdieu, P. (1986) *Distinction: a Social Critique of the Judgment of Taste,* London, Routledge.

Brecht, B. (1967) 'Über die Malerei der Chinesen', in *Gesammelte Werke,* vol. 18, Frankfurt-on-Main, Suhrkamp.

Brown, C., Kelch, J. and Thiel, P.V. (1991) *Rembrandt: the Master and his Workshop,* New Haven, Yale University Press.

Brown, T.M. (1958) *The Work of G. Rietveld, Architect*, Utrecht, A.W. Bruna.

Bruna, D. (1988) *On My Walk*, London, Methuen Children's Books.

Brunsden, C. and Morley, D. (1978) *Everyday Television: Nationwide*, London, BFI.

Bryson, N., ed. (1990) *Visual Theory*, Cambridge, Polity Press.

Burgin, V., ed. (1982) *Thinking Photography*, London, Macmillan.

Chatman, S. (1978) *Story and Discourse*, Ithaca, N.Y., Cornell University Press.

Clarke, G., ed. (1992) *The Portrait in Photography*, London, Reaktion Books.

Comolli, J.L. (1971) 'Technique et idéologie: camera, perspective, profondeur du champ', *Cahiers du Cinema* 229: 4–23.

Coupe, S. and Andrews, M. (1984) *Their Ghosts may be Heard: Australia to 1900*, Melbourne, Cheshire.

Dance, F.E.X. (1967) 'A helical model of communication', in F.E.X. Dance, ed., *Human Communication Theory*, New York, Holt, Rinehart & Winston.

Deleuze, G. (1992) *Cinema*, vol. 1: *The Movement Image*, London, Athlone Press.

Dondis, D.A. (1973) *A Primer of Visual Literacy*, Cambridge, Mass., MIT Press.

Dragt, H., Hofland, W.A. and Tamsma, R. (1985) *De Geo Geordend*, Amsterdam, Meulenhoff.

DSP (1991) *Arts Literacy*, Sydney, Disadvantaged Schools Programme Report.

Dyer, G. (1982) *Advertising as Communication*, London, Methuen.

Eco, U. (1976a) 'Articulations of the cinematic code', in B. Nichols, ed. *Movies and Methods*, vol. I, Berkeley and Los Angeles, University of California Press.

—— (1976b) *A Theory of Semiotics*, Bloomington, Indiana University Press.

—— (1979) *The Role of the Reader*, Bloomington, Indiana University Press.

Fairclough, N. (1992) *Discourse and Social Change*, Cambridge, Polity Press.

—— (1993) 'Critical discourse analysis and the marketisation of public discourse; the universities', *Discourse and Society* 4(2): 133–69.

Finch, C. (1968) *Pop Art: Object and Image*, London, Studio Vista/Dutton.

Fiske, J. (1982) *Introduction to Communication Studies*, London, Methuen.

Fiske, J. and Hartley, J. (1979) *Reading Television*, London, Methuen.

Fresnault-Deruelle, P. (1975) 'Du linéaire au tabulaire', *Communications* 24: 7–23.

Gauthier, G. (1973) *Initiation à la sémiologie de l'image*, Paris, Cahiers de l'Audiovisée.

Genette, G. (1972) *Narrative Discourse*, Oxford, Blackwell.

Ghaoui, C., George, S.M., Rada, R., Beer, M. and Gerta, J. (1992) 'Text to hypertext and back again', in P. O'Brian Holt and N. Williams, eds, *Computers and Writing: State of the Art*, Dordrecht, Kluwer.

Gledhill, C. (1994) 'Towards a genre analysis of abstracting', paper presented at the twenty-first International Systemic Functional Congress, Gent, 1–5 August 1994.

Goffman, I. (1976) *Gender Advertisements*, London, Macmillan.

Gombrich, E. (1960) *Art and Illusion*, London, Phaidon.

Goodman, N. (1969) *Languages of Art*, London, Oxford University Press.

Gregory, R.L. (1970) *The Intelligent Eye*, New York, McGraw-Hill.

Habermas, J. (1984) *The Theory of Communicative Action*, vol. I, Cambridge, Polity Press.

Hall, E. (1964) 'Silent assumptions in social communication', *Disorders of Communication* 42: 41–55.

———— (1966) *The Hidden Dimension*, New York, Doubleday.

Hall, S. (1980) 'Encoding/Decoding', in S. Hall *et al.*, eds, *Culture, Media, Language*, London, Hutchinson.

———— (1982) 'The determination of news photographs', in S. Cohen and J. Young, eds, *The Manufacture of News*, London, Constable.

Halliday, M.A.K. (1978) *Language as Social Semiotic*, London, Edward Arnold.

———— (1985) *An Introduction to Functional Grammar*, London, Edward Arnold.

Halliday, M.A.K. and Martin, J.R. (1993) *Writing Science: Literacy and Discursive Power*, London, Falmer Press.

Hartley, J. (1982) *Understanding News*, London, Methuen.

Hauser, A. (1962) *The Social History of Art*, vol. 2, London, Routledge.

Hermeren, G. (1969) *Representation and Meaning in the Visual Arts*,

Lund, Scandinavian University Books.

Hill, J. (1980) *Introductory Physics*, London, Macmillan.

Hjemslev, L. (1961) *Prolegomena to a Theory of Language*, Madison, University of Wisconsin Press.

Hodge, R. and Kress, G. (1988) *Social Semiotics*, Cambridge, Polity Press.

────── (1993) *Language as Ideology* (2nd revised edition), London, Routledge.

Hogg, J. ed. (1969) *Psychology and the Visual Arts*, Harmondsworth, Penguin.

Honzl, J. (1976) 'Dynamics of the sign in the theatre', in L. Matejka and I.R. Titunik, eds, *Semiotics of Art: Prague School Contributions*, Cambridge, Mass., MIT Press.

Hughes, R. (1969) *Heaven and Hell in Western Art*, London, Weidenfeld & Nicolson.

Humphrey, S. (1992) 'Exploring the language of school geography', unpublished research report, Sydney, Disadvantaged Schools Programme.

Iedema, R. *et al.* (1993) 'Media literacy report', unpublished research report, Sydney, Disadvantaged Schools Programme.

────── (1994) 'The language of administration', unpublished research report, Sydney, Disadvantaged Schools Programme.

Iser, W. (1978) *The Act of Reading*, Baltimore, Md., Johns Hopkins University Press.

Jaffé, H.L.C. (1986) *De Stijl: 1917–1931, Visions of Utopia*, Oxford, Phaidon.

Jakobson, R. (1971) *Studies in Verbal Art*, Ann Arbor, Michigan University Press.

Jenkins, C. (1990) *Science Scene*, Book 1, Melbourne, Edward Arnold.

Jennings, T. (1986) *The Young Geographer Investigates Mountains*, Oxford, Oxford University Press.

Joos, M. (1967) *The Five Clocks of Language*, New York, Harcourt, Brace & World.

Kress, G. (1977) 'Tense as modality', *UEA Papers in Linguistics* 5: 40–50.

—— (1985) 'Ideological structures in discourse', in T.A. Van Dijk, ed., *Handbook of Discourse Analysis*, New York, Academic Press.

—— (1987a) 'Educating readers: language in advertising', in J. Hawthorn, ed., *Propaganda, Persuasion and Polemic*, London, Edward Arnold.

—— (1987b) *Communication and Culture: an Introduction*, Sydney, University of New South Wales Press.

—— (1989) *Linguistic Processes in Socio-cultural Practice*, London, Oxford University Press.

—— (1992) 'Explanation in visual communication', report to the ESPRIT II Basic Research Project on Explanation, Working Group 326.

—— (1993a) 'Media literacy as cultural technology in the age of transcultural media', in C. Bazalgette, E. Brevort and J. Savino, eds, *New Directions: Media Education Worldwide*, London and Paris, BFI/CLEMI.

—— (1993b) 'Against arbitrariness: the social production of the sign as a foundational issue in critical discourse analysis', *Discourse and Society* 4(2): 169–93.

—— (1995a) 'Representational resources and subjectivity', in C. Coulthard, ed., *Critical Discourse Analysis*, London, Routledge.

—— (1996) *Before Writing: Rethinking Paths into Literacy*, London, Routledge.

Kress, G. and Trew, T. (1978) 'Ideological transformations of discourse: or, how the *Sunday Times* got its message across', *Sociological Review* 26: 755–76.

Kress, G. and Van Leeuwen, T. (1990) *Reading Images*, Geelong, Deakin University Press.

—— (1992) 'Structures of visual representation', *Journal of Literary Semantics* 11(2): 91–117.

Lakoff, G. (1987) *Women, Fire and Dangerous Things: What Categories Reveal about the Mind*, Chicago, University of Chicago Press.

Lakoff, G. and Johnson, M. (1980) *Metaphors we Live by*, Chicago, University of Chicago Press.

Leibovitz, A. (1990) *Photographs 1970–1990*, New York, Harper Collins.

Lindekens, R. (1971) *Eléments pour une sémiotique de la photographie*, Paris, Didier.

McKenzie, A.E.E. (1938) *Magnetism and Electricity*, Cambridge, Cambridge University Press.

McQuail, D. and Windahl, S. (1993) *Communication Models*, London, Longman.

Martin, J.R. (1985) *Factual Writing*, Geelong, Deaking University Press.

Martin, J.R., Wignell, P., Eggins, S. and Rothery, J. (1988) 'Secret English: discourse technology in a junior secondary school', in L. Gerot, J. Oldenburge and T. Van Leeuwen, eds, *Language and Socialisation: Home and School*, Sydney, Macquarie University.

Martin, M. (1968) *Le Langage cinématographique*, Paris, Editions du Cerf.

Merritt, P.C., ed. (1984) *Book of Flowsheets*, New York, McGraw-Hill.

Metz, C. (1974a) *Film Language*, New York, Oxford University Press.

———— (1974b) *Language and Cinema*, The Hague, Mouton.

Modley, R. and Lowenstein, D. (1952) *Pictographs and Graphs*, New York, Harper.

Morris, D. (1977) *Manwatching*, London, Cape.

Mukarovsky, J. (1976) 'Art as semiotic fact' and 'The essence of the visual arts', in L. Matejka and I.R. Titunik, eds, *Semiotics of Art: Prague School Contributions*, Cambridge, Mass., MIT Press.

Mumford, L. (1936) *Technics and Civilisation*, New York, Harcourt, Brace & World.

Myers, G. (1990) *Writing Biology*, Madison, University of Wisconsin Press.

———— (1994) *Words in Ads*, London, Edward Arnold.

Nash, J.M. (1974) *Cubism, Futurism and Constructivism*, London, Thames & Hudson.

Nattrez, J.J. (1976) *Fondements d'une sémiologie musicale*, Paris, Uge.

Nitzschke, V. (1990) *Politik: Lernen und Handeln für Heute und Morgen*, Frankfurt, Diesterweg.

Novitz, D. (1977) *Pictures and their Use in Communication*, The Hague, Nijhoff.

Oakley, M. *et al.* (1985) *Our Society and Others*, Sydney, McGraw-Hill.

Ohman, C. (1989) *Historia*, Uppsala, Esselte Studium.

Ong, W.J. (1982) *Orality and Literacy: the Technologising of the Word*, London, Methuen.

O'Sullivan, T., Hartley, J., Saunders, D. and Fiske, J. (1983) *Key*

Concepts in Communication, London, Methuen.

O'Toole, M. (1994) *The Language of Displayed Art*, Leicester, Leicester University Press.

Panofsky, E. (1953) *Early Netherlandish Painting*, New York, Harper & Row.

———— (1970) *Meaning in the Visual Arts*, Harmondsworth, Penguin.

Pask, R. and Bryant, M. (1982) *People in Australia: a Social Geography*, Melbourne, Edward Arnold.

Pierce, J.R. (1972) 'Communication', *Scientific American* 227(3): 30–42.

Poynton, C. (1985) *Language and Gender: Making the Difference*, Geelong, Deakin University Press.

Riley, J.W. and Riley, M.W. (1959) 'Mass communication and the social system', in R.K. Merton, L. Broom and S. Cottrell, eds, *Sociology Today*, New York, Basic Books.

Rimmon-Kenan, S. (1983) *Narrative Fiction: Contemporary Poetics*, London, Methuen.

Ringbom, S. (1965) *Icon to Narrative: the Rise of the Dramatic Close Up in Fifteenth Century Painting*, Abo, Abo Akademie.

Sacks, H. (1992) *Lectures on Conversation*, Oxford, Blackwell.

Saint-Martin, F. (1987) *Semiotics of Visual Language*, Bloomington, Indiana University Press.

Sale, C., Friedman, B. and Wilson, G. (1980) *Our Changing World* Book I, Melbourne, Longman Cheshire.

Saussure, F. de (1974) *Course in General Linguistics*, London, Peter Owen.

Scannell, P. (1994) 'Communicative intentionality in broadcasting', unpublished paper.

Schapiro, M. (1973) *Words and Pictures*, The Hague, Mouton.

Schramm, W. (1954) 'How communication works', in W. Schramm, ed., *The Process and Effects of Mass Communication*, Urbana, University of Illinois Press.

Selander, S. (1994) 'Pedagogiska texter och retorik', in S. Selander and B. Englund, eds, *Konsten att informera och övertyga*, Stockholm, HLS Förlag.

Shannon, C. and Weaver, W. (1949) *The Mathematical Theory of Communication*, Urbana, University of Illinois Press.

Sharples, M. and Pemberton, L. (1992) 'Representing writing: external representations and the writing process', in P. O'Brian Holt and N. Williams, eds, *Computers and Writing*, Dordrecht, Kluwer.

Shepherd, J. (1977) 'The musical coding of ideologies', in J. Shepherd, P. Virden, G. Vulliamy and T. Wishart, eds, *Whose Music? A Sociology of Musical Languages*, London, Transaction.

Sontag, S. (1977) *On Photography*, Harmondsworth, Penguin.

Suffolk Coordinated Science (1978) London, Longman Educational.

Theewen, G. (1993) *Joseph Beuys: Die Vitrinen*, Cologne, Walter König.

Thibault, P. (1991) *Social Semiotics as Praxis*, Minneapolis, University of Minnesota Press.

Thompson, P. and Davenport, P. (1982) *The Dictionary of Visual Language*, Harmondsworth, Penguin.

Threadgold, T. (1988) 'Stories of race and gender: an unbounded discourse', in D. Birch and M. O'Toole, eds, *Functions of Style*, London, Pinter.

Trew, T. (1979) 'Theory and ideology at work' and 'Linguistic variation and ideological difference', in R. Fowler, R. Hodge, G. Kress and T. Trew, eds, *Language and Control*, London, Routledge.

Tufte, E.R. (1983) *The Visual Display of Quantitative Information*, Cheshire, Ct., Graphics Press.

Uspensky, B. (1973) *A poetics of composition*, Berkeley and Los Angeles, University of California Press.

—————— (1975) 'Left and right in icon painting', *Semiotica* 13(1): 33–41.

Van Leeuwen, T. (1985) 'Rhythmic structures of the film text', in T.A. van Dijk, ed., *Discourse and Communication: New Approaches to the Analysis of Mass Media Discourse and Communication*, Berlin, Walter de Gruyter.

—————— (1986) 'Proxemics of the television interview', *Australian Journal of Screen Theory* 17/18: 125–41.

—————— (1988) 'Music and ideology: towards a sociosemiotics of mass media music', *SASSC Working Papers* 10(2): 199–220.

—————— (1989) 'Changed times, changed tunes: music and the ideology of the news', in J. Tulloch and G. Turner, eds, *Australian Television: Programs, Pleasures, Politics*, Sydney, Allen & Unwin.

—————— (1991a) 'Conjunctive structure in documentary film and television', *Continuum* 5(1): 76–115.

—————— (1991b) 'The sociosemiotics of easy listening music', *Social Semiotics* 1(1): 67–80.

—————— (1992) 'The schoolbook as a multimodal text', *Internationale Schulbuchforschung* 14(1): 35–8.

—————— (1993) 'Genre and field in critical discourse analysis: a synopsis', *Discourse and Society* 4(2): 193–223.

Van Leeuwen, T. and Humphrey, S. (1993) *Learning to Look through a*

Geographer's Eye, Faculty of Education, University of Joensuu.

Van Leeuwen, T. and Kress, G. (1992) 'Trampling all over our unspoilt spot: Barthes' "punctum" and the politics of the extra-semiotic', *Southern Review* 25(1): 27–38.

—— (1995) 'Critical layout analysis', *Internationale Schulbuchforschung* 17(3): 25–43.

Van Leeuwen, T. and Selander, S. (in press) 'Picturing "our" heritage in the pedagogic text', *Journal of Curriculum Studies*.

Van Sommers, P. (1984) *Drawing and Cognition*, Cambridge, Cambridge University Press.

Veel, R. (1992) 'The language of school science', unpublished research report, Sydney, Disadvantaged Schools Programme.

Voloshinov, V.N. (1973) *Marxism and the Philosophy of Language*, London, Seminar Press.

Watson, J. and Hill, A. (1980) *A Dictionary of Communication and Media Studies*, London, Edward Arnold.

Whorf, B.L. (1956) *Language, Thought and Reality*, Cambridge, Mass., MIT Press.

Williams, N. and Holt, P., eds (1989) *Computers and Writing*, Norwood, N.J., Ablex.

Williams, R. (1977) *Culture and Society 1780–1950*, Harmondsworth, Penguin.

Williamson, J. (1978) *Decoding Advertisements*, London, Marion Boyars.

Wolkers, J. (1965) *Een Roos van Vlees*, Amsterdam, Meulenhoff.

Wollen, P. (1982) 'Godard and counter-cinema: vent d'est', in B. Nichols, ed., *Movies and Methods*, vol. II, Berkeley and Los Angeles, University of California Press.

Index